River Ask Me Why

Into the West on Two Wheels

March 27, 2024
Virginia City NV
For Rick & Roslyn
w/ deep thanks
& appreciation

SHAUN T. GRIFFIN

JUNIPER

First published in 2024
Juniper is an imprint of Southern Utah University Press
Cedar City, Utah

© Shaun T. Griffin 2024

ISBN Paperback: 9780935615586

Layout and design by Jessie Byers
Cover photo by Cody Griffin, Yukwah Campground, South Antium River,
Oregon
Cover design by Chris Younkin and Robert Blesse

Acknowledgments

The author owes a great debt of gratitude to so many friends, writers and family who helped make this book possible. To my late editor, Margaret Dalrymple, you were there when it counted for almost three decades. To my writerly friends both here and abroad, thank you for keeping me in the grain: Gailmaire Pahmeier, for your endless support and belief; Robert Reid, it meant something to walk in the Arctic together; Douglas Unger, you never stopped believing in the old man beneath this story; Richard Wiley, you were a lightning rod of clarity when I needed it; Lindsay Wilson, you came into the room like a song from these mountains; Chris Coake, always on the window of what it means to care; Robert Blesse, publisher, stalwart friend and believer; June Sylvester Saraceno, caretaker of all things words in the mountains; David Winkler, endless believer in the dream of the written word; Izzy Santillanes, friend now of three decades you have finally arrived on free soil; Dave and Jan Lee, how could I do this without you; Paulann Petersen, you have been there all the while my friend; Sam Green, who makes books and words we need in the Northwest and beyond; Michael Branch, because you are the real thing; Mary O'Malley, Michael Coady and Brendan Flynn—

you handed me the torch when I landed in Connemara; Howard Levy and Baron Wormser, you reached for my hand at long-ago Frost Place and now I reach for yours; the late Hayden Carruth and Joe-Anne McLaughlin—not a day goes by without you most enduring friends; Tom Meschery, peer of so many years and poems, I can't thank you enough; William O'Daly, your voice, a persistent reminder of grace in the Western Sierra; Rick and Rosemary Ardinger—your presence is felt throughout the Intermountain West and here—you ushered us into the Sawtooths; Erica Vitale-Lazare, seeress to those in the margins and friend I hold close, always; Gary Short, old friend, how long has it been since we started making poems; John Irsfeld, who never stopped believing and helping—even now in farthest Texas; John Garmon, compadre and poet who opened the prison workshop to me; William Douglass—your call in Stanley, Idaho, came like sweet nectar; Steven Nightingale, you welcomed me into the room with Lorca; Gabriel Urza, Nicky Laxalt and the late Robert Laxalt, I have been ever thankful for your presence in these, my listing years; to the late Richard Shelton, I would have never gone into the prison without you; to John Rember, thank you for your help and permission to use your references in Stanley, Idaho; to Dan Turner—you brought my bike—and so much more—back to life; to Randy Collins who sold me the Bianchi Eros bike years ago; to Gary and Carley Hansen Prince for your warmest welcome in the Corvallis sun; to Joe Curtis, who made our great t-shirts and upon returning from the ride planted the seed: "So when ya' gonna write a book about it?"; and finally to Ric Shrank, who rode with me as I writhed—neighbor, biker, beacon.

To Debby, Brenna, Suzette, Xavier, you were there riding with us always, keeping us upright when the wind and weather wanted more; to my late father and mother—your example lives on. You learned to love early; I have spent my life trying to follow.

Thank you to the entire team at Southern Utah University Press, Chris Younkin, Jessie Byers, Matthew Nickerson and Trudy Widup, for your belief in this book, in the possible West we rode into.

Contents

"This is… a paean to doing one single thing with,
as the Bible puts it, "all thy might; for there is no work,
nor device, nor knowledge, nor wisdom, in the grave,
whither thou goest."

—Ursula K. Le Guin

"Once more my deeper life goes on with more strength,
as if the banks through which it moves had widened out."

—Rainer Maria Rilke

"Think where man's glory most begins and ends
And say my glory was I had such friends."

—William Butler Yeats

for

Nevada and Cody who made the journey
one a father will never forget

Scott and Joe
who knew why long before we left

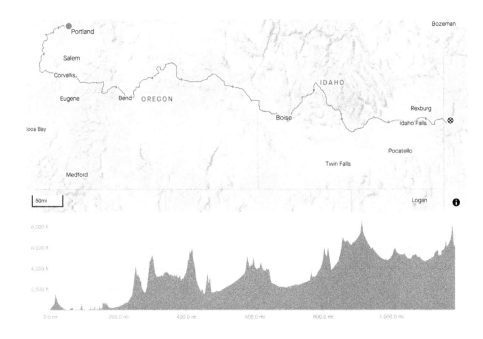

Preface

Distance: without end
Elevation: unknown
Great Basin, 2019

Something turned inside, something I was not aware of. A silence crept in where once there was noise, where once there was clutter. My days before leaving were filled with preparation, with worry over what could and could not be done and with the endless details of turning to the road. I called or texted my sons daily, wondering if they too found what they needed: the right tires, lights, racks, lightweight bag and pad. Of course this was the small stuff, the things that consume a mind. The real worry was the pedaling—would I be able to last and would they be gracious enough to *let* me be last in the long push over the western ranges?

Last fall a friend asked if I would like to go on a bike ride in the West. I thought about it for two minutes and said absolutely. Then I shared it with my boys, who are not boys at all but men. Nevada is thirty-five and Cody is thirty. Both are married to loving partners, both work too hard at their jobs and, I imagine, saw this as an opportunity to break free. Whatever qualities have been attributed to freedom, those found on two wheels are the slowest to reveal themselves. In the months of planning and organizing, the realities of being on a bicycle for several weeks were just outside our awareness. We could articulate what we *thought* it meant but not the experience of it and that difference became our journey across three states in the American West.

I have believed since I was boy that a bicycle was a winged spoke and wheel, that with very little effort you could pedal to extreme joy. I never believed it could also be a form of transport, a way into the silence of mountains and rivers and jagged lava flows. I never understood how it could alter your presence in the world by asserting its privilege over your attention. I never thought I could surrender to two wheels for most of a month and recover in the comfort of my home weeks later. I never wanted my legs to freeze up with lactic acid; what I wanted was winded exertion, a quality I valued but rarely chose.

The morning we rode out of Bend, our first as a father and sons, was what I had prepared for: to be alone with them, to be against the elements in a saddle on two wheels. To live without an explanation for the brief moments together in June. I cannot say what brought them to the ride, only that it was a reckoning with their vision of physical and mental stamina. Of course, each of us would reckon with so much more and that became a parallel road we traveled.

Late one afternoon after miles on a two-lane through an Idaho hayfield, Cody said, "I just spent thirty minutes trying to figure out what I will do with my sons when I'm sixty-five." That other road would shift and move in and out of consciousness but it was never far from each of us. Some days I traveled for hours without recognition of being in traffic or behind my sons. Some days I floated that other road to sanctuary. I trust they did too, but it was their sanctuary. Just as we must worship at different altars, the bikes forced us to quiet our minds and be in the presence of what was passed by: tree, flower, water. Water grew to surround us, these few riders from the driest of basins in the West. Water followed to its origins, to the River of No Return where the Salmon begins and dozens of others. Water in a West without water. It was such a juxtaposition from our home: the Great Basin of forty-five north-south mountain ranges and few rivers, few navigable waterways, most of the water underground. A watery landscape yet to be revealed. We hear words like the

Humboldt Sink to define the disappearing Humboldt River. The Carson Sink similarly swallows the Carson River. And our trapped bodies of water in the north—Pyramid and Walker Lakes—they survive the carnivores of sun and salt. This was the frame of water we took down the highways, this frame that grew with every passage until water finally became something we saw, fished and laid in.

On a rock in the middle of the South Santium River, I laid in the setting sun for over an hour. I heard the whip of Cody's Tenkara fly rod in the distance. The water was warm, and few fish were biting. It was our first day in the wet. I looked into the western sky and felt like we had arrived at the precarious place of quiet. Nothing spectacular, just a river and a granite boulder to lie on, but we had spent many days hoping to find this small corner of respite. Cody's job was in busy L.A. This must have seemed like stepping into another universe. We started to unwind.

> Last night, under a moss-draped Western
> Hemlock, you hugged me long.
>
> Somewhere in the branch of history,
> a river rose. Today, roadside, fern gloss,
>
> we lie in pine needles and listen
> to the gathering quiet.

Scott and Joe joined us on the road to Prineville—just out of Bend. It was Scott who had asked me to ride months earlier. Joe and Scott gave us the levity we needed as we set off into the Cascades. They had ridden long distances many times. They wanted to do this ride because it had been so pleasurable before. My sons were new to the experience. At the end of the second day Cody said, "I've never been on a bike for seventy-four miles in my *life*." By the time the other three had joined us Cody and I had been riding for a week. We were almost used to the stiffness, the sweat, the billows of diesel smoke and the unexpected hands that joined us everywhere. I told Nevada it would take days to let the hayfields, osprey and trout find their way in. Slowly, the tissue began to build among us. My sons were able to be with Scott and Joe as men, not in the shadow of their father.

I was grateful for the quiet that accompanied us through the striated canyon in Central Oregon. The walls looked like coral ribbons stretched to the summit. Miraculously, none of us fell on the gravel and sand highway. The clouds that night were beyond painting—burnt orange puffs feathered the sky. It looked as if the creek flowed from fire. My watercolor postcard could barely start to show the beauty. I tried each morning to write a few words and sometimes paint in the palm of my hand. Weight again—the portable watercolors were not enough. And there was no time. At night, it was no different except we were hungover with fatigue. A shower if there was one, food wherever we found it and sleep before the sun went down. Another ritual of dreams and restless worry of weather, mountains and road stops until dawn. Each day was a separate film, a running narrative of unexpected and profound revelation. Four of us carried fly rods and coming out of Dayville, we stopped on the John Day. Joe got out his journal and wrote from the bank above the river. Cody hit it from the start—small rainbows flew and the more he cast, the more he caught. It was like watching him return to the boy in the mountains of Jarbidge where he and Nevada learned to fly fish. Swallows darted in and out of the willows. I set down my rod to paint. Joe set off to get a head start.

We caught up with him at the gas station. Several Canadians were riding motorcycles over the same stretch of highway. A slow affinity began with them and others who rode on two wheels. These strangers you meet on the highway, these outposts of reflection. You get to know people on a long ride, their grist, their grit.

Scott never planned on being stuck with four outliers; he's a scientist for whom a poem is like a veil on the face—the background isn't quite revealed. I, meanwhile, quoted haiku written during the last ten miles. Joe teaches with him at the university, in the dreaded humanities, and yet, laconic, full of free-range humor and a serious student of literature, Joe did not parse words. It was Scott who revealed what we were riding through: "Do you notice the algae in the river? It's percolating up from the plates. The coastal crust is being subducted under the continental crust. As it rises up this causes volcanoes and it brings nutrients in the rocks from the ocean—which increases the algae bloom." In the Painted Hills, he named the striations, the geologic formations that made them happen. He anchored us to the physical world we rode through. His bike was a touring bike he bought in the Netherlands and he had every tool with him. My sons began to appreciate his science when they needed his chain oil.

When you leave on a bike you try not to imagine what could go wrong; this was doubly so with my sons but three soon became five and the questions ran away. If we had the gift of inches between cars and panniers, that was enough. On the good nights we texted our spouses, made it to camp. When we were out of reach of a cell tower we sent a note on the way to our camp site. All the noise began to fade—the news, the interruptions, the constant hassle of Now slipped into the distance. In its place was the mountain before us, a mountain we had never seen, and despite its contoured presence on a topo map, a bicycle was like a butterfly cresting its summit. Soon we understood that we were ephemeral.

The trees were scattered like bowling pins from an avalanche; a guard rail of quarter-inch steel was twisted flat. This is what we rode through: detritus of snow and water. At the summit there were rocks on the outhouse roof, so much snow had fallen from the ridge above. We were minimal in this place, without purchase, without mirror. The occasional car seemed to come from another time zone, not the one of material energy that broke trees in half and tore rivers from their path. Each of us tuned into the foment of natural strength. The switchbacks to the summit wore through us and we listened to what flew overhead. The raven's shadow looked on.

Sometimes the wind was behind us—the day into Mitchell—and others, in front like a hurdle. No matter what we did the wind came with us. We learned to live with its covenant of dust and surgical precision. It cut the road ahead and behind like it was cloth. When we turned into the corn rows, the killdeer distracted us, screeching at our proximity: their eggs were on the ground. I learned to live with the birds; they followed us every mile. So did the hooves and horns and tails: Cody happened upon a herd of big horn sheep, Nevada an elk, and I looked up to see red-tail chicks standing as their mother fed them. What a gift slow travel provides! The elements of wind and sun reveal how close things are. We lifted our heads to examine much beyond the wheels. This was our place of rhythm for weeks and it became a winnowing rhythm. It took us from our lives and poured us into this new one. At first we were unwilling to let go of that other regimen but soon there was little choice. The sheer stamina it took to cross miles of lava, hay, mountains and river valleys required us to pay attention, to be present, without affiliation. This was what we left for; this is what we left behind.

Trochilic—

Adjective: relating to the wheel or the rotary motion.

Etymology: from Greek trochos (wheel), from trechein (to run),

which also gave us troche (lozenge) and the metrical trochee.

Earliest documented use: 1570.

In the Province of Clouds
I

Distance: 55 miles
Elevation: 8,400 feet
Sierra Nevada, Spain, 2008

When nothing else is above you but sky and you imagine the faint distance as a peak with a thread-like path to its summit, when you turn into the switchback and nothing is behind or in front, when the stillness of high altitude brings you close to the rails you ride on, when the bones begin to turn as if of their own volition, you believe this is the lone place in which to defy sweat and start. I looked back at the young *ciclista*—half my age on a bike that weighed under eighteen pounds—and he yelled *animal* in his best, tormented Castilian and I smiled, having never been chided for riding too far. But it was the kind of bravado that cyclists trade in: the one more pass to climb and then I'll find the word for losing all thought to its devotion type of bravado. I asked a few people at the ski resort high above Granada, Spain, how much farther to climb. No one knew really, save the geologists who were working on its flanks. Maybe eight, ten miles I heard, but nothing of certainty. In the gift store the woman offered her best maternal face: *Ten cuidado. Hay mucho viento en la montaña. Be careful, there's much wind on the mountain.* By then I had heard enough to believe there could have been dragons at the top of Pico de Veleta, Spain's third-highest peak at 11,142. There could have been hobbit-like villages up there for all I knew, or there could have been silence. I was about to find out. On an old crappy mountain bike with most of the gears working— except when they didn't—I had enough sprockets to try, which was probably part of the reason the young cyclist, up for the day from Granada—a fair ride without other distractions, took one look at me and surmised: he doesn't know shit. The water bottles clung to the rack under bungee cords and I had no windbreaker, no way to dodge the wind. I trusted the woman in the gift store to send a good weather request to whatever god she prayed to, surely a Catholic God in this part of southern Spain. I trusted all of the gods and goddesses to transport me to this summit I could no longer see, so steep had its flanks become. And I started on the switchbacks without much else but intention. It had gotten me to this place of trying things and if something came of it, so be it. If I flew down the mountain without so much as a sweat, I had ridden into the clouds and the clouds stretched to the Mediterranean.

These were airplane clouds, things you see from the window of a Cessna, like the corn fields, the poplars, the tobacco that stretched to Malaga and through the villages of Federico García Lorca's childhood. We had ridden into those villages as well, my best friend and lover, more than once. One summer day Debby and I turned the corner into Fuente Vaqueros to see the town gathered in the square, surrounding the bust of the great poet. He was born here, two years before the dawn of the twentieth century, to educated parents and a loving family. He studied piano as a boy and was precocious, a savant who could hear things in the wind, the same wind that woman in the gift store warned me about. And that bust grew in size the longer we looked at it—so garrulous it could have been life-like—but he, in life, was diminutive and not outgoing. He wanted, rather, to find a way to express what he saw in the community of gypsies and peasants and people loyal to the land. They were his compass, his magnetic north through his many iterations as poet, playwright and reluctant spokesperson for the Spanish working class.

I looked down on that valley and wondered what stories were emanating now, what flights had come from those tobacco sheds where the leaves, larger than elephant ears, dried in the hot Spanish sun. And I kept pedaling. Some of the switchbacks were so steep I could only see the next hundred yards but my ignorance was a thing to be prized: I would have never attempted to outlast such earthen strength as a mountain, alone in the province of clouds. A place to begin training.

When my neighbor, a true *animal*, asked if I would accompany him on a ride in the Utah mountains, it sounded like fun or at the very least, an adventure. I was always up for an adventure and said, without much thought, sure, I'll join you. After the realization of distance and elevation set in, I had to do something: ride hundreds of miles to prepare, this time in Spain, so that when, in the darkest of the two a.m. night I was exhausted and wanted to sleep, I could keep on through Bryce, Zion and Escalante National Parks. I didn't know any of this then; it was preamble to another type of learning— abandon what you know and start over. Start here with no knowledge of the body, its temperamental rhythms, its torment when the water dries in your cells and the oxygen runs from your lungs. Start here when you have nothing but miles to ride—in wind or dust or rain. Start here when the sound of a bird is the greatest distraction you will enjoy. Start here when the saddle you sit on becomes ligament to your legs—and the bars appendage to your arms. Start here when sweat is an insect running over your lips, onto your tongue and you breathe without thinking, without preparation for less and less oxygen.

I sat at the elbow of another switchback trying to digest my dried bread and warm cheese, hoping to find enough in them to push on. Nutrition was just a word then, it was not what you ingested to gain strength; it was a noun, devoid of any properties that might help you in this endeavor. If you hit the wall—the proverbial deadness that sets in on such a ride—you laid down in deference to its calling. You gave in to the wind or sudden eclipse of strength in your legs. And sometime later, you rose to start again. Start here, as if it had never happened.

I crested the last hairpin to a boulder field. Shale and cut rock to its summit. There was a microwave tower and not much else. No path, nothing resembling a way forward. I hoisted my bike on my shoulder and bouldered up the next hundred yards. It was still of an angle I could not process. Only the haze of the valley below me and the faint outline of rock above. My aging steel bike with the water sloshing in the bottles in my pack, my arms small cylinders that cradled these wheels, my eyes dry under the afternoon sun, my legs shifting on the tennis shoe soles until I stood and dropped the bike, my pack and yelled to Lorca's home—I'm here! High on this ridge, where nothing seemed alive but then a sparrow came, and a honey bee, and they stayed and I was friends with them in that moment. Another man who hiked up raised his palm, a Dutch hiker, and we sat on the ridge as if on top of a pole overlooking the continent. To my back were the small mountain villages whose *acequias* or water canals dated from Roman times. Hiking trails crossed the ridges to meet them. And I exhaled all the oxygen I had, drank water, and laid down, thankful to the woman in the gift store for keeping the wind away, to the worn tires for not bursting, to the granite for letting me ascend.

This is how I started to train for the ride with my neighbor, and we rode that ride that was really a race and did all right. But I didn't know that then; I just went along. I have been infected with this need to be on two wheels as long as I can remember and it has taken me places, lovely places like this, sitting in thin air, looking down on all southern Spain to see what daylight appeared on a farther horizon. I kept that view close when I went away, back to my room, my wife, my work, my family. I kept the view inside where special things live and nurtured it to travel with me so that I may never forget how long it takes to climb a summit. Because in the miles that pour out from the plateau there will be the disregard of the elements, sure, but more than that, you must pass through the barren land and unwelcome eyes to answer what it is that drew you from your station. This was the question I tried to acknowledge when my sons asked if they could join me on a ride across the American West.

The Estuary Beside Her
II

Distance: 8 miles
Elevation: sea level
Southern California, 2018

When my sons and I met in Orange County it was not to ride a bike into the West. It was not to feel the fall air of September. Nine months before we rode off, we stood around the hospital bed of my mother. She had been transported from her assisted-care facility because her heart was failing. She was gasping for air. I did not know if she would pull through but I could not watch her starve for oxygen. Helpless to change the chemistry of the oxygen levels in her blood, the staff called for an ambulance to transport her. Once in the emergency room, despite all of the attendant worry, she was feisty and wasn't going to lie in wait for death. Nevada called me and asked if he should come. I told him it was his decision but I could not say whether she would be here for long. He stopped everything and flew across the country to be with her and her children. She was in and out of consciousness for a week. All of us spoke silent hymns to the unknown and known healers. When they transferred her to a room in ER, the doc asked us to come outside. He said she had a "do not resuscitate" message on her medical directive. He looked at us plaintively: "I can do surgery... but at 89 it will cause more harm than good. Her quality of life is what matters. You must decide what to do." By then, we realized, we had already violated her instructions: she had had transfusions to increase her oxygen levels, and we did not want her in this place any longer than necessary.

Nevada and Cody worked in health care and knew what we were facing—no easy way out—but her stamina, her resilience fought through over and over. My sisters were riddled with grief and my brother could not find a way to articulate what had happened. An imperceptible sound came from her room: *I am here*. When she was transferred to a private room, we sat by her bed looking at the coastal skyline, the beauty of the place she had been in for the past twenty years. We found a hotel near the hospital and settled in. Out of the chaos came routine.

Our decision came after looking at her: we wanted to honor who she was—a seeress, a woman who taught farm kids music, reading, writing and art. A woman whose paintings were in her room at the assisted-care facility. A woman who gave the seeds of art to my sister and me. A woman who took those seeds from her mother and passed them down. Art's subtle movement across time. A woman who had been on a boat with my father on the Sea of Cortez and up and down the coast of Mexico. A woman who learned Spanish to ask for the ingredients to cook in La Paz. A woman whose life had been attenuated by raising four kids and working and never having enough time. This was the woman we stood around, we watched while she slept, we helped with soft food and water. This was the woman whose choice it would be to survive.

This was the woman who taught each of us a reverence for life, for the little man, for the person in the margins. This was the woman whose empathy ran down halls, chasing children, keeping them safe, loving them through twenty-eight years of teaching. This was the woman who did not know how to cook, clean, and sew when she married my father fresh out of college. This was the woman whose beauty and earthy smile and empathy cut men down like rain. This was the woman who brought us up without ever asking why or how or if. She just did it.

People often think of compassion as a doorstop to lesser humilities— losing one's grasp on love, on touch, on patience—and hers was a compassion that knew no bounds. I talk about her compassion in the past tense, but it was in that time when we felt it most, because she had given it to us endlessly for six decades. Which meant, of course, it had circled back to envelop her as she might envelop her school children. My father had been gone over two decades; she had navigated many countries in that time. To this day she keeps his letters in her bureau and rereads them as if for the first time.

We never fully understand why we must leave a place, let alone a place where the hydrangeas bloom year-round, the bougainvillea is on most every street, and the maples sag under the weight of irrigation. I went to college in Southern California, did my internship in this place where she now resides. It was eerily perfect then, but now, driving the freeway from our hotel to the board-and-care home she lives in, I could not feel. I was a desultory fragment; I wished for nothing but the present as I sat with her and the others watching daytime TV. Some ghost of what we had become spilled from the screen: people dressed like it was a play they were in and not real life. All day the ratchet of make-believe, which is finally what it became, this place of show and tell.

Our first night, my wife and I, weary from the drive to Southern Cal, landed in a bastion of well-heeled diners. Nearly every employee was the very person being spat upon in the media—the newcomers, the immigrants, the Latinos burning down the wall for jobs. All of it was lost in the rush to be seen in this place. A Black jazz pianist set down some riffs. I staggered into the hotel, which became a kind of sanctuary because there was a woman at the desk whose mother was also dying. When Debby went downstairs to ask for another night, and then another, the woman at the desk asked why. Debby just started to cry and Maria gave us a discount, gave us nearly everything she could because that was her job: to be nice no matter how intimidating the tall buildings outside.

For one week we lived across the street from the airport, not knowing if the sound of planes would arrive at dawn and leave, like us, when the day ended. Cody asked us to stay with him and we tried but his home was an hour from my mother. In L.A., traffic is not a paradigm for floating above the cars. It's just driving the two taillights in front of you until the exit, which will not be found without effort. People take umbrage at being told L.A. traffic is bad, or normal, or even exciting. It doesn't matter; what it means is time that is taken, time to be with her, time to sit, strange as it was, on the couch with Sam, Chris, Angel, Sofia and the blessed caregivers, Rick, Gloria and Susan. We believe time is a threshold for having more time, enough time to be frivolous with time. When we stood in cardiac ICU at my mother's bedside, those equations became meaningless. This was the last time she would be in the hospital: the doctor had asked about her quality of life. The four of us siblings looked at each other, at her and knew it should not be like this, and so made the unwanted decision to follow her directive and start hospice.

This is not new; people die every day. What is unthinkable is death's insatiable appetite, and each of us was now in its orbit. A great fiction writer, a Joyce, might parody such an idea, but it was not amusing. When we met the hospice nurse, he pointed to all the drugs that would soon become friends. I recognized morphine, the rest were not there in any real sense because I knew morphine meant goodbye. Morphine disrupts pain's last door.

Almost every good person we met said you did not play God; you did what she wanted. It did little to assuage the feeling of turning into an alley of last resort. Nevada walked the halls in thought. Was there something else he could do, some tool he could offer us in the blur of medical questions? He and Cody had seen the inside of the medical profession from their separate coasts, but this was too close, too much like loss. There was no path to describe what their grandmother had begun to experience. And so they did what young men do: they helped her from the wheelchair to the bed, they brought food, they listened as the doctors came and went and translated for us, her siblings in a stupor.

Miraculously, a few days after coming home from the hospital, my mother got her spunk back and began to give me her usual fireworks—"Oh, Shaun, you have such a way with words, and I don't believe any of them!" On the banter went until she finally released us from the moment of not knowing, and we were together again. Because if you're always worried and never present, she loses again—not just time, but you, and then it really is stealing. I resolved to sit with Steve Harvey and answer another dumb question with his feuding families. We both got better as the days went on. The exercise people came into the room in the afternoon, tossed balloons from one hand to the next. Singers came too: minstrels with no road to follow save this one in a living room of octogenarians whose favorite songs were "This Land Is My Land" and "Don't Sit Under the Apple Tree"—music my mother taught in school and played at the house when I was young. My boyhood friends had come to listen as she regaled them on the grand piano my father restored, and they wondered how anyone could master the chords that jumped from its depths.

Music was tonic for my mother. She hummed rhythms and lyrics while cooking, knitting and painting. The visitors at the board-and-care home asked who did the paintings, and my mother, stoic in her pride, in her assessment of what art meant, smiled. She did not have enough time to paint more; she raised us, taught, and taught my friends to read and write when she got home. Their parents were jealous that such a beloved woman lived in our house. I didn't understand; how could I? She had given those gifts to me, and so I had left her and my friends to the piano, the grammar and spelling.

The waterfall strokes had dented her prescient memory, but she held me like I was without love. That was what she needed to say—the bones rubbing through her thinned flesh. Her arms were splotched with bruises from the IVs and blood-thinners. I traced their unruly shapes on her wrists and hoped they would dissipate before we left. She kept asking for her watch, which we had put in my sister's purse at the hospital. Once it was back on her wrist, she knew where she was, how she was: in the present, with us. Not much else to report: "Oh, Shaun, I'm fine," her daily retort, and so I stopped asking and became her son who sat on the couch beside her. Sam leaned over and said, "She's fine," and I believed him.

On the fourth day, I needed to find another sanctuary and rode along the estuary to the beach. A red-tail hawk circled overhead. In the sea grass were two egrets and a great blue heron. What was it they were trying to tell me with their thin, white legs? What was it I could not understand? I remember in Chile, when my father died, the egrets would not leave me, and finally I decided it was he, still in the tidepool, trying to stab the minnow. How these bird images came together two decades apart, how they strung a life of marital friendship into the bold declaration of love, I will not know. I got off my bike in the harbor. A boat like the one my parents floated away on was anchored there. For four years they were at peace in the Pacific, almost without anchor on the shore of Mexico. Is this what love becomes: a journey to the marsh of your first words? The next day I walked the estuary with Debby, wanted her to see the birds, to feel them beside her so she might be released from this tide that pulled at us.

In the mornings, before I went to see my mother, I walked to the bagel store and a middle-aged Mexican woman served me with equal portions of Spanglish and warmth. I wondered who took the most from the store. Each day they gave me more and by the time I left I needed them, not the other way around. I needed their perfect understanding of loss, their near-remarkable ability to carry on despite a border fifty miles to the south. I needed their recognition of mutual despair: they were not free beneath these buildings. They hid in the shadows and read English headlines announcing their absence. On an earlier trip down to visit my mother, my sister took me to a restaurant in San Juan Capistrano, the earliest Jesuit settlement in California. Pat and Richard Nixon smiled down on us from a black-and-white photo taken after he left office. Now we lived in the nexus of fear and its ethereal messenger, greed. Now we traded barbs on the stock exchange: will he build the wall, won't he, and Mexico lies in the footnotes like a woman who cannot be had.

I hugged my mother goodbye for an interminable moment, her earring post stiff at my cheek. Debby and I headed up I-5, the freeway clogged from downtown Los Angeles north. Arteries, I said, arteries. What she didn't have enough of—clean, fluid arteries. The cow fields, the grape fields, the oil fields. It was a strange paradise we drove through. In Sacramento, I pulled into my old friend's house, the one whose driveway I would cry in when we left a day later. I knew him from high school, when I was a tyrant and my mother could not find the right path to my heart. Here we were, fifty years on, talking about death like it was a gardenia growing in his beautiful garden. Friends do not know what to say in this moment but he and his wife, a former hospice nurse, know too well what can become of silence. They held us close for long periods of time, like my mother did before we left. This is how I remember being with her, with them, with my love that walked the estuary with the herons, the gulls and the thrushes. Native species of the habitat earth. What we want to remember even as we divide its colonial shipwreck for our children.

Mother, I give what little I have: words and a few articles of paint. When we moved you for the last time, you handed me my books, because you were no longer able to read. I did not want to take them, wanted to leave their paper skeletons behind. But they gather now at my feet, in the dust of this room where I begin to spell your name without. Where I look east to reside in the weeks before I return to sit with you on the couch and hope Sam and Chris keep you happy, or at least that you win one round of *Family Feud*.

Our lives sharpen to this point, this end-stop, a hyphenated word in poetry, Mother, where you become the riddle of a life juxtaposed for meaning. End-stop; what each of us children would give to take this ending away and go back to our lives, which thankfully, we absorb with alacrity because you showed us how. Love is really the dying down of two hands, then one. My sisters, brother and I will trade hours to be with you, trade almost anything because it is the only time we have to be alone with you. Alone with your breath, your food, your sleep. Your whitened blouse, your reddened lips, your Dean Martin. This is our transfusion, Mother, this is how we put the blood back into our lives. In the morning when Cody comes to visit, please tell him what you told me: "Oh, Cody, I'm fine," and he will laugh, know you're lying, and drive home satisfied that nothing has changed.

The Last Ride in the Hollywood Hills
III

Distance: 15 miles
Elevation: 1,800 feet
West Los Angeles, 2019

Cody and I sat in the living room of his apartment. We had just returned from visiting my mother. She was settled into her new living quarters and stable. It was early spring. The ride was starting to take shape. We knew where we wanted to go but not the route. He opened up his bike application, Strava and Google Earth, to look at what we might encounter. For three hours we watched the TV screen—scrolled from one camp site to another and the two-lane highways we might ride.

It was hard to visualize what we would ride through. Even though the road seemed fairly innocuous, there was no "real time" way to understand the unknowns—traffic, weather, distance to shade, detours—things that would matter once we started pedaling. Cody did the best he could. He plotted a rough average of sixty-five miles a day, which we imagined would be possible. Of course, that was all we could do: imagine what would come from this time together. This time alone on two wheels. This time to settle into a routine. He was very busy at work and, like Nevada, trained on the weekends and an occasional weeknight. They were both consultants in competing firms. Nevada focused on health care solutions and Cody on strategic decision-making to improve the bottom line. The idea of pedaling for a day was just that: an idea. Only I had ridden for long distances, but they were young and whatever we could not envision, youth would overcome. That's what we told ourselves sitting on his Mid-City couch that Sunday afternoon.

Each day became a series of graphs: distance, elevation, campsite, motel, food and water. I rode for years without any such preparation. If I found food, so much the better. If I didn't, I rode hungry or tired but rode on. This seemed surreal—to have a three-dimensional map of our route. But it was beautiful to see, to visualize what we would be doing. It was like being in a theater watching what was about to unfold. Neither of us believed the ride would take this exact path but the process of laying out the maps, trying to find rest stops, water, food and bike stores, made it something we could see. I sat with the physical maps of Oregon, Idaho and Wyoming, and tried to find the smallest highways from point to point. Cody, of course, was ahead of me on the screen. If I got lucky and found a place that looked inviting, he was already there, noting its convenience or lack thereof. We tried to stay by rivers because this meant time to fly fish. What more could we want than to be alone in a stream with the whip of the rod? That was another reason for doing this, or at least part of it. Each day the question became, can we fish here or somewhere near here? It was a fool's game because we would be tired and without a local knowledge of the stream or lake, but we wanted to dip our rods, not worry about what would come of it. In this way, fishing is like riding a bike—you must pretend to like it long enough to find the one moment of joy when the rod bends and there's something below.

The short film, *The Fly Highway*, gave birth to this longing to be by rivers on Highway 20 across the West. There was no end to what they could catch in the film. And therefore, no end to what we could catch. This made the anticipation even greater. I spent days in the fly shops picking through dry flies, trying to sort the right combination of Adams and other small insects. The Tenkara rods we took did not have reels—less weight and easier to set up. The downside was they did not cast far—the fish had to be close. A risk we took because the extra weight was more than we wanted.

Catching fish wouldn't matter. To be by a stream was the real gift. Sitting on the couch with Cody, I did not know that. I did not know how to sit in a cold stream out of sheer exhaustion, hoping it would soak away the sun and dirt. I did not know how to lie on a granite stump at sundown, waiting for stars to claim me. I did not know how to surrender to the river. But we chose rivers nonetheless, chose to abide by their strength and the beauty which could ravage and calm, not unlike the road we would ride. We chose the water because it would sustain us. If we had no food, we could still drink the water from the stream. We chose the water because at one time the three of us lived in a dry land, a land without water. And so coming to its banks through the mountains and watersheds below was like coming to spring. There was no getting over its sustaining gravity. We needed this water, needed to know it was close by. In camp, in the mornings, in the crushing daylight, it was water we needed most. No amount of food or energy drinks could replace water. That there might be fish *and* water was a bonus unthinkable to us then, sitting on the couch in LA.

Cody slowly added the miles—it was close to a thousand—which seemed much more than the distance from Portland to Jackson Hole. It seemed like an endless stretch of miles and the elevation, equally so—about 50,000 feet. What does that description really mean? Is it something we climb over or can we ride to the top? Both of the numbers had an obvious significance: the journey would take us into the mountains, across many rivers and above the trees. The trees that guide and shelter would disappear from view, moving away from us to release hundred-mile views. And although we did not know it then, when we stood atop the headwaters of the River of No Return, we could plainly see what that view restored to us. We could see what the water became. We could see far enough to belong to sky. We could ride without weight at this elevation. We were part of an environment that was greater than any one person could create. We were small, infinitely small in the valley below. Our bikes became insects on a path through its floor. We felt released from the ordinary.

In those three hours on the couch, we might have hoped for some of this, but we did not know what to expect. The graph would change and we with it. The graph would become an outline, something we laid on the road before us each day. Stubbornly I brought a real map, which did prove to be useful when there was no power, no way of accessing the world outside. And stubbornly it refused to make the ride any easier.

It was redolent of what was to come every day. I relied on it as you might rely on a cane or prescient glimpse of the road ahead. The peaks, the twists up the inclines, the cities where the lines grew larger. The map informed me and sometimes presented real difficulty: Cody could not find a way from Boise to Idaho City without taking the freeway for twenty-five miles. None of us wanted to do this; but that didn't matter. It was an unavoidable consequence of a journey by the river on Highway 20. In order to stay on our small highways going to the Tetons, we needed to give up something in return.

Cody sent the tentative route to Nevada who was three time zones away and traveling for work. Nevada's job didn't permit the kind of attention the route deserved. He frequently left on a Sunday to live the next four days in a hotel and returned on Friday. He trusted Cody to make the right decisions. I did too. I had little concern for the exact coordinates of place and time. What I wanted was to be alone with them in a place of quiet. Maybe a deer, a raven, a trout in a pool but little else. All the things that make quiet possible. A way to insert myself into their lives that we might coalesce on a journey from one point to another.

The next day Cody and I rode into the Santa Monica Mountains: a short ride through gorgeous hilltop homes to a dirt path that followed the mountain ridge to the San Fernando Valley. I was tired but happy to be out of the traffic below. Cody told me he did this ride two or three times successively to train. I knew already he was miles away and I must have seemed an anachronism in the distance.

Both of the boys had been gone for over a decade and Debby and I were used to the rattle of living alone, or more correctly, living without them. In a perfect world, she would have been on the bike with us and their spouses would. There was nothing special about riding through this wilderness. It was just an idea to leave the daily-ness of our lives. It was just an idea to surrender to another rhythm before I got too old. It was just an idea of letting go in the middle of their high-stakes jobs. It was just an idea of living without much at all: a few snacks, some mac and cheese, water, sleeping bag and a couple pairs of riding shorts. It was just an idea of having very little to sustain us save each other.

Fathers and sons do not get long together. The first eighteen years collapse like a rubber band when released, and then the calendars resist reunion. Jobs, spouses, friends and creating a life of one's own all take precedence. This was turning back the clock, renaming what we believed for a few short weeks on a bicycle. I believe in them. There is not much else to decide as a father. You give your children breath; your lover and their mother gives them breath. Together you raise them, hope for some understanding of consequence, hope in that same breath that they learn your voices so that they may be recalled when the storms come in. You break rules to confide this passage of unknown hopes and lies. You break into their stories long enough to slip in and leave a bit of yourself but not too much. Their own story must resolve the storm that awaits. And they look forward to it, look forward to breaking the mold you have set for them.

I was born in the stifling 1950s when we conformed and grew up in the 1960s when we rebelled. That time still seems more real than the surreal time I'm living in: a president who could not say three things to quiet the mind; a leaderless leader trying to secure points on the stock market. In the five decades since the 1960s, the world has moved to other stories, but we cannot absolve ourselves. We cannot do away with reason any more than I could negate the need to leave with my boys on this trip.

The darkness beckons day in and day out. It beseeches us to relent, to stow away in the gridlock of supplication, it beseeches us to obey. And what if we do? What if we do? I never asked my boys what they might do if confronted with such a choice. I imagined they might become men who resolve tough questions with tough answers, imagined they might learn enough without me or their mother, imagined they might start another course on the highway ahead. A course that would free them of some of the ugliness of our journey through Vietnam, Civil Rights and discovery of the very real consequences of not caring. John and Yoko's billboard in Times Square doesn't seem so irrelevant now: War Is Over (if you want it).

In the middle of a very dusty patch in Oregon, there was a marquee outside a café and gas station: "The steaks are blue, the bacon is red, and the poems are hard." That became our motto—where the bacon is red and the poems are hard. How that phrase landed on a one-horse café I'll never know, but it stuck. More would ensue from that poetic entrée and from a hundred others that intimated possible futures, even ones as unprovoked as blue steaks, red bacon and hard poems and resisted immediate interpretation.

Even the paints I took were not enough to convey our journey. And the watercolors I did were ephemeral—more colored dreams than paintings. The only thing that seemed adequate for the trip was the haiku form. I could create them while riding. They added no weight; they asked nothing. I rehearsed and rehearsed until the syllabic form met the clouds and the cornfields with precision. And if they were worthy of telling, I shared occasional haiku at our rest stops. Sometimes they were more than haiku. Sometimes they were lines across our faces—the gathering points of two generations locked in the temporal quest of growing old and growing away. An unwanted destiny but one that gave urgency to our departure. We could not wait much longer. My body would defer to these mountains long before theirs and I would only watch the outlines of their bodies climbing the summit from the distance. I was not worried about finishing the ride; I was worried about the little things—breakdowns, discomfort, unforeseen hiccups. They, I imagine, were worried about me: could he finish? could he keep up? complete this story we were creating? This story we told ourselves to get up in the morning on the days we rode to practice. This story we believed long enough to say yes. This story we cajoled and coaxed from what was really being done: without the literal confines of adulthood we rode into a vacuum of isolation and extreme physical effort, which rubbed us clean of any notions of being adequately prepared.

When Cody got married in the fall, my mother insisted she come. My sisters, Cody and I tried to plan it so they could drive up from Orange County, stay for a couple of hours and return to her board-and-care home without excessive difficulty for her. It was a gamble—she might need the bathroom, might not feel well, her pulse or oxygen could fall. When she rolled up in her wheelchair, resplendent as the new morning sun, we knew it was the right thing. There would be no second chance—and even though she was not certain of the place or the many people, old friends comforted her for the afternoon. Again, she rose. She was the *doña*, after all.

When the celebration started, Nevada toasted Cody by saying he was his mentor—despite being five years his junior. But I knew what he meant: Cody trusted his intuition to move in the busy streets of L.A. and the equally busy throb of work and love and self that never disappears, only goes underground for the duration of a ten or twelve-hour day. He lived for the joy that outlined so many of his choices—to surf, ride his mountain bike and back-country ski. Nevada loved these things too, loved them before Cody knew them, but he was on the East Coast and it was harder to access them. What he really said and Cody heard this, was I respect your choices. I respect how you've cut your free time from the obligations.

A few days before the wedding, the three of us rode into the Hollywood Hills. We left late and people crowded the twisty roads home from work. I remember the two of them saying we had to pick up the pace; it would get dark soon and we needed to get home. I looked at them and said "I ride like I ride," meaning I could never keep up with them. It was almost dark when we started down the hill. By the flats, it was black. None of us had lights. I worried as only a father can: keep the stray car from their path. A half hour of unsettling darkness. I looked at them when we returned: promise me you'll never do that again. Both of them ride their bikes to work when they are not traveling. In big cities with people on their phones, texting, eating and dozing. I block it from my mind. I block it, thinking as any reasonable person thinks—don't let something into their path.

It was a snake Debby and I wrestled with and one which any conscientious person does—but patterns of risk and reward grow down to meet you and it was crucial they form their own. When Nevada left for college on the Hudson, Debby and I knew that he would root there. Those roots would take him places—to Central America for a summer internship as part of his graduate training in public health and most important, into the arms of his partner and her Costa Rican family. He also went to perfect his Spanish. I remember him holding the cue cards with the nouns on one side and their meanings hidden on the other side. It wasn't long before Cody found his way into that same language and tonight Cody embraced his new bride who understood the long tendrils of her Spanish culture. Her grandmother lived in Chihuahua and sometimes she visited her to listen and learn from the *doña* of her family.

There was a pattern between my sons—a yin and yang of lead and follow—and it alternated through the years. When they were boys, Cody was the blusterer and Nevada the socially adroit, thoughtful one. As they grew, they migrated to their respective middle-selves and in the throes of long nights at the consulting desk, they relied on those attributes of character and each other's counsel. They grew to be an amalgam of each other, yes, but their own men as well. Nevada hewed to task, determined to finish with perfection. When Nevada was still in college, sometimes he would call from the library and Debby and I would tell him to go outside, rest a little, play a little. Cody called from the library too, in a hushed voice. He had entered its hallowed halls for the first time. A double helix of thought and emotion—the twin selves that spread out on this land—as far from home as they could be.

The wedding drew us into many lives, many hands pressed to our palms. We danced until late in a makeshift party building. Next door a young Black woman was celebrating her sixteenth birthday. The two Eritreans trying to shoehorn a livelihood in the city were painting the building when we showed up to decorate it. They offered to come back and clean when we finished. They did not know Cody or Nevada and yet they did not treat us as strangers. At 11:00 p.m. the owner stopped by to ask if we needed anything. He couldn't believe how happy the boys were and how good the place looked. I thanked him for his kindness on Pico Boulevard and watched him trail into the night. Eritrea—some mountains from here. Mountains I would not cross on my bicycle, but mountains that he would not forget in this new country of his. Mountains he would lie on in the brisk L.A. night. Mountains he would retreat to before coming to see us the next morning.

We too retreated before we came back together. Our trip before the wedding was the last time the three of us rode our bikes together before the long ride. We did not know if we could do this together, only that we had tried to train for miles without traffic, for miles without interruption. It was something we thought about for the next seven months, thought about it always because the road would not ask if we were ready. It would only relent to our thin tires crossing its surface. Reluctantly, Debby and I said goodbye and we released them to that light over the ocean and made our way home up Highway 395.

To Hell with the Questions
IV

Distance: 33 miles
Elevation: 2,538 feet
Northern Nevada, 2019

As I had lost something—if time with my sons was something—I had the most to gain from the ride. In my small corner of thought, I believed this time would be like when they were still a daily presence in my life but of course that was fantasy. They were men now. What it did give me was time without interruption. Each of us came with some desire of mind that needed settling. Desires speak with very different voices but the voice beneath our conversation, our time together, was a constant of kinship. We could not have done this otherwise. It was a risk to spend this much time as father and sons—we had changed enormously from the days of living in each other's orbit. Still, I trusted this lost time together might somehow be restored by the physical act of being together. We loved each other and that smooths countless bumps in the road. But it was the other bump that most concerned me—would we find our way back to that easy give and take of years before, not the staccato communication of phone and text? Would we find a renewed depth of feeling, riding together for miles at a time?

Like them, I agreed to pedal into a fog of questions rooted in memory. How do you return to some other time, how do you switch roles to create an extended friendship on two wheels, how do you remake the bones of a relationship? The rivers would not answer, the water we had learned to live without. The endless mountains would only stand, implacably, as we rode into them. For such silence, there was no preparation. I thought of the Japanese poet, Matsuo Bashō, wandering with his knapsack, poems and bread, alone on the path across his island landscape. In all time, travelers have told us not to fear the unknown, to embrace it, but this unknown was found in the two men I loved most. I would pedal with them, I would learn the silence of miles. I would dress at dawn and undress by the moon. And I would sleep in the tent with them. If nothing else, proximity would bear down on us, make us vulnerable to the empty horizon. I tried to share this with them and I tried to hide it like a kid with a new toy. I tried to tell them my only reason for going was to be with them but I don't think they believed me.

At some point, I said to hell with the questions and started to train. It was six weeks out and I filled my panniers with twenty-pound barbells. Forty pounds with water should come close to my riding weight. I picked a pass in the Eastern Sierra and started. About twenty miles to the summit and 2,500 feet of elevation. If I could do this, I reasoned, I could do the ride.

It was cool when I started out of Genoa and slowly I rose up Kingsbury Grade, the homes, ranches and valley which spread to the Pine Nut Range. I remembered earlier times on the grade without weight which still felt hard. But it was a good road to climb—not much traffic, a wide shoulder and mostly respectful drivers.

Once I start pedaling, something quiets inside—my breath becomes a stroke at the end of each downward rhythm, my eyes fasten to the rib lines on the front tire, my hands and shoulders clutch the handlebar to pull the incline beneath me. I listen to what is out there: mosquito, deer, wind ruffling the aspen. I listen to the downshift of a truck, for the tire tread crossing the median grooves. I listen for the restless spoke, the thorn that will cut my tire. I listen for the red-tail hawk who circles, the raven whose shadow follows on all roads. I listen because it is all I can do.

There are two false summits on Daggett Pass and when you climb the first you swear the pines lied to you: you are not done. You must go on. I was sweating; the wind choked my lungs like a thief; the indifferent sage sat at the road edge. It was just the bike and the summit ahead. I kept pedaling, foolishly thinking it would translate to being able to climb the mountains ahead. I was elated at the summit and sipped water, ate an energy bar and then sailed the descent into Genoa. The last five miles through the valley, everything hurt though it had only been a short ride. But I had started. The deadline of departure made me a believer: we were leaving.

Twice a week I found another path in the mountains near home. I lived at elevation so, also foolishly, I believed this would equip me for the trip. Mountains speak their own language. You must assent to their counsel if you go into them. I tried to follow a regimen, all the while wrenching the bike, which broke and broke. It made me think I should have listened to Debby: "Let me get you a new bike." Mine is fine, I told her, but the rear hub was not fine. My bike mechanic gave me his until I returned. It was like floating on a metal wing but shards were falling away. Brakes, shifter, bar grips, chain, seat—all had to be trusted without thought. Thought was not your friend on the bike. You needed complete focus or you woke up somewhere unwanted.

I kept my ornery green fifteen-year-old steel Bianchi Eros out of spite, and my sons kept their carbon fiber bikes. I knew I was finished. Their bikes were like cotton compared to mine. How would I keep up? And what if theirs broke? Again, they researched and talked with bike guys and bought panniers to fit their frames, and said, "What the hell, I'm going with what I have." We were stubborn, a given if you ride more than a day.

I made oatmeal this morning with the last four packets from the ride. It is cold and snowing lightly. Days ago, I took my seventh ride since returning. It was still sunny; it almost seemed like fall would last. The sunlight on Geiger Grade was low; an auburn hue hung over the ridge. At times, there was no one on the grade. I rode alone, into those same questions, but now they were tempered with the distance of past tense. Now they were ephemeral and I was back on the bike training, or trying not to lose what strength I had. I remembered the repeated rides up the grade before we left, the stares at my overweight apparatus. Sometimes I talked to people, told them what I hoped to do. Sometimes I just kept riding. Once, a garrulous middle-aged man rode by, cheering me on and I got a little testy, started pumping harder and caught him at the summit. See that, I thought to myself and refused to believe competition had crawled into the ride. When I shared it with Nevada, he said "We're f—ed!" I laughed because it didn't mean a thing. Of all the things I ride for, to prove myself is not one. The same is true for my sons and Scott and Joe—they ride for pleasure. Riding for other reasons can kill the joy faster than you can say my name. I have friends in tight pants who race, churn the wind and see their peers in the distance. But I am not one who cares a flick about speed for speed's sake. And I'm careful to ride with those who think joy first, speed last. A bike is a place of quiet. A place of being apart from the tinsel of worldly things. Each time I rode, the training became witness to the limits we might find in the Sawtooths, the Cascades, the Coast Range.

I took my bike with me everywhere and rode in between the days and the hours: on the highway to Tonopah in the middle of the state, I parked my car. The sign to Silver Peak read twenty-three miles. I thought I could do it and still get home in time. Time, that ledger we keep in our heads, against which we push and push hoping for middle time, or time without borders. It was May, a gorgeous high desert afternoon. I rode in complete peace, just the wind in my ears. I was completely alone—a car every ten or fifteen minutes. I could see to the southern horizon. There might be a moon out there, might be other places. The globe mallow at the road side bobbed in the light wind. I remembered teaching poetry in the lithium mine town, the school a first stop for green teachers. One of my students was crying when I returned to class after school. Her teacher excoriated her for asking a question without raising her hand. I looked at him and could not understand. "I asked her to speak," and I moved between them until she calmed. That day, I learned how children come so easily to a thing like poetry and how hard it is to return after such sorrow.

I kept riding; the more I pedaled the easier it became; the road behind me fell away. I could barely see my car in the distance. It felt like I was free of the physical world. At the summit, I stopped and looked at my phone—I needed to head back. The first shift at the mine would end soon and I wanted to avoid the trucks and cars heading home to Tonopah. I wanted to keep riding, wanted to ride into Silver Peak and see the eyes of the students again. I did not want to return to mother time. There are a handful of days when you can be completely present on a bike and I was. I thought about riding until dark, riding under the stars in the desert. A sight you cannot describe. No light pollution, no sound, just the whoosh of the wheel against the road. When my neighbor and I rode through the Utah desert, I watched those stars. It was two-thirty in the morning, every constellation in the northern hemisphere overhead. I could see the stars in back of stars and knew that something other than us was out there. That is why I wanted to keep going. There were so many paths to ride in this part of the desert. So many I had yet to try.

On the way back to my car the men drove into the opposite lane to give me a wide berth. They were speeding home but conscientious. These things matter on two wheels. I imagined they thought it was a miracle of perception—a bicycle on their isolated two-lane highway to home. And maybe they thought something altogether different, a distraction, an outline against the mountain. I put my clothes in the car, loaded the bike in the back and started the drive home. A calm had come over me. I needed nothing as I watched the light play across the desert. The mountains were seething and bold, the bitterbrush gathered at their heels. The riverbeds were quiet, no water to fill them until the next season and then only for hours. A flash flood of brown water had left its shawl on the road. But this is what water looks like in the desert. It has no place of origin save the sky. It comes down to start a motion of gravel and sand. It comes into to a place with force and just as quickly, it leaves. It leaves gutters filled with debris and stones and glass. The makeshift particles of something washed away. Something once held in place. Something without a home.

My sons and I have ridden these roads for decades. Rarely is there water to define them. Rarely is there the outline of trees. Rarely is the desert more than it appears, except of course that it is always more than it appears. We do not take water for granted. Water is underground here. In the states we would ride into, we could see it, smell it and give thanks for it. But seeing this landscape daily, seeing its acrid outline, let us know how important liquid in the streambed was. We hoped to find water everywhere on our ride. We hoped the water would be a reward for hours in these middle desert mountains.

The light grew into softer and softer hues of brown until the mountains finally gave way to the dusk. And I put my bike in the garage, my clothes in a bag upstairs. I tried to calculate how far I had ridden. It didn't matter. The distance wasn't important. The distance would come. Being in the saddle was its own gift. Slowly, I turned from preparation to enjoyment. An hour or two on the bike was the time I gave to the wind. In a few more weeks, the wind would return that time. Although we could not know what was really needed in those first few days outside of Portland, the wind would follow, prescient traveler, at our side.

On Hayden Mountain Summit
V

Distance: 12 miles up Geiger Grade, over and over
Elevation: 2,300 feet
Northern Nevada, 2019

We were down to weeks. We couldn't let go of the list that grew every morning when we awoke to the fear of not having what was needed. We called, texted and compared notes from other bike gurus. They made suggestions—get this pump or that snack bag. You'll need special lights, a waterproof sack for the sleeping bag. What bike shorts are you using? Who will bring extra tires, tubes and food? Did you get your Tenkara rod and flies? Who has a patch kit? We'll have to get stove gas in Portland. I have first aid, duct tape, extra bike tools. Despite having no room in my panniers, I stuffed my paints, watercolor postcards and a small journal into them. Every time I thought I was close, the list slipped away from me. I still couldn't get the derailleurs to shift properly and needed my bars taped. I kept wondering if the old bike would hold up. I kept thinking my stubborn insistence would get the best of me and I would break down long into the trip—the one whose bike would fail. I tired my poor bike mechanic just walking into his shop. He'd look at me and ask, "What is it?" and I tried to humor him, but there isn't humor in a broken bike. There was only my desperation disguised as impatience, and I did not know how to assuage his concern. He worked and worked on it—replaced most of its moving parts and assured me it would be fine. I had to trust him, I had to trust his endless savvy around spokes and hubs and bearings. He was not worried; he didn't have a doubt the old bike would hold up. So he put two new tires on, mounted a pump, ordered the snack bag, the lights and kept smiling. In the end, my trips to his shop became something of a ritual. I needed his calm, his earthy wisdom. He had worked on bikes for over two decades, had the most unorthodox store in the region: old bikes, retro bikes, tandems and dozens of aging touring bikes. He still rode in the BMX competition—a big man—and led a team at the local track. He had some cred in the bike world. Opinionated, happy-go-lucky and real. The kind of man I gravitated to. For years his sister sat on the couch in his shop watching him. She was developmentally disabled but as sweet a woman as I have met. I said "Hi" to her on every visit and asked about her brother. She always gave him grief in the loving way family members can do. She was the anchor to many things in his life—and to his patrons. Not tolerated but loved for who she was— the faithful sister who believed in him. If you didn't like the bike boxes that lined the path to the counter, the gear clusters on the glass shelves, the dusty frames in various states of disrepair, you just didn't go in. You didn't ask why things were in disarray; this was his way of being altogether present in the low-tech world of two wheels.

When I last went into the store before the ride he had begrudgingly accepted the advent of electric bikes—one of his customers loved the fact that they could glide up a hill but he thought it was damning, a disgrace to bikes and his livelihood. Commerce dragged him into the twenty-first century, but his VW Bus remained firmly planted in the one before it. This is what happens when you decide to leave on a journey: you must find a few people who will suspend disbelief to join you in believing such a thing is possible. You must search them out before beginning because you will need them and I needed him. His presence became a cyclical force in my life. As I'd start to prepare for a ride (this was one of many), he would roll his eyes and ask again, "How can I help?" What he helped with was not questioning why this was important. He accepted such things and honored them with his attention to detail. He made sure every part of that bike was ready like it was his own. I promised myself to text him from an Idaho summit knowing nothing would make him feel better.

I called my mother and told her we were leaving the next day. She was happy for us but still did not understand why we wanted to do such a thing. Her ninetieth birthday was coming up. I apologized in advance for missing it but promised I'd call from the road. Silently, I promised to be there if anything happened in the interim. She came first to each of us—and we would return in a minute if needed. I told my sisters not to worry. They could reach me on the phone for most of the journey. I told myself there was no better time and asked the night sky before we left to watch over her, to keep her close while we were gone. In some maternal way, she was letting go of us, much as I would learn to let go of any notion of permanence.

Nevada was worried about Cody and I starting the ride without him. He could not get off work until we were in Bend—a week after beginning in Portland. It didn't matter when he joined us. I only wanted him to experience that first day; to know the exhilaration of starting on something so unorthodox as this. We talked on the phone, assured him we had everything we needed. He just had to show up with his bike and camping gear. Somehow those words seemed hollow in far-away New York. Somehow they seemed inadequate. He was struggling with how to keep on at his current job—a lot of pressure and expectation. All we could do was acknowledge his concern: once on the bike that other life would disappear. Or maybe that's what we told ourselves. None of us really knew what was ahead. It didn't matter; he wanted to be with us and we held his place close, as if he was with us.

Scott sent a last text from abroad: "Highway 20 looks a little bakey"—shorthand for hot and dry— "maybe go north out of Bend." This would mean we would miss the roadhouse with the poetic marquee. Scott was ever the realist and we needed that. In the days to come, heat would bend Cody and me to the pavement, draw a circle around our backs and slow us to a crawl. Scott brought perspective to the road—he had ridden many long journeys and was anxious to join us on ours. He and his wife were cycling in Western Europe, which could not have been more different than the Intermountain

West. He also told us Joe would be joining us, his friend from the university. I trusted Scott implicitly—his friends, judgment and knowledge of the natural world into which we were pedaling. If Joe was coming, he would bring something large to the party. Part of leaving what you know is respite from the ordinary. Part is the thing you cannot fully articulate—something lies ahead. In a few short days, Joe reached deep into those things we could not say.

I packed the car with extra parts and tools and put my bike on the rack. In a day, Debby, Laurie and I would leave for the airport to pick up Cody, who was flying into Reno with his bike. My sons and I had stopped training and reached the end of preparation. It was a relief—a punctuation mark in the months of anticipation. Whatever we lacked we would address on the road. There wasn't a way forward without some discomfort. I walked into the house and told Debby I was ready. She had been patient with the months of tedium and graciously agreed to drive us to our first stop—Portland. It was time to let go. There was nothing more we could do.

Cody flew in at 9 a.m. He was excited. His bike arrived in the case without any problems. We stuffed his duffle bag and bike case in the back of the Jeep and started north on Highway 395. I wanted to exhale, wanted to find another way to be on the highway for the day's drive. Heading out of Reno, the fields opened to piñon and juniper. When we turned out of Susanville, the two-lane stretched for miles without cars and interruption. It was a place to begin. I looked at Cody and jokingly said, "Maybe we should start here." We passed lakes and mountains and climbed ridges. It foreshadowed the ride, and we were eager to be doing what we had prepared for. In Canby we stopped at the fairgrounds. It was bucolic, empty but for the intrepid bicyclists about to eat on the lawn. Cody and I tried not to speak about the ride. We wanted to be present. Laurie was happy to be with us and it made Debby happy to have someone along for the drive home from Portland.

Laurie is a woman who has been tested; she doesn't ask why getting up each day is a gift. She lives on the heels of what has been lost—a two-time breast cancer survivor. She loves her three children, her health and her drums. Music keeps her close to the rim of satisfaction. And she has learned how to give it away—to use music like a wing into the lives of others. I think of her as a woman unwilling to let a single day pass without stretching it as far as it will go. She kept us grounded as the road unfolded to the horizon.

On Hayden Mountain Summit, we stopped for a drink. There were plants, stunted, in small containers. There was a man sitting outside the store. He said they had two feet of snow the night before. This elevation—4,705—seemed so low, but it was a harbinger of weather to come. Snow was not on our graph and we did not have clothes for real cold. We would ride if the clouds let us through. Snow made us small, ephemeral, like dust.

The man reminded me of the poet Hayden Carruth sitting on his stoop in upstate New York when I used to visit. This would be a place where Hayden would settle. And my wife, in her magnanimous mischief, brought him along. She made t-shirts with an inverted line from his poem, "Paragraph 25": "ivy league to cavalier, to smart ass— never who I was." The stanza continues with "Say it plain." She did this out of fealty, what someone does who loves a poet. I have recited those lines innumerable times. They have kept me grounded—never take yourself or your art too seriously. Leaving on this ride, it was the most important line to remember. This is nothing more than a pedal into the West. It is not groundbreaking, is not heart-rending. It is only a wade into a big, lost river. You must not pretend it is anything more. To do so, would be to tempt invective—it would take every bit of good luck to get the five of us in and out of this West so big. Whether my sons and Scott and Joe felt any of this I cannot say, but I did. I had to pay attention to what the poet intimated: the road is not yours. You must set upon it with care. Treat it as if it were something given, something earned. Treat it as if you were on it for the first time. The rattles of regard will come soon enough— speeding cars, log trucks and people. I knew this and I think my companions did too. But some things cannot be shared. They will wither when spoken.

Above the poet's words on the t-shirt was the motto we had hoped to find on Highway 20 in hottest central Oregon: "Where the bacon is red and the poems are hard." We promised Scott and Joe it was a real place and it became so. I doubt the roadhouse will ever see the gray t-shirts, but I still want to see it.

We arrived at Debby's cousin's in late afternoon and schlepped our bike stuff into his garage and heaved a sigh of relief. We had made it to the destination, a path into the West that in a day would become real. Debby's cousin, Rob and his wife, Christy, put out a huge spread and we snacked and drank and talked for most of the night. I think Rob wanted to come with us. I would have welcomed his gracious spirit. Cody and I knew we would be tested—Rob's peaceful demeanor would be welcome after the first hundred miles in the saddle.

The next morning we put Cody's bike together, loaded it onto my rack and laid everything else out on the garage floor. There was more bicycle apparatus than I had ever seen.

It looked like we were having a yard sale for two-wheelers from another country—the country of what might be necessary. Rob came out of the house and saw the mass of equipment: "Are you sure you have everything?" he half-joked. Cody and I steadied ourselves with the assurance that we had most of what we needed. Portland was sunny and after we double-checked for any missing things, we left for downtown. I couldn't resist a return to Powell's Bookstore. It's probably a good thing I don't live there—I would have to surrender to the poetry section as a clerk. But I did allow for one purchase— the *Cosmic Canticle* by Ernesto Cardenal, Nicaragua's late and best-known poet after Rubén Darío. In all the chaos on the ground when Debby and I worked briefly in Managua, his voice was the anchor, the refuge for a country running from its former liberator.

In the Rose Gardens, there were thousands of blossoms, every color and shape. There was even a black rose—something I had never seen. The gardens are terraced on the hills above Portland. We could see the Cascades we would ride into and north into the city. It is a place of calm, of sanctuary for the visitors who come from all points. Like us, they walked the grassy rows. The soil is enriched beyond any soil in our mountain home. The roses grow as if they could take flight. They mushroom up from the ground, hybrids and floral prints that might have been painted. The roses also have the rain water that feeds them year-round and keeps them returning each spring. I kept thinking of the roses that night, kept hoping they might accompany us when we started. Not the physical roses, but the image of wild color and fragrance just beyond our reach, on the edge of perception. A floral river beside us.

The Tillamook Ice Cream Takedown
VI

Distance: 55 miles
Elevation: 2,707 feet
Portland, Oregon, 2019

Rob stood in the morning light, sipping coffee. He asked how I felt. "Ready," I said.

Yesterday, Cody asked me the same question. I flippantly answered, "I've been ready since we left for Portland."

"Noted—"

Rob poured me a cup and I sat down at the kitchen island. No more preparation, no more waiting. In a few hours, Cody and I would be pedaling. I hugged Rob goodbye as he left for work and stood in the window light until Cody came downstairs.

"This is it, Pops."

"Yep, it is."

I quickly realized there was never any getting ready for the day of departure. Debby and Laurie dropped us off at a gas station in Banks, outside of Portland. We didn't want to straddle the freeway on our first day. It took us about twenty minutes to load the panniers, sleeping bags, food and water on the bikes. We turned, hugged, kissed them, and rode off. About a hundred yards later I realized I left my lights in the car. Frantically, I waved and rode in their direction to head them off. Debby stopped and I retrieved them from the wheel well in the trunk.

The morning was strangely calm. Miles of hayfields just minutes from the city. It seemed like we were riding into the middle of the country, not western Oregon. It was green everywhere, so unlike the brown high desert of home. The air was filled with ocean moisture and there was no wind. We had found the right way to start. My bike felt good—nothing was pushing me right or left. The weight was there but it was not overwhelming. Cody's bike looked like it was on a rail and he was happy to be in the quiet of this rural place. Highway Six connects Portland to the coast and we were headed for a campsite south of Tillamook. By the time we hit the Coast Range, the sun was overhead. Our first climb of many—and we did not yet know the muscles that tightened with each successive pass. Cody began to pull away. He rode in a higher gear—much like Nevada when he joined us. I couldn't pedal that fast, but he was never out of sight, or if so, not for long. When I arrived at the summit, he was waiting. There were some kids in a car, smoking, wanting to find a place to get away. A whiff of pot swirled around the parking lot. Cody and I sat on the retaining wall, sipping water and eating the first of dozens of energy bars. Welcome to Oregon, I thought. The day before, in downtown, the city had been filled with pedestrians as the sun was out. A great omen for a city in the Pacific Northwest.

We felt good—the pass wasn't that difficult. Naively, I imagined the training had helped, that I was close to being ready for the trip. All that preparation—what I thought I could do—had yet to be shown. The mountains claim us quietly. They help us to lay down our bloated notions of preparation. It would take weeks before we understood: what you perceive to be difficult, it will change with each passage up and down the mountain's spine.

Cody pointed to a dirt road off the highway. There was a river down below with a bridge. We sat in the sun and ate lunch. A motorcyclist pulled in to rest. The first biker of many who became a motorized shadow to our journey. I never would have imagined such proximity between their bikes and ours, but being exposed draws you together. Everywhere we stopped they were curious and likable. They became another perspective on this black road across the West. I walked down to the water, washed my face and dripped my bandana into the cold. It felt good on my neck, which was getting red. The water ran slowly; I couldn't see any fish but it was still early—perhaps they had not spawned. The motorcyclist almost got stuck trying to turn around and go up the hill to the highway. Then we were by the water, alone and lying in sunlight.

This is what I had left for. This is what I hoped to find. It takes very little to calm a traveler in the natural world. The threshold was a riverbed, the stones small orbs against my feet. I started to drift off and Cody said we should get going. I pushed my bike to the highway and we started again, mostly downhill to the coast—which, deceptively, made the ride easy. We averaged 10-15 miles per hour, unthinkable in the mountains and pedaled into a wilderness of green and wet and flowers. A haiku for the roadside:

Green, white, brown; donkeys
in the yarrow. A fawn
in the stream of leaves.

My habit became the count of syllabic lines—five, seven, five— sometimes less. The haiku masters were less constricted by form than image. If the first line held four syllables but was breathtaking, it stayed. Translation usually made that leap even harder. My rudimentary culling of syllabic notes from the land was all I needed. I could not go far without seeing another image. It was more than a distraction; it was a record of light and color and smell. I didn't intend to write on the bicycle. In fact, I had hoped to let go of words, having just finished a book of essays. But the perception of such floral hints would not leave and as we coasted down the summit every ravine was bathed in the afternoon light. The forest on either side of the highway was gorged with deciduous trees and evergreens. It had not been cut for some time and because of the moisture, almost all roads up and out of the canyon were dark with undergrowth. In just a few short hours we had been transplanted to a landscape unlike our own—a fertile ground, a place of florid density.

Foxglove, larkspur, daisy,
what halo of color have I
come to lie in?

Towards the coast the wind picked up. The fog was right on the ridge coming into Tillamook. We put on our windbreakers, the bikes slowed, and we wove along the road edge for the last ten miles into Tillamook. I had called my good friend Dave Lee—Utah's finest poet—now retired in Seaside an hour to the north. I had hoped to have dinner with him and his wife, Jan, that night. At the stop light in downtown Tillamook, I called again—"Let's go to the Mexican place. Can you come to the campground and pick us up?" I was thrilled that Cody was going to meet them. Dave is unlike most poets—he has an accessible, narrative style suffused with a depth of knowledge and candor that makes him widely read and deeply respected.

Cody and I wrestled with where to camp. To keep our pace of sixty-plus miles a day, we chose a site ten miles south for the first night. But we could not get back in time for dinner. And then I looked down—my pump was missing. I either dropped it on the ride into Tillamook or left it in the car. We rode into town and found a Fred Myer store, hoping they might have a bike pump. I got lucky and found an even better pump and then bought ten dollars of quarters to shower at the camp site just outside of town. When we rode into the camp along the estuary it was almost empty. We registered with the woman that was living in her trailer for the summer. She told us to fill out two forms. Cody told her we were father and son. She said, "You look the same age." We doubted her but laughed just the same. There was grass throughout the site and it wrapped around the waterway leading to the ocean. I imagined we would wake to shore birds. Our first night would be peaceful.

As soon became his practice, Cody set up the tent and I fumbled in my bags for a change of clothes. We made some tea and snacked in the waning sun. I hoped the fog stayed at a distance. Dave and Jan pulled up in their red Toyota Prius. "He just does this" he said to Jan, getting out of the car.

The Mexican place was hidden on a backstreet—if any place can be hidden in Tillamook. This, too, suddenly felt like home—the Spanish in the background, the smell of carnitas from the kitchen, the families after work. Cody and I ordered more tacos than we could eat; he finished my plate and still we wondered when hunger would return. Dave and Jan were the welcoming people that strangers hope to meet—without pretense, puff, or circumstance—despite having returned from immersing himself in Shakespeare's collected works—a birthday gift from Jan—in Spain a week earlier. This was maybe his third or fourth careful reading of the master. More than I will have read by life's end. Dave was trying to reconcile his mind with the serious flight from civil discourse and failed leadership in our country. Spain had its faults and they, too, were not far from a dark past but after three months abroad, both of them were in culture shock.

How they found their way down Highway 101 to meet us for Mexican cooking I will not know, only that kinship drew them in. Kindred spirits in the far fog of the Oregon Coast. They were kind enough to drive us to the Tillamook Creamery for some real ice cream and, sufficiently bloated, dropped us at our perch in the grass. I said goodbye to my friends and hoped not much time would pass before we would see him again. But poets wander and he, with books coming out and children on both coasts, has a full life. It would be months before I heard his voice again.

What we didn't tell Dave and Jan followed us into the next day: our ride became ten miles longer because we had chosen to sleep in town. We imagined it would be all right to go a little farther the next day. So much for planning; the graph became fluid. It was just the two of us—we could manage a small change in the itinerary. Besides, the coast road was mostly level—or so we believed.

We put the food away, tucked the panniers under the tent and settled in for the night. Fog would crowd the moon out before long. I hadn't been to sleep by 9 p.m. in a year, but the moonrise became the hour of lying down. I was anxious to hear the birds, the other animals that might move in the dark. Only a few others joined us in the campground. It was preternaturally still. I stacked my long johns to make a pillow and said goodnight to Cody, the first day almost eclipsed by moonlight. I thought of Bashō again, alone, by the side of a road in rural Japan with stars overhead, and over four centuries later, those same stars were over mine. I wanted to capture them in a painting, wanted to record the celestial orbit of something greater than us. I listened carefully for Bashō—might he be walking into this century? I listened for the haiku to end the day. All that came was silence. The endless, dark swallow of night.

The Raven at My Back
VII

Distance: 74 miles
Elevation: 3,400 feet
Tillamook, Oregon, 2019

I awoke to the taste of salt in my mouth and moisture inside the tent flaps. Everything was wet. I couldn't see as far as the bathroom. This is what it felt like to be with fog: a damp light obscured the sun. The grass faded into gray. There was no plain in the landscape, no horizon to seek out. All details faded to a moist lens, a lens I had not seen coming from the arid Great Basin. I tried to remember being wet as a condition of living; I could not. It had escaped me after years in the dry land. It had left my hands, my feet, long ago. They were whorls of skin without this gray topography. Slowly, I had moved into a morning of dampness.

Cody found the coffee filter and fired up the gas stove—our first fire of the trip. I heard the sizzle from the valve. In a few minutes he handed me a plastic cup filled with dark coffee. Somehow he had managed to bring real java. I sat in the fog and sun trying to name what we had started. He made oatmeal and peanut butter, our last protein for the morning. I was stiff but not overly so. We laid out the tent on the picnic table and went to wash up. The morning ritual had begun. The clock started: we rose by sunlight and tried to find every last bit of strength until it set. I packed my bike and tried to keep the seat and sleeping bag dry. We rinsed the dishes and put them in Cody's front pannier. He carried the cooking utensils and I had the extra food. We said goodbye to the camp host and rode back to Tillamook. I expected that the morning would be calm, a slow pedal down the coast.

We got about twenty miles out and came to a long stretch of sand. There was a man with a tandem recumbent bicycle gathering sea water in five-gallon buckets to *pedal* back to Portland. His wife was lying on the beach. I had never seen such a bike and could not imagine pedaling that much weight back to the city. He wanted the salt water to use at home. Cody and I looked at each other as if to ask, is there a shortage of salt in Portland? We wrote it off to our first encounter with the highway outliers. He was happy enough. Maybe pedaling salt water for three days kept him fit, who knows? A short while later, I punctured my front tire. Thankfully we had purchased the pump the night before. It only took a few minutes and we were on our way again. We had lunch in Pacific City. A part of me wanted to stay there. The sun was everywhere, and hot. We ate in front of a coffee house and filled our water bottles for the next twenty miles. Each stop became a mark in the day, a gathering of necessities yes, but also a way to breathe in the specific landscape. We were relatively clean and untouched by the road. The little things that surface after miles were hidden from view: the stillness, the rhythm, the highway opening before us.

Cody was ahead of me and reading the route from his phone. He found a detour to get off the main highway south and out of the traffic. In Neskowin we took Slab Creek Road to Otis, about six miles and an additional 660 feet of elevation. Nothing really to fret over. The dense growth was so thick that light barely shown through. Slab Creek wasn't visible in the canyon below. It was almost a one-lane road. We didn't see a car the whole time. Our words tapered off in the dark green light. My body started to stiffen. I could feel it inching up from my legs. I ignored it and stood on my pedals, pushed into the ferns of this canyon, imagined my legs running above the creek as preparation for what was to come. What we could not yet see. What the road would take from us. My legs wore down to posts. I could feel the oxygen leaving me. I understood then this was the bargain you set yourself against. This was how a canyon of sanctuary tormented you with physical effort. This was how it undid your rhythm. This was how you came to accept what the road took from you. I looked for Cody. He was up ahead, climbing into the green mist of light and I thought his torso was like the boy who used to be at home but now he was a wind of strength on a carbon wing. He sliced the air like a sail. And I let him go into that fern-draped light. This was the wedge of effort—my legs were coming to a stillness. I wanted to tell him to stop but could not. I tried again to right my wheel, to turn into the mountain so that what little momentum might come from the zig-zag across the one lane might propel me to ride on, might stem my stiffened limbs, might move me out of the fog. Slab Creek became the script for what was ahead: the burning regimen of riding the mountain flanks. I turned up the switchback, exhausted and not knowing how much farther we had to go, dropped my bike and lay on the pavement. I lay there looking up through the pine needles until Cody returned to ask if something was wrong? Did something break on the bike? "Just need to rest," I muttered.

"Take as much time as you need."

This was a helluva way to start—I'd never finish the ride, let alone get to the campground that night. I pulled my bike up from the asphalt and got back on. Cody was as patient as the evergreens overhead. I fought to the summit and into Lincoln City. I looked at him and half-seriously asked "Were you trying to kill your old man, you motherf—er?" That pretty much ended the calm of Cody's 'hella' detour (our slang for going off the beaten path).

He was unflappable: "What do you need, Pops? Get you some ice cream?" We spotted a convenience store and bought an ice cream bar, a protein drink and coconut water. I consumed them and we rode on. The next twenty miles to Beverly Beach State Park were beautiful. It was late in the afternoon. There was a sea breeze and for the most part, the highway was level and we were able to do seventeen miles an hour. Cody found another four-mile stretch of single-lane road on the ridge above the water. By then, the food had helped and I was flush with adrenalin. The sun was setting at our back. Cody turned and saw a raven and he snapped a photo from his phone. The raven became the bird that tracked our path from that day forward. Floating the thermals of the ocean cliff, the carrion bird became a symbol—not just of beauty but of empty unease as well. The scavenger of what we could and could not see. A last hill into the campground and then I exhaled. With all of the furious pedaling we had arrived, not quite initiates yet, but as travelers in a suddenly serene landscape. The grassy camp sites were filled with hikers, touring bikes and tents. To our left a trucker sipped his coffee next to his bike, free from the cab and highway at last. Toward the north end of the area, there was another couple touring from Armagh, Northern Ireland. They had flown here to ride the coastal highway to San Francisco. And then, two young women walked in, twenty-five miles from Lincoln City. Somehow, we had gathered on this knoll—disparate travelers yoked together by the open road.

I took a shower in the camp washroom below our site and Cody left for the store to find more protein for the mac and cheese. I tried to write in my journal. My thoughts wandered. If I could have written in longhand, I would have. Instead, a haiku from the road south:

Down the coast, over
the estuaries, a raven
at my back

Our second night in camp. Cody surprised me with red licorice, bacon and eggs from the store. Suddenly the mac and cheese became something to be cherished, hot and salted with bacon bits and cheddar cheese. After all the miles, the pasta soothed what was left of the day. It pushed the sweat and tumult of Slab Creek into the recesses. I thanked Cody again, not just for putting up with me but for making the dinner, the morning coffee, the daylight last.

"I feel ya' Pops. There's going to be days when it's time to lie down."

"I guess. Sometimes you think it will go as you planned. And then you find out. Guess you saw just how ready I was."

"You knew what to do. You knew it was time to stop."

We put most of the food in our panniers and hoped the rodents found other camps to raid. I crawled into the tent and stacked my long johns for a pillow, the perfect complement to weary eyes. This is what I couldn't explain to others when I said I wanted to ride. This is what I couldn't share: out of exhaustion comes resolve and then calm. Nothing intended, nothing spoken. A consequence of miles, of repetition.

A Breath Not Easily Taken
VIII

Distance: 70 miles
Elevation: 2,661 feet
Newport, Oregon, 2019

The raccoons left the crackers on the picnic table. The sun was hidden in fog above the ocean and the other campers were stirring. Our trucker friend loaded his bike and pedaled away in hiking boots. The hikers left to push further south. Cody made bacon and eggs, and I ate three of them. I never imagined hunger could be so tangible; every bite of those eggs was delicious. We cleaned up and packed our bikes, turned on the lights and zigzagged along the back roads through Newport to get to Highway 20, the beginning of the infamous *Fly Highway*. It wasn't romantic; it wasn't even quiet. People were on their way to work, log trucks towered over us, and we couldn't hear each other. Up the canyon, we were little more than bark on the roadside. This is when I started to chant my hymn—bubble of light—so that, without him knowing, Cody would be surrounded in this imaginary light, much as Nevada and Scott and Joe would be when they joined us. It was the only way I could be alongside the weight of diesel rigs with logs stretched high above the twin axles. It was the only way I could live in fear and not fear. Bubble of light, I said to myself, over and over so that it became a mantra for the few feet given to us on the road edge. It became a place of relative distance—enough to provide passage, which was all that was needed. One more note in the long epigraph to my sons— there is obvious danger out there but we move through it. We move beside it. We move into the morning without hesitation.

We rode into Toledo for a respite from the log trucks. A logging town at the far end of Yaquina Bay, this watershed extends fifty-nine miles from the Coast Range to Newport. We were not prepared for its quiet slough, its meandering thread of salt and fresh water. High above the piles of wood waiting for the mill, the fog rose in puffs of broken light. The tide was out; a few boats meandered in the estuary. A thousand years Before Christ, the Yakon clan lived in this valley. Long before any notion of bridges and mill saws, the estuary was home to migrating birds and waterfowl. We followed the river through the hot day ahead. This river was the shadow river we took inside ourselves to start up the mountain. This river became the water we crossed and re-crossed on two-lanes over many passes. And it ran without instructions to this place in the fog of Toledo. We swallowed its wet song for days.

After another stretch of Highway 20 Cody found a parallel road to the base of the Coast Range. Crystal Creek Loop was not a hella detour but rather a peaceful one, and we followed the stream through the morning sun. There had been a fire and the stumps climbed the canyon walls. The slash piles were stacked for burning. We were in logging country. This is how people made their living. What more was there to do? It was rural, miles from a city, and if you liked the calm of the country it was home. There weren't more than ten houses on the long stretch of two-lane road. I knew why these people lived here. It was the same reason we lived on the side of a mountain— respite from a busy place. An unobstructed view. A way forward to the horizon. I'm not foolish enough to believe that everyone can live like this but it is a living I choose. It settles in the way this bike ride settles—without fanfare, without interruption.

After the first two days I thought we were doing pretty well. A little soreness but nothing to speak of. Only the hunger never stopped. No matter what we ate, it was always time to eat again. When we were in Tillamook, we had bought groceries at the Fred

Myer—bagels, peanut butter, honey, nuts and cookies. We had eaten the bagels with peanut butter for lunch both days and today, following Crystal Creek, I was looking forward to finding a rest stop. Slowly the sun rose overhead. The creek bed was bucolic with ribbons of sunlight from the south. We snaked around the canyon and came out once again on Highway 20—out of the city in a pine forest. There was a bus stop on an auxiliary road just before we started up the grade, and we paused. The temperature was about seventy degrees. Cody was out of water, but there was a farmer on his tractor when we arrived, and Cody walked up to the farmer's house. In a few minutes he came back with ice water in his bottles. I made a blueberry bagel sandwich for us and we ate slowly. It was going to get hotter. I walked up to the farmer's house. He and his wife were inside with their puppy. He was happy to fill my bottle too. The ice water was like rain going down my throat. I asked about fishing Crystal Creek. He said his son was a guide but now was not the time. "Later in the year," he motioned. "Salmon aren't running yet." Good people. The kind you wanted to be your neighbors. We must have looked like we parachuted in—funny clothes, sweaty from the ride, yet it didn't matter. He knew why we were out there—he would have joined us if he could. It wasn't for the exercise or the distraction; it was for the long breath in the saddle, the one that comes after days and days of riding through small places like this. A breath not easily taken.

We left for the highway to the summit. The road did not provide much shelter from the sun. I thought this would be a relatively easy climb—we had crossed the Coast Range two days earlier. But it had been cooler then and this was mostly uphill, not downhill like the road out of Portland. After a mile I felt the heat squarely on my back, my neck. This was going to burn. I looked up to see if Cody had stopped but had to mostly keep my head down, pulling against the bars. I poured water on my face and was thankful to not know how hot it was. I guessed in the high-seventies but we were only at the beginning of the incline. The traffic had thinned to the occasional log truck and locals. The sun was glinting off the guard rail like an unwanted companion. I turned my head and pushed the pedal down, focused on the few feet before me. Suddenly the trip broke open into thirds—the calm of the first day, the physical test of the second day, and the heat of today. Was this what was ahead—the rolling unknown? I didn't know if I'd make it to the crest. I stopped and looked up again. Cody was in the distance, patient, waiting. He soaked his bandana under his helmet, trying to keep cool. I worried this intense heat might stop us miles from the ocean and Corvallis was still four hours away—we had to pour water down. If we ran out, so be it. I didn't know. He didn't know. I rode another hundred yards, leaned my bike against the guard rail. We found some shade but didn't say much. The sun was its wearying self; speech seemed superfluous. "We gonna be all right?" he said. I nodded, hoping that was true. The heat didn't care, didn't listen to what we thought. It bore down, made us choose—which way, up or to the coast?

If you want this, you must give what you didn't know was inside. You must pour yourself into the bike, not separated, not apart, but one element, steady, in a rhythm, without distraction. You must disguise pain, pretend it does not exist. You must put the heat in a room where the cold lies and let it suffer like you are suffering now. You must disengage from the mountain because in this heat the mountain will eat you.

I climbed back on to start again, the only refuge I knew. To start again in the sweat and stiffness of midday. There was no wind, only the occasional car and the two of us, leaves on the roadside. We had no position, we took what little space we could, dodging the shards of glass below, the errant bolts from rims, the gum wrappers that eluded small hands. We were like debris—without knowledge of what lay ahead. I rode until the guard rail was in the shade of a pine. Cody was ahead. Intuitively, he knew I would rest when I needed to. He needed no explanation when I caught up with him—"You do you," he said, recalling those same words spoken when we rode in the Santa Monica Mountains.

Now—four months later as we pedaled in this hot air—those same mountains were on fire. A flame so large it consumed hillsides and houses and everything in its maw. How is it we rode through that scrub forest just months earlier and never imagined such infernal heat? That fire would consume that dry landscape was an eerie reminder we were not important. The natural world was much larger, would last beyond this time and would take many things with it. It would be days before we rode into the Sawtooths where avalanches uprooted trees and guardrails, but every mile of the highway we understood: you were small, insignificant in this place. The mountains and forests belong to another map, a map of reckoning that we cannot fully comprehend. It is beyond our temporal knowledge, this register of the physical world. Every day I read the science that dispels our truth and recall the ancient Chinese master, Tu Fu, from "Clear After Rain":

> Once dry, these wildflowers bend and, there
> where the wind is sweeping, fall.

There was no wind on Highway 20. The sun was at our backs. I pedaled another mile and stopped. More water on my face and head. Cody squirted the bandana on his neck and head but I couldn't keep cloth around my head. The heat was excessive—maybe 90 degrees. Four miles to the summit. I looked at the guard rail to my right, tried to keep enough distance and pedaled slow, constant strokes. The cars and log trucks blurred what little I could see out of my peripheral vision. There was no other route, only up. This was the third day, the real test of my limits. Would I last, would Cody be all right with my stops, my water breaks? Of course I had little choice. All I could do was push on. The rhythm of two wheels up the mountain. At times, my bike seemed to crawl and the mile markers were no closer. I was lost in the orbit of exertion.

When I looked up, sometimes I saw Cody, sometimes he was gone. But I never worried about him. He waited for me—made sure I was doing all right. We needed that give and take—"Everything okay on the bike? Enough water? Need a chew?" It became a dialogue of reflection. The things that were said and not said: "You going to get there Pops?" And then—"You sure as hell are."

"You going to wait for me Cody? Of course you are." We squandered vanity in the heat and occasional dust from the passing cars. The log trucks tilting the curves. We believed in what was ahead.

At the summit—words I didn't believe I'd say. Somehow the road let us into to its confidence, measured what was left in our frames and permitted passage. I had no thought, could not say what we had ridden, could only lean into the pine needles and dust of the road. We laid the bikes in a turnout and sipped from our bottles. It was 95 degrees and just out of sight, coming up the other side of the Coast Range, was a bicyclist towing a trailer. He was on a mountain bike, and it looked as if he had tied, roped, and wedged his entire belongings on the bike and trailer. *Inside* the trailer was a sixty-pound pit bull—unbelievably quiet, given the confined space. In the milk carton basket on his bike was a Coleman Stove, a coffee pot, a shovel and gallons of water. It had to have been over a hundred pounds. How he pedaled up that mountain I will not know. He was nonchalant; "It wasn't bad. But I lost my wallet and money in Corvallis. Going to the coast for a few weeks to camp." He was fortunate—it was downhill from there and he might make it if his rig held up. The frame member holding the trailer to the bike was inches from the ground. One bump and it would collapse, but he probably knew that. I think he had done this before. I think he lived on the road. His dog was his partner. And he seemed almost happy, whatever the outcome. Who was I to judge what he had or didn't have? We said goodbye and wished him luck. I trust the beach he coasted onto kept him from harm's way. I trust he found shelter by the ocean. I trust he didn't get hassled for having nothing but a bike and a trailer and a little food and water.

It seemed wrong to ride away from him when I knew he would struggle no matter where he landed. I didn't like that feeling; Cody didn't either. He was with us clear into the next the town where we stopped for Gatorade before we rode into the hills and hay and houses of Corvallis. The sun was unrelenting and the road was without end. About five miles out, Cody stopped and found a bike path that got us off the highway. We rode through the backyards of the city and crossed the streets into the late afternoon hustle of commuters trying to get home. Cody had made a reservation at a hotel. We staggered in, sweaty and reddened from the day like strangers in the air-conditioned lobby. We pushed our bikes into the elevator and collapsed on the beds. The day's riding was done. We had come to our first rest day, bent in service to the road.

Serendipity called us to dinner. Cody's former babysitter lived in Corvallis. She and her husband had settled there after leaving Nevada.

She taught radiologic technologists and he was an electrician. They were people who cared first and asked why later. She had a depth of humanity I have rarely seen and Cody understood that their time together was special, something not to be taken for granted. She picked us up outside the hotel. Even though it was a mere three miles to their house, after that push up the Coast Range it would have been a long ride. Her husband was remodeling the house to install a master bedroom downstairs and a salt bath to relax in, with elevated salt content to float you and buoyancy to perform its magic. She made a large salad and we ate at their kitchen table. He came up from the crawl space to join us. He was working on the plumbing after working all day. Labor of the hands, labor of the mind.

She brought out a picture of their wedding; Cody was in my arms—maybe seven years old. Such a change of place, person, and context. A child had become the man now sitting next me. Larger than me. And she had been a young woman about to take a young man to spend her life with all these many years ago. Thus we shape our lives and turn back to important moments for reference, for gravity.

Cody had colic when he was young, but she never winced when she took care of him. Debby and I were convinced that she was already a mother, had already intuited what love could not design. I knew her parents well; without their help we would not have been able to build our non-profit organization in northern Nevada. Trust in one another let us start a program for youth and families. Thirty years later, it was a central part of the social fabric of rural northern Nevada. Her parents had made it possible to watch our program grow—to take our leap into this unknown future—and she had done the same for our children— making them that much more humane.

As she drove us back to the hotel and we said goodbye in the hot June night, Cody and I wondered at the circumstance that led us to her door and which would lead, now, to the doors ahead. We walked into town looking for some dessert. At the Dairy Queen, Cody ordered a cheeseburger and fries. I settled for ice cream and promised not to tell his babysitter. She wouldn't understand that we were never satiated. We just pretended to be satisfied and hoped the next stop was not too far along. At the hotel there was a message.

Cody had left his sunglasses at her house. We turned off the light and waded into dreams.

A Roadside without End
IX

Distance: 5 miles
Elevation: flat ride into town
Corvallis, Oregon, 2019

Our bike clothes stank and we needed some food. The bagels were gone and the chews were swallowed. I was so happy to awake in a bed. The pad and sleeping bag were fine—I'd slept on harder things—but convenience was something I could not forsake. We slept in and found the last clean clothes. At breakfast I stared into eggs but knew they would disappear after the first few hours of the day. There was a group of tourists from Texas. We sat across from a couple who told us about their journey. They had been through the northwest and were slowly heading back home. This was their annual vacation. She spoke softly, had a tube inserted into her throat but it seemed normal enough, the minor distractions of age. He hardly noticed and translated for her when she could not elevate her voice. When they rolled out of the lobby I told Cody I had just seen a glimpse of the future. "Can't imagine that being how you spend your days, Pops."

Maybe he was right—I'd traveled on some buses, made the journeys north and south. But I'd rather ride into that same distance, into the horizon with a last star overhead. Age is a storm that lives in our lives. Only when we slow do we notice its coming presence.

I thought of my mother, alone in her room in Southern California. What she would surrender to speak without memory loss. What she would give for an afternoon out with friends. What dresses she would dance in if she could. Just five years ago, I sat before a stage and watched her tap through the chorus with her octogenarian friends, so lithe was her body. This woman who did not believe in the curse of her leaving, this woman who nevertheless spoke to me and all her family as if we were her one, constant concern. I went up to the room and called. She was fine—always—"I'm fine Shaun, how are you?" Her question was not one of intent but of love. She knew I could not come to see her and she could only imagine our time on the bikes. "How's Cody? Is he all right?"

"Without him, I would have already turned around." She laughed because she knew my white lie was for her, for us, for the time I was away. "I'll keep calling, Mom, and if I get a chance, paint a postcard for you. Maybe it will arrive before we finish. Maybe it will bring some light from the mountains."

Cody and I rode into town. We looked at the map, tried to find out if we could get to McKenzie Pass. It would require another detour. At the bike store, we asked if McKenzie Pass was still closed to cars. They thought so—until this weekend. One of the guys had ridden it the previous weekend. We bought some bars and chews, inflated our tires to 100 pounds and oiled our chains. This would be our first real climb—4,000 feet without cars. From the forest floor to the lava beds above. We would take the detour up Tombstone Pass and then down to McKenzie Bridge, spend the night and start up the pass the following morning. Something to look forward to, something to consider: a way into the quiet of the Cascades. This would mean a second climb after going up much of Santium Pass on Highway 20, but it would get us into the forest, out of traffic and onto a fern-draped path up the mountain. Scott had told us about McKenzie Pass: the ride opened to that parallel view you could only see on a bike. Apart, alone, set in the rhythm of two wheels.

At the hotel we found a small bag at the reception desk: our dinner host had delivered the sunglasses with a dozen homemade peanut butter cookies. They were hot and we sampled. What a gift to savor. I packed them carefully so they would not break. I found the washer and dryer and spent the afternoon lobbing quarters in the machine. Clean clothes, another gift to savor. Cody found a movie on the tube and I drifted off, happy to have the soft blankets at my back.

For the first time I could recall what we had ridden through. I pulled the slim, handmade journal from my panniers and started to write. The pages were soft—there was a scarlet macaw on the cover. Nevada's mother-in-law had given it to me; it was from Costa Rica. She knew I loved the birds. There was a group of them that flew in the early morning and sunsets at their home in Jacó. I was transfixed by their perilous screams and rocket-like flight. They hung for hours in the trees peeling the almonds. Hung like magistrates at the dais of the floral kingdom. I knew it would make her happy that her journal was at my side:

> Thankful to be scrubbed from noise back home.
> This takes a singular focus—one pass at a time.

The journal felt like home, a place for the record of our days. I transcribed the haiku and remembered how little we had done: there were mountains ahead I could not imagine. Barely days into the journey, the rest felt as necessary as water. Again I wondered if it was possible to do this, or more accurately: was it possible to do this without feeling the weight in your limbs? I did not think so. What we spent getting over the Coast Range was our passage into the foment of exercise and exhaustion. It tired us in a way we had not been tired and quietly took us out of our former lives and into this one. The physical effort was preparation for the visual—I began to see and hear the road beside me. The smallest of flowers, the squeak of killdeer, the heavy, insistent throb of blood to the limbs. And the endless hayfields we rode into. A perception of wilderness outside of our awareness. A roadside without end.

Cody found a McMenamins and we rode over there for dinner. I remembered the same boutique hotel and restaurant in Edgefield, outside of Portland. Debby and I had spent a long weekend with our friends sipping beer, sitting by the fire and watching a film in what seemed like our private living room. When I walked out onto the grass it was foggy and our friends were going to play golf in the mist. I looked upon the manicured lawn and flowers—how could this have possibly been a refuge for Oregon's poor at the turn of the century? When the bottom fell out of the economy, the state made their sustenance a priority. They worked in the fields, harvested their crops and found a labor of dignity. Whole families lodged in this building that now housed us, wayfarers of another time. By the fireside with my dear friend Ben, I wished for similar compassion in this time, something that would propel us to kindness without question. A state could see this obvious solution a hundred years ago but we seemed trapped in our divide, unable to forgive or more importantly, provide access when it was the most obvious choice for a family. I have written many poems on the blood coursing through veins that slowly calcify through unwillingness to care. Sometimes the contrasts were beyond reckoning. Sometimes they hovered over us and we made our way back to the fire where, in the smoke-filled room, there was an hour or more of unrelenting warmth.

The sun was going down and we ate slowly. The waitress couldn't believe we were on bikes. That became a joke we readily acknowledged—it would have been far easier to start the ride in Corvallis. The food did not disappoint and we made our way back to the hotel. I packed the panniers with the fresh food, careful to put the cookies on top. Our legs had almost recovered. The Tenkara rods were the perfect antidote to the lactic acid. We rolled and rolled our thighs and AT bands. Without stretching, they would surely tighten and slow us in the morning. We could not find one piece of equipment to leave behind. We had chosen the right clothes, tools and supplies. My map was frayed, but we had only come a small distance: there was so much more geography to cover. I still did not know how or if we could push through two more states after Oregon. And yet, it did not matter. The peeling away of expectation had already begun: the good, saturated, tired before sleep. Cody called out from the dark. "Night, Pops. It's been good so far. Nevada will like this." I agreed in the dark. A night whose welcome we embraced.

This sliver of recognition between father and son. We had ridden three days, rested one, and would ride three more before the elder son would join us. Each day became its own circular revolution, its own spinning desire. Practice was letting me down into something I could not possibly see in my busy, other life. And it was placing son and father in a place of equanimity, of careful, thoughtful, passage into and out of relationship. A grown man at thirty, curiously happy on a thin line stretched across the West.

The Water We Knew
X

Distance: 59 miles
Elevation: 1,600 feet
Corvallis, Oregon, 2019

We settled up, said goodbye to the desk clerk and rode out of Corvallis. I texted our friend to thank her again for the soft peanut-butter cookies. I promised her I'd return before the next twenty years passed and Cody was riding through Oregon with his kids, not the other way around.

In the bag she had left us a note: I could drive you to Bend. It's not a problem—just a couple hours—and then you could start fresh when Nevada joins you. We were tempted by her offer—surely her kindness would keep this body from wear—but equally tempted by the pass ahead: a climb into the forest without cars. Some bicyclists drive for days to do this and it had fallen into our hands. We could not pass this up. Strange as it is to articulate, the passage up is so much more than physical effort. It is a kind of leverage that you must exert to participate in the summit. And the car, while easier, did not have that leverage. We rode in a car to Portland. We left our car to do this: to turn without its convenience into the mountain West.

We rode into the Willamette Valley on an almost perfect day—low 60s, no wind and a view of Mt. Hood to the north. A day for pedaling. Cody found a route through neighborhoods that kept us off Highway 20. There were old Chevy's and Fords parked in people's lawns like yard sculpture. I wanted to stop and look at every car, the patina of rust pushing through the morning dew. Cars, the very thing I'd sworn off for this time, were commanding my attention. Cody reminded me that we were a long way from home; I could not tow one on the back of my bike. But in the haze of stepping down from the non-profit, I once again returned to my indulgences and coveted the never-to-run-again rust buckets in the weeds. It's what I'd done for thirty years; I was practiced at observation, the first tool of being a poet. Not a contradiction: the words grew from the same source—a love of what was possible. In art there is a mind apart. Seamus Heaney wrote "The end of art is peace." Not unlike this labyrinth through the hayfields in this valley.

I looked south to the valley's end—nothing but hay and sheep and green patches. It was flat, very few cars, and the ravens followed overhead. On the telephone wire they looked down. We must have been out of place—tractors and farmers and field hands belonged but not us—foreigners in a green land. It had been a good season for growing, this was probably their second crop of hay. If they were lucky, they would harvest through the fall. What water provides. That there could be a place without dryness was an anomaly to us. This watershed from the Cascades we were about to pedal into. This downstream current of snowmelt. It was beyond imagining. A dry land was what we understood; its absence was the measure of home. Here, water became a presence of miles: moisture made dry land an altogether different land. Water—we were without a language to absorb its content. After decades in Nevada, water was without us and we without water. It may as well have been a dry lake that fed this valley. That is how the dry lakes fed the valleys of home—once every winter after a hard rain or snow, they gurgled to life and gave six inches to insects and coyotes and bighorn sheep. And then receded to outlines, places where water was. This was the water we knew. Not a valley of green but a valley of thorns.

Cody pulled off the road to grab a snack. I was close to being filled with sunlight, not sore or tired but filled with light and air. We ate slowly, quietly, a heron off to our left. At the corner, we found a place to pee before we started back on Highway 20, the log trucks pushing into the mountain. Each time we traded for the quiet of back roads the day grew more inviting—we rode without worry in our solitary travel. Then the highway became manageable, not the distraction it was leaving Portland but the necessary give and take of riding. The backroad was its analogous twin, a parallel road on the map.

Day five and we had finally come to the place of calm. We rode into Sweet Home looking for a place to eat. At the market a young man was cooking ribs. We gave in faster than rabbits. The young man cooking kept checking the thermometer—were they ready? We promised him we had all the time he needed. Cody left to find some money. I had to go into the store and asked a woman if she'd watch the bikes. She was smoking, thin, my age, whispering to the man waiting in her car. "Sure," she said, staccato, and I walked away. It was probably not smart but I was tired of the presumption of theft. I had to let go, had to trust this woman on the bench beside me.

She was still smoking when I came back. I liked her reticence. She asked where we were going. When I told her she almost laughed. We understood—it didn't matter how far it was. A bike was only so good and if you were on it, so be it. "Have fun," she offered walking to her car. We shook our heads. She was as much a part of this place as its hay. A stem of a woman who was near her final harvest. A part of the West where she rode out her days.

Cody rode back and looked at the rib man: they were ready. "Give me two half racks."

He handed one to me and I felt their heat on my thighs.

"You must have planned this, probably called ahead and found a rib joint."

"Just for you."

"Now it's starting to smooth out—the road, the food, the company," and I nudged Cody as we ate on the bench outside.

A Chevy van pulled up. A man got out and walked with a cane into the store. He asked us where we were going. We mumbled and he said, "I used to ride a bike like you before RA. I'm fifty-four, enjoy yourselves, you never know what's coming." We ate slowly, not knowing what we would hear next. I cleaned up, filled the water bottles inside and lathered sunscreen on my legs and arms. We started to ride out. A guy got out of his truck with his wife's help. Almost into the wheelchair, he looked at us and had to wave, despite needing his hand to slow the descent. He crashed into the chair, satisfied that his signal was received. I turned to Cody—"Did you see that?" He nodded. An affirmation, a recognition of something more than the metal he rolled into the store. The bike was a treadle into people's lives. Somehow it gave them permission. They did not worry about a simple exchange. We had no metal skin to protect us, no way to drive off if things didn't work. Two strangers in a Safeway lot felt compelled to move from their lives into ours. They drove off, had time to reflect on the minutes together. Just when the busy day strips us down and we become less in its order, we sat on a bench in Sweet Home, fat with ribs and listened because there was nothing else to do. The calm after exertion let us hear their admonitions: I'm here, I'm alive, even though life's not perfect. A storm has come to my body, but I make do. I get to the store, do my errands, go home just as I did before the storm.

Maybe it was the unorthodox welcome we needed.

A slow climb up the Santium River Gorge out of Sweet Home. An easy day. The sun was at our backs and the traffic was light. After the push into Corvallis this was almost what we expected—mostly uneventful cycling. A long day of quiet in the June light. Nothing to disturb us. The next twenty-one miles we said little, the echoes of the two men at the store were not far behind.

Cody was on the hunt for a place to camp. We rode into the circular drive of Yukwah Campground. There were very few people and several good sites on the South Santium River. We leaned our bikes against a Western hemlock and went to the river. A family floated in a truck tube. We headed west and found some granite boulders in the middle of the water. Cody got out his Tenkara rod. I laid down on a boulder. The sun was on my face. Not a sound save the whip of Cody's rod. I dozed off—this is what I came for—this quiet by a river that could not be easily had. My muscles relaxed; I was without tension, present on the warm rock. Cody didn't have any luck—it was early, and the fish were small. He laid down on the boulder beside me. We were there for an hour in the late afternoon light. I saw the hatch on the river—nothing rose to strike but the bugs were plentiful. We walked back to the campground. Cody set up the tent and I blew into the pads. A rhythm of preparation—camp stove, cups, spoons, water to boil—effort split easily with two of us. He cooked mac and cheese with tuna. Each night it got better with sprinkles of chili and salsa from Cody's spice bag. I made some tea and started to write in the journal. The forest was dense with moss and needles overhead. I didn't have a book—too much weight—but the journal sufficed. I recorded the ebb and flow of the day. We cleaned our cups, which doubled as bowls, rinsed the cooking pot and tried to stay awake at the camp table. The dark crept in. A few stars overhead. The river moved to the valley of hay below. I laid down on my bag, as soft a cloth as I could hope for—or so it seemed at day's end. I slept for the owls and nocturnal ones outside. Nothing disturbed us until first light. This was our pendulum, our daily restoration, our time to return from night to day.

It wasn't cold—we were still at low elevation—and the mountains were a day away. I fumbled for my lightweight down jacket and walked to the outhouse. The man next door lit a fire outside his RV. His wife walked the dog to the shrubs. We dismantled the tent and pads, cooked six packs of oatmeal with peanut butter and sipped coffee at the table. The ride was as much about this routine, this repetition of small tasks, as it was pedaling. In time, and time had slipped from us, the set-up and breakdown of camp, the meals from a cup without many words, the occasional cookie, became a separate pleasure. Something we depended on to mark the end of day, the return to sleep when exhaustion was its own reward and hours later, to signal the outline of morning sun.

Waking by Lost Creek
XI

Distance: 45 miles
Elevation: 3,830 feet
Yukwah Campground, Linn County Oregon, 2019

I awoke thinking of Tombstone Pass, our first real push since the infernal climb over the Coast Range. There was very little sound—our neighbors were outside with their dog. Cody made me coffee. I thought about Bend, where Nevada, Joe and Scott would join us. The journey would change, how I did not know but it would alter this chemistry of two. I heard Scott's voice again: "If you want to do this with your boys—" but I knew he and Joe would ease us into a friendship of peers, temper my resolve to keep my sons from harm and, more important, humor us with facts of science and literature. Best of all, both sons would ride with me from there to the Tetons. That is what I most wanted, the unscripted time with them and the universe beneath our wheels. It is a quality of mind they cannot know, not being fathers, that constantly circles to their presence. When you love someone from birth, you live in the uncertain belief they are there—full, present, lives—whether or not you can be with them.

Scott and Joe knew this also. This made their arrival a kind of magical moment. Sure, Cody and I were in sync, but they were too. It was why I wanted to go on the ride in the first place: Scott's peaceable manner—"I'm going on a ride in June. Want to come?" It took no more than that—he wouldn't have asked if the twine between us wasn't right. I imagined Joe was equally enthralled, and Nevada was almost born on a bike. It was, in the parlance of the saddle, almost natural.

Cody packed up our tent and I washed the oatmeal from the mugs. We looked at the map—about thirty miles up Highway 20 to Tombstone Pass, then down to Belknap Springs. Not so bad, I thought, not so bad. About ten miles up the road we stopped at the last store before the grade. A woman was smoking outside in a lounge chair. She said we should take the fire road to McKenzie Bridge. She went inside and brought us a topo map, told us she and her husband cut wood up there. Cody looked at me—"Want to give it a go?" We thought hard and almost took the turn but didn't want to get lost and chose the highway. It would have been fun—assuming we found the road out. I saved the topo map, our first of many markers of place, of circumstance.

Tombstone Pass is 4,219, not a staggering push from the valley floor. Happy to do most of it in the morning shade, we pedaled another seven miles to Fish Lake. Cody went to fill our water bottles and I fiddled with the sandwiches. The day-campers and weekend anglers were at the shore. What could we possibly be doing among them? One of them told us about spring water at the ranger station. We left immediately—it was too hot to fish at midday. The house sat up on the hill beneath a dense forest cover. It was an old family cabin, a summer home I could live in. Cody yelled, "I found the icy spring water." By then the sun had risen overhead to seventy degrees and the liquid soothed our dry throats. We loaded the bikes up for the second half of the day and pedaled off. But maps deceive—what looked like it was downhill was up and down and well into the forest. The scrim of road dust, sweat and thirst were close behind. I was close to hitting the wall, but I promised Cody I would not lie in the street. We made the turnoff for Limberlost Campground and found the last spot. No water, no electricity and somehow it didn't matter. Exhausted, cold with sweat and hunger, Cody looked at me and said "I'll ride into McKenzie Bridge and get dinner." He was gone before I could answer. I peeled to my bike shorts and stepped into Lost Creek and splashed my face and torso. Tremulous, the frozen water ran down my back. I toweled off and went back to the picnic table, blew up our sleeping pads and put them in the tent. The ritual of nightly preparation.

I sat while the nearby campers drank in the late afternoon sun. I was fading—the sun and distance had taken all of me. I ate the last bar I had—it tasted like rope. I needed salt, fat, carbs. Cody rode into camp with a grin: "I got burritos," he said, and we fired up the stove to heat them. We fished salsa from Cody's spice bag. It was as savory a meal as I have had, and I started to recover. Cody knew exactly what to do—get some food into me. I surrendered—my vanity lying in the pool of water at my feet. "You feel any better? I'm riding to the hot springs. You coming?"

I could almost imagine pedaling back to the springs—and a hot shower. "I'm coming."

We took our panniers off, stuffed our wallets and suits in a bag and rode off. At the hot springs there were kids, dogs, beautiful people and the raging McKenzie River. Even the cops were there—some guy had hassled a young woman in this bucolic place. What desperation in the background! Campers and trailers were squished into every corner of the park—the spectacle of camping with convenience.

I stood in the shower for minutes and let it scald the sweat from my body. My legs were stiff, my arms sun burnt, and the water felt like balm to my skin. We sat on the steps of the pool and listened to the river at our backs. In two months, Debby and I would return to this camp with friends. It seemed almost surreal—a time so far from now with the very real road ahead. Cody found some Moon Pies in the gift store and we ate them, delirious with the hot steam after a long ride. We coasted back to camp and settled in for the night. I looked out the tent flap—it was not yet dark. Dusk took us into its arms.

I drifted off thinking about Mom—it was nearing her ninetieth birthday. I promised the crows overhead I would call her on her birthday. They didn't care. The moon crept in—there was nothing left to give this day. "Thanks for saving me from hunger again."

Cody laughed, "You'd do the same."

Yes, I thought, if I could. This slow evolution from father to son to caretaker of the one who once was father.

Lost Creek seemed appropriately named—or maybe it was we who were happy to be lost at its side. It is referred to as a "losing stream" because it disappears into the water table as it flows downward from the Collier Glacier in the Cascades. The headwaters of White Branch stream follow a glacial trough underground before they resurface to join Lost Creek, a tributary of the McKenzie. Over and over, I kept asking why we were by water and this time, by water that flowed underground like the rivers in Nevada. Water that was cold enough to freeze the skin on my legs. Water that had come from the glacier we were about to ride into. Water I used to boil for coffee. I put all my clothes on—it was chilly, maybe high thirties—and the sun would not shine down here for another hour. The campground was quiet—most people had left before we awoke. A few heads poked from their rigs of bedding and heaters and pets. Again I sat at the picnic table and wrote briefly in the journal. Today would be the first real climb. Today we would learn a little more about ourselves. Today we would discover how absolutely serene it was to be on a windy mountain road with no cars. I thanked the bicycle mavens in Corvallis for our good fortune. By the time we pedaled out it would be just the right temperature for the push to the summit. If left to us, we would have ridden out of our way every day to be able to be alone on a road like this.

I was starting to get my legs back. In the scant hours that we slept my strength had returned. It's hard to understand how fast a body recovers, but it does and it does so quickly. I wasn't completely back, but I was close. A little nutrition, some sleep, and water: the same cold water from Lost Creek. After a few minutes with Cody's Steripen filter, it was in the pot for oatmeal. Then I wondered—who had been here before us? How did they follow this underground creek? What led them to its source? If I think of the early explorers— certainly Lewis and Clark in this region, it was water they followed west. Water drew them from a midland shore to another. I wondered who or what quieted their minds on such an undertaking. Strangely, I felt their presence north of us, heading west on the Columbia, looking for a route to the Pacific. It's difficult to understand what takes hold in a person, what beckons them to follow water. But I couldn't let go of the notion that we were not alone—this Lost Creek at our feet would eventually join the Willamette River and flow northwest on to the Columbia before reaching the Pacific Ocean. And surely, there were many lost in its tracks, not least were those who had lived here first. Cody was already packing his bike. He snapped the bungee cord on my sleeping bag and hollered, "Time to head out, big man. We got a hill to climb."

"A hill to climb," I said. "Is this what you imagined, rolling into the mountains with the old man?"

"I didn't know what to expect."

"The job leave you yet?"

"I'm still thinking about it—but it's starting to fade. You know, almost no one at my firm takes a sabbatical like this, even though it's offered. The culture just doesn't support it. There's just too much to do, too many deadlines to meet for the client."

"Your mother and I worked for ourselves but we served other masters—grants, funders, commissioners. Sometimes the people get lost in the equation, even the people you're supposed to serve."

"You guys cut your own road. Nev and I talk about that a lot. Starting a firm with our backgrounds in health and business. We'd probably kill each other though."

"Working together is not easy. It tries a marriage. Tries anyone. You think about payroll, the people working for you, their lives like small stones in your pocket. You never forget them."

"I don't know if I'd want that responsibility."

"Nobody ever does. It sneaks up on you and one day you're paying thirty people and you wonder how you got here."

"There's thirty people on my floor and two hundred in my office."

"A payroll I would not want."

"That's why they charge so damn much."

"I wouldn't know. Our idea of a consultant is fix it yourself. The non-profit world is many things but the turbulence of high income is not one of them."

"You're such a tool—"

"I'll give you a tool—" and we pedaled into the wet fern forest.

Rotiform

Adjective: wheel-shaped.

Etymology: from Latin rota (wheel).

Earliest documented use: 1816

A Worthy Contour
XII

Distance: 59 miles
Elevation: 4,667 feet
Blue River, Oregon, 2019

We put on our windbreakers, leggings and rode off. It was about 8:30 and not knowing how long it would take to reach McKenzie Summit we got an early start. There were no cars and we pedaled through dense forest, moss draped from the fir and cedar branches overhead. On the long, slow climb to the mountain's base, an elderly couple whizzed by on an electric bike, so happy they could not contain themselves: "Have a nice day."

The two of us looked at them and smirked, "Try this—" and we hunkered down for the next miles. I stripped off the extra layers of clothing as my skin warmed in the first sunlight through the ferns. Then the switchbacks started. The density of the forest was comforting; I could not see far enough to know how much farther the summit was. My eyes were on the front tire, the rim and the occasional leaf caught in my brake caliper. I took the fenders off before we left Portland to cut the weight but the aluminum brackets rode right above the tires. The pebbles scuffed as they followed the rubber to the metal. It kept me listening: if something grated on the bracket, I was pedaling, moving up hill. Some measure, faulty as it was, of progress. An occasional car startled us. Cody waited for me after ten minutes or so. I trusted him to pause when it was right. By now he understood: there was no race. This was altogether different—an exploration of distance and time but nothing to do with expediency. This was two people alone on a small patch of asphalt, with the weight of their necessities on pedals and rims. "You all right, Pops?" I nodded and took a sip of water. He always thought I didn't drink enough, but I swallowed as if it were some other liquid, some cure for the constant thirst.

Lost Creek occasionally surfaced in the canyon. With water nearby we didn't have to worry. And the heat was far overhead. Shadows crisscrossed our path up the road. The farther we climbed, the closer we came to the mountain's flank of dark and shaded trees. Again, I listened—what lived there, out of sight, nocturnal, wary, undisclosed? No doubt the bobcats and the owls who hunted as we slept were nearby and the others, quiet, hard to distinguish: the snakes and rodents and rabbits—the prey of the forest floor. I tried to see through the latticed light, but it was difficult to know if what I saw was anything more than a chimera.

Cody stopped by the road edge. "Time for a snack, Pops." I was starting to learn the limits of intake and output. We could only go so far on a breakfast of peanut butter and oatmeal. I never ate enough. I was hungry before we rode off, but the edge was gone. Cody kept an eye on the approximate distance—"Think we have about ten more miles to the plateau before the summit. We can have lunch there."

We hit the gate that kept cars from going up the mountain and exhaled: nothing to distract us now. Just as we settled in a road biker flew by, having already summited that morning. It was hard not to feel intimidated but I pedaled back and forth, across the road to cut the grade. It was a push—maybe 5-6%—but not overly so. Something I would do at home out of joy and here, with no cars, it was an excursion into silence, to notice what was all around. There were so many shades of green a painterly eye could not capture them. And the bird calls—different from those I knew—fluted from the air overhead. At my back, the ruffle of skin on nylon, a hush of breath: the day-cyclists came by, grinning, lighter. Their haste made no difference. This was not a hurried ride to the summit, this was not an outing. I still could not entirely define what it was, but I knew the quick ride was what we might have done with less time. We were opening an aperture, a place in which to perceive this volcanic mountain on whose back we climbed. The rock below the road was porous, just like the light through the trees. We were little in this place, nothing of consequence. The interior of the forest was metaphor enough—an interior I grew more attached to with each successive pass. I remembered Crystal Creek coming up the Coast Range—the logging debris, the forest after a cut—the slash piles, what was done for work. This wood we rode in took millennia to grow, an era of forest tumult at the base of a volcanic summit, this wooden landscape that was unchanged but for the elements. I looked down at my gooseneck to the words on my red aluminum cap: *all work and no play is no good at all.* I had given it to my neighbor at home who rode daily and thought it might help him on his long-distance rides. But he returned it so that I might have a recourse of humor on this one. "Maybe three more miles, Pops—" and I smiled: my son the stenographer in the virtual world. Thank god he could read the phone and ride. I couldn't read it without my glasses and they were not handy with the sweat and exertion of a climb.

"I can do three more—" I yelled. It wasn't overly difficult, more a consistent climb, a steady motion of effort. It was a worthy contour of steep and shrouded woods. My legs were holding up and the water, too. The shade kept us from getting too hot. For what seemed like minutes we were alone in the silence—the occasional murmur from Lost Creek below but little else: all that I had imagined was before me. Cody saw it in my face: "Pretty nice, eh?" He was starting to come down from the hail of work to the pace of the ride. He was close to these woods and their calm. We didn't need speech. Just to breathe with each crank of the pedal, little more, to acknowledge one another.

At the plateau there was sunlight and scraggy pines. Snow was deep here in the winter, and the water had pooled at the roadside. We were thankful to have made it out of the green and into the blue. The landscape looked like it was shaved from the mountaintop; Belknap Crater Volcano had been active between 1,500 and 3,000 years earlier—a minute in geologic time. The Three Sisters, also part of a volcanic range, were to the south, and the blue light shone on their peaks. We pulled off the road to eat but the bottle flies would not leave us alone. We stood and finished the last of the sub sandwich purchased the day before in the Safeway. The meat and cheese had lasted. The bread was moist but it didn't matter—it was food and we needed some.

We began to depend on the elements for our refrigeration. We bought just enough to last for a day or two and then found the next stop with something to refresh. This, too, was a comfort. We were not alone or struggling in any real way. The only nuisance was the flies. We rode on to Dee Wright Observatory where we met a hundred cyclists who had come from both sides to this ridge. The observatory is made of volcanic rock; it is a shelter and a place to view the major peaks of central Oregon. We were at home with nothing but two-wheeled compatriots for the midday rest at the summit. I sat on the stone and looked out from the ridge at an endless horizon of sky and peak and snow.

We started down the long slope into Bend. Fire had taken many trees and turned the land barren. Almost the opposite of the western slope, this area was spotted with trees but nothing dense or dark, save the dead stumps from the burn. It was a nice descent after the push and then a long flat ride into the outskirts of Sisters. Cody noodled around for the right path into Sisters and once again, we were on a highway with motor homes and happy visitors. We found a coffee shop and he ordered me a matcha latte—which is a lot of green things that refresh—and we sat outside in the heat of the afternoon. We were back in the convenience of cars and food and cold drinks, our bikes anchored at the curb. Some part of the day I would not recover in speech would stay with me. The aperture to the parallel journey had opened.

We left Sisters for the last hot miles to Bend. A completely different ride—motorhomes and trailers and people looking for a place to get off the two-lane. Cody noodled through the routes and found one along the river that put us into the backstreets of Bend. Families were playing in the Deschutes and I told Cody we would be back to fish the following day. The sun was at our sides as we rode out of the valley, up the switchback into town. We found the hotel and pushed our bikes into the room.

Our first week in the saddle, a rhythm of riding and sloughing noise from the mind. My mind, Cody's mind. We had let go of the worry, the preparation, the coming departure. We were on the path and the path was yielding something altogether different—a nexus of being outside and away from the throb of little things, the jester in the flat screen and the roil of news. We showered and found a McMenamins for dinner and ate outside. It was still warm and the sun was almost over the ridge we had just ridden. There was quiet between us, not much to be said. We had given our words to the road. And the road had given us one week together—that unbelievable length of time as two. Nevada was supposed to have joined us but missed his flight out of New York. He got a room in Portland and drove down the next day. Scott and Joe were close behind, coming up from Reno. The rhythm was about to change—from two to five— from this relative idyll to a boisterous timbre neither of us yet knew.

The next morning, I painted the first of three watercolor postcards for Debby—a childlike picture of Cody and me atop McKenzie Pass. Her letter was at the hotel desk when we arrived: "But most important is that in Bend, Oregon, on this Father's Day, you are with them." I told her we had made it to Bend and that Nevada was joining us. I hoped that when my postcard landed in her post office box, some part of her worry would let down and she could exhale with us, however far away, knowing that her sons were together. No doubt Cody and Nev felt the same way—they were with the old guy now. What could possibly go wrong? Debby and Cody's spouse had received arrival texts from Cody for a week already; now Nevada's spouse would join them. The three women in our lives had summoned the willingness to let us ride. A break in the middle of my son's lives, a break in mine, but together it was still more: we dipped in and out of the consciousness of a family, yes but also of three men on a thin line through the West.

Nev pulled into the restaurant in Bend, happy to be off the road at last. "Hey guys, what's up? You don't look too roughed up." We laughed. The three of us—not quite a dream but close. I never imagined we would be together for nearly a month at this time in their lives. It just seemed so improbable. But we were. I looked at his face against the window—resplendent and ready. He was still weary from the late flight but happy to have put the work behind him. "Bikes working okay? No real issues?"

"All's good. The first week was relatively painless except the climb over the Coast Range. Just too hot. McKenzie was outrageous. You should have seen it. No cars after the gate. Just bikes for twenty miles. Pretty sweet." We got him back to the hotel and he started to unpack, sort through his bags to find what was missing. Nev packed and repacked and Cody and I lazed in the air-conditioned room while the laundry washed. It would take a few days for the work and the travel to wear off. He had been running for months at his job and was trying to find this open space in which to breathe. He brought a hammock rather than a tent, hoping the lesser weight would pay off. "You can climb in the tent if we get rain," Cody assured him. Mostly, we'd dodged bad weather, but we weren't really in the mountains yet. Beneath the flurry of activity was tension: now the ride started for Nev. No doubt he could see in our faces the weather of exhaustion. But he was in the best shape—this came naturally for him. "You'll be fine, just make sure you stop for me," I joked. He put his bike together on the hotel floor—it took about an hour—then rode off to test it out. He asked Cody repeatedly about the rack on their carbon-fiber frames: "No problems? Hold up okay?" The staccato word-smithing of two wheels. Fortunately, his bike made it in one piece and it rode fine. He loaded the panniers and took another run. "This is a little different." He felt the weight that followed each of us, the weight that ebbed with stores and rest stops and cheap food in the gas stations. The barnacle of being on the roadside. At some point, it was just food and no more. Just liquid. Just filling the tank.

At the bike store, we filled tires, oiled chains and adjusted derailleurs and sleuthed more directions. Was there any special place to ride? How far off the route was it? Until it became a pattern—the planned journey was no longer the plan but rather something like an outline, a reference for what we *might* do.

Nev called his wife and told her he made it and she sent him off like Cody's wife had sent him, into the hayfields of central Oregon.

We mailed Nev's bike crate back to Debby and went out for tacos on the other end of town because we still had his car. Joe and Scott texted to say they were in town. They'd meet us tomorrow for a late lunch and join us on the following day's ride to Prineville.

We headed to the Deschutes the next morning. The families were at the shore, dotting the rocks and wading in the pools. I couldn't see any fish but threw my line in—a small rainbow jumped for the fly. It was still early. All of us scattered downstream. My once-boys knew what to do without me: even though their lives had taken them to cities, fly-casting came back like walking or singing. I didn't see them again—they were entranced with the riffles and the occasional deep pool. If this day gave them no more, it gave them its time by water and the solace of its movement to another watershed, the outline of moisture that we followed. I hoped the whipping motion of the Tenkara rod would quiet their hands and I knew no fish would rise to keep them as they were already slowing to its watery surface. This was all I could ask of our second afternoon together—some way forward in the stream, in the warm sun. We walked back to the car with little to show for our time but the sun's red lines on our backs. We drove into town and found Scott and Joe at the hotel. What a joy to see them after these many months of planning. Scott turned to me and then my sons with a hug. A reunion of sorts. A reunion to ride out of Bend into the Mill Creek Wilderness as five.

For the first time in over a week I looked up to a TV in the Deschutes Brewery: a hundred migrant children were being escorted off a bus at a McDonald's in Deming, New Mexico, its poorest town. A desert community about thirty-three miles north of the Mexican border and sixty miles west of Las Cruces. The kids were dazed: where are we, how did we get here and why now? I tried to imagine being on that bus, what must it have meant to watch the miles go by—where is my family, what have they done to them? The ministers and the non-profit leaders scrambled to find something for them—shelter at the county fairgrounds, food from donations, and a welcome to their unwanted home. I yelled at the screen—"Goddamn them"—meaning the feckless ones who put the children on that bus and Joe added some words of his own—"The bastards are going to take this country apart." What Faustian bargain brought these children to this corner—for me to eat I must risk capture. The ICE transport van appeared like a new moon to bequeath its fulsome presence at 721 Pine Street. The apologists were apologizing because it was the "right thing to do," almost freed from their trope of officialdom.

It felt like we were back in the tumult we had hoped to leave behind. The immigrants staggered on to waiting hands in the town that, despite having almost nothing to offer but poverty, welcomed them. This was not what any of us wanted at our first lunch but it was a reminder—we were away but we had not left. We live in this country which is more than a border, more than what its leaders proclaim, more than a corner in southwestern New Mexico. By now, the porter was flat and I told the guys I'd wait outside and I tried to find room for the children who walked from the bus to the vans in the Deming desert.

I thought of Wendell Berry:

> In the dark of the moon, in flying snow, in the dead of winter,
> war spreading, families dying, the world in danger,
> I walk the rocky hillside, sowing clover.

I also knew that no poem would save me from the tendrils of the decision to move children into a desert without notice. We were two states northwest of those children. What would they say to us now, riding by on our bicycles? Even if I couldn't understand what they came from, what they left, I understood they had lost the ones they love. It would take months to reunite the children with their parents.

This is how I met Joe—and liked him immediately, not because he felt as I did but rather because he made no effort to impress. I also knew that my sons were on their own—they would form their opinions and move into one another's lives as men. They would form a relationship with Scott and Joe as separate people, two individuals without pretext. What they said, how they thought, whom they emulated, would evolve in the miles ahead. They waded into another layer of depth knotted together by this road ahead. The conversation had just begun.

High Above Ochoco Pass
XIII

Distance: 82 miles
Elevation: 3,410 feet
Bend, Oregon, 2019

We spent two days in Bend getting ready for the next week on the road. And we grew by three—now the full complement of raconteurs were riding. We put our clean clothes in our panniers, cinched down the sleeping bags and pads and checked out of the hotel. Water bottles were full, food was stuffed in every crevice. We rode out of Bend, the three of us in the morning traffic. Scott and Joe joined us on Highway 20 into Prineville.

We rode into the rising sun, something I enjoyed almost without parallel. Nev cautioned, "Put some sunscreen on." I told him I already had but my leathered skin looked haggard. As the days wore on, each of us grew darker until the sunscreen seemed almost pointless. Our ribbon tans were like striations on a hillside—covered by dust and wind and exhaust. We draped bandanas on our necks and tried to keep the sunscreen on but sometimes the sweat just made it an oily mess. We found Highway 20 and turned south. It was about twenty miles into Prineville, which made me think the late John Prine would be there to greet us. And damned if I didn't hear him high overhead. The name stuck: it was one of the great place names in Oregon—had to be from his family tree, at least in my mind.

We turned a corner to find our friends close behind—they had slept on a friend's porch north of Bend—and now our centipede was longer: we were five rolling shadows on the roadside. I wondered how long it would take to find the subtle rhythm of riding together— when to slow, when to stop, when to call an audible? Scott and Joe were old hands at this; it just took time for my sons and I to grow along with them. There was palpable joy—we had spent months working toward this day, this intersection on a two-lane in the West—and it was finally happening. Unlike Cody and I, Scott, Joe and Nevada were fresh, although the two days of rest put us close to them. I was glad Cody and I had the time to warm up to the ride—it let us wind down and let the road come to us. There was no hurry now, only pedaling and where the bike took us was just fine.

Joe pulled off at the *panadería* in Prineville—"I need a *pan dulce*," and we looked at each other and agreed: yes, we all needed one. You can do things like that when you ride all day. You can do it most of the time if you don't care how much the middle wiggles. I laughed at us, standing in the parking lot—just miles out of Bend and we were stuck in the sweet Mexican dough—and then took the obligatory ride to the bike store which doubled as a brewery. Almost every bike store in Oregon doubled as a brewery. I looked down at my rear light—a nice arc had been rubbed from the plastic, the mount had slipped over the tire, and for the last week I had pedaled the plastic away. I bought a new rear lamp that needed charging every night but it flashed, and on the road that flash took eyes off cell phones and pointed them to our backs. "Lights," we hollered at one another every time we started. Another ritual that drew us together. The owner of the bike shop asked where we going. "To the campground on Ochoco Pass," Cody shot back.

"Well, you know—" and by now we did—"if you go a little farther, there's a bike hostel in Mitchell. And it's worth the ride." Cody and I were reluctant to speak—we didn't want to commit the others to a long ride on their first day. Scott said, "I'm game. What about you Joe?" He nodded in his taciturn way and Nev was fine. He could have jogged to Mitchell. Having little choice (there being few stops until Ochoco Pass), we ate lunch next to The Good Bike shop. I thought it couldn't get much better and hoped the others felt similarly. It would take a lot to dissuade us now—we were primed with *pan dulces* and real sandwiches from a mom-and-pop deli. Into the hayfields we rode. Miles of hay—like small green masts waving in the wind. It wasn't too hot, the wind was at our backs, and the traffic was minimal. Central Oregon was a wide open plain of cultivation and harvest—farms supporting a culture of cattle and livestock. It's hard to script what green does but here it made a valley thick with crops, birds, and insects. It made farming possible—rarely producing more than what was needed and often less—but enough to survive. A script for leaving one's land to the generation that follows, for giving them calluses and hay fever and wood smoke.

Joe pointed to the Ochoco Reservoir as if it were an apparition and we followed Ochoco Creek upstream. Dammed shortly after World War I, the reservoir fed irrigation troughs in the valley below. It was part of the Deschutes River Basin—something I could now imagine: water running through a landscape, water of a place, water originating in the mountains we rode. The creek is a thirty-mile tributary of the Crooked River—a name that symbolized the tension of liquid when all we knew was thirst.

"You must have known Robert Laxalt," Joe said in the wind. It was more an opening than a question.

"I did. For the last decade of his life I spent a great deal of time with him and Joyce. I miss him terribly."

"He's Nevada's finest—he and Clark." Again, I acceded. "You read *Track of the Cat*?" he would ask months later fishing at Pyramid Lake.

"No, but like so many books that I have yet to open, it's waiting with the others for my time." Joe laughed.

"Damn kids, I ask 'em to read and they just look at me. Getting so hard to teach. If it were on the phone" his voice trailed off. I knew he was going to be my literary companion before the summit.

Scott muttered "I thought you two would get along." I smiled. Scott's intuition was a thread throughout eastern Oregon. The easy wrangle of conversation on a bicycle brought us back to what mattered: the give and take of points not known, not read, not seen.

Scott looked at us both: "All right, you two: tell me what the hell existentialism means. I can't understand a damn bit of it. Science has no use for this crap." Well, I may have exaggerated. He probably said dung.

"It's a choice, a decision you freely make to take responsibility for your actions."

Joe was doing just fine. He didn't need a poet to come in for the close. "It's not something that happens to you. It's a way to navigate the myriad questions: Sartre never wanted a simple answer. You must choose with every action what it is you stand for and why."

Scott teased him back: "So if I want to lower temperature for climate change, I choose it."

"Just like that. You fricking science guys are all alike. It has to make sense. If it isn't logical, what the hell? I can't say a damn thing without you refuting it." Cody and I were laughing at the scholars— two good men on opposite sides of the brain. Thank god I didn't have to try and explain poetry or we'd still be in Prineville.

The miles disappeared in conversation as the sun rose over our backs going up Ochoco Pass. This was the first push into the mountains since McKenzie, which the three guys had not ridden— and so it was their first pass over 4,700 feet—almost 1,900 feet of elevation out of Prineville. But the wind was at our backs and we sailed. It made the first day of riding together exceptionally calm— an airy pillow pushed us up the ridge into the pines. Long stretches of gradual climbing. I hoped Joe and Scott were not too tired or worse. A first day is usually the day for settling in: making sure the bike works, nothing rattles, the clothes fit, and the real reason for training: the body feels good after miles of pedaling. Scott had just come from many long rides and Joe had ridden miles in the Sierra Nevada and the valleys on its eastern flanks. I knew they were strong but I also wanted them to have a couple days to get used to the routine.

Nev was out front. Scott turned and said, "Guess we'll see him in a while."

"Yeah, he's riding, he's finally riding." This trip was less a challenge and more a release for Nevada. He would be tested, we all would, but his public health consulting had pushed him equally hard and this time away, even though he was moving to the West Coast and starting a new job, was such an unexpected release from the threads of New York. After seven years in a 60-plus hour a week job, he had made the difficult decision to leave the gilded bracelets. Time finally became something he no longer spent on planes and hotels. Time finally wore into his consciousness—you must choose the way forward. No one else will. His Brooklyn home of nearly four years was shrinking in the distance. His wife worked until she flew to Jackson Hole. The miles of black top in front of him were miles he spent saying goodbye to a way of life. He had risen fast in his company, was deeply respected and could have stayed until he retired. But the choice to relocate, to choose another path, was as invigorating—and challenging—as this ride.

We decided very quickly that he would ride point. On the good days, the wind took him miles from us; on the bad, he broke the wind so we might keep up with him. Our bodies became tools to wedge the obstacles—whether wind or moisture or cold. We tried to ride single-file to keep the cars at bay and the elements at a minimum.

The gift of a tailwind made this first day exceptional. At the summit we ate a snack and asked how many more miles? Cody and Nev glanced at the Strava app and said—"About twenty. You still want to go or you want to camp here?" We looked at each other and nodded. Joe said "My knees may not want to go but I do." He had some soreness that he rode through and hoped it would not return. We rode on, slow, the sun lowering at our backs. Mitchell—a town I had never heard of—was on the TransAmerica Bike Trail. But still, a bike hostel in a former church? I didn't know such a thing existed.

Cody and Nevada were first to arrive in the three-house town—a brewery, naturally, the hostel and a restaurant. Sounded perfect. I saw my sons in the late afternoon shadows—they were off their bikes, relaxed and happy. Nev said, "Park it here." And I did until the proprietor, Pat Farrell, came out: "You want Death by Chocolate or Death by Chocolate and Vanilla?" A kind of a devil's choice, except it was about ice cream. I knew we had come to the right place thanks to the good omen at the bike-and-brew shop in Prineville.

"Bring your bike inside," Pat said. "Put it in front of the bunk where you'll sleep." Just like that, we had arrived at the Spoke'n Hostel. One of the truly cool places to rest your head on the highway. I looked down the road to Scott, happy to have finished the first day.

Joe was in the distance but steady as the hour hand on a watch. We went downstairs in the former chapel, and Pat served large helpings of sweet frozen cream. We were incredulous—the very thing we craved night and day on the ride was here as our welcome gift. This was the right choice. I showered out back and by the time I returned to my bunk, Jalet, Pat's spouse and fellow innkeeper, had calligraphed my name on the end of the bed. A welcome I could not have expected after an eighty-mile day. How these two made a living deep in a mining canyon of a small town I didn't know. The occasional car almost never slowed and the only route in or out was the same mountainous two-lane. A hitchhiker was across the street. He was waiting for a ride to Bend, I can't imagine for how long. We took him some energy bars and water. It looked forlorn on that side of the road. And I thought back to the corner in Deming. The corner that would not let us alone.

We unpacked our panniers and settled in. Pat said the restaurant and brew pub stayed open till eight. We were starved—which became a euphemism for "Is it time yet?" There was never enough food but that was beside the point: smoked chicken wings and a microbrewery were a hundred yards away. The sun had not yet set. The brilliant light shone down the canyon. We grabbed a table outside. Our waiter, complete with a bowie knife, long beard and black vest arrived to declare, "It's all good—I'll be back." Somewhere a pirate ship was missing one of its crew. We nodded—and stretched our legs on the iron chairs. The brew pub was an old gas station—his father's, he would tell us—and they decided to turn it into a retro eatery and pub. Lucky for us—two brew pubs in the same day. My fellow cyclists tried the hoppy IPA and I sipped something cold although I missed the sour brews. My sons let me taste each time we arrived, so I was close to being part of the brew tour.

The chicken wings were smoked all day and we ate every kind—hot, spicy and barbeque—until we couldn't eat any more. The beer followed each serving and the sun drew a long shadow on the canyon wall. What a place to settle, to eke out a living. We kept asking ourselves *how* they made a living—Pat and Jalet, the waiter and the others who called Mitchell home. Maybe it didn't matter. They were close enough to town if they needed something. In Nevada, eighty miles was nothing to drive for convenience and it sort of made sense in that isolating way: this was a choice of being for something, not against. A choice of relative independence. Pat and Jalet were lay ministers in the church-come-hostel and they wanted to be here and did other odd jobs to make it. Strangely, they depended on cyclists coming through the canyon for donations. Their business ran completely on kindness. An anti-capital establishment, yet another paradox, but it worked for them.

Rain clouds were in the sky when we turned out the lights. It was a good thing we were in a room and not in our tents. When we awoke, the rain was coming down. We looked at each other and decided to delay our start. Sometime in the night, Pat called out to the hitchhiker and he slept in the hostel. He was gone before we rose.

There was coffee, pancake mix, cereal and more downstairs. We huddled by a big table, sipped black coffee, and I wrote in my journal, thankful for a morning without the rush to ride. Scott asked no one—"Do you think we're getting out of here anytime soon?"

I looked at the clouds, the rain on the window. "Nope." We read the magazines in the lobby. Jalet showed up about ten: "I'm so glad you haven't left. I was afraid I'd miss you." We took the sheets off our beds, packed our panniers and put our rain gear on. Pat motioned south. "If you go back a few miles, there's a beautiful dirt highway through the Painted Hills. It's not far. You'll be fine on those tires. Lots of cyclists take that route." We looked at each other, by now almost prepared for the change in routes. "Why not?" we laughingly said.

Serendipity had followed us to the hostel: the one night it rained we were sheltered. It had also given us a bed—which meant Scott, Joe, and Nevada could settle into the ride without an early start the next day. There was a certain euphoria to the morning. None of us discussed it, but it looked like the rain would stop, so we said goodbye to Pat and Jalet and rode off. I don't think we saw five cars in the time we were there. Maybe that's what drew them—the silence, a way to live without distraction. A way to serve.

The River Like It Was
XIV

Distance: 43 miles
Elevation: 3,585 feet
Mitchell, Oregon, 2019

I couldn't look up because the rain spat at my face. I trusted the others—it would stop soon—and tried to focus on the road ahead. We slowly separated, each of us alone with our thoughts. Day two as a whole group and my sons out front. I wrote several haiku but nothing captured this wet morning heading into the clouds. Nev and Cody found the Bear Creek Road turnoff and were gone. Scott, Joe, and I pedaled slowly, the dirt and ruts kept us from moving fast. At the cattle guard, Cody had his bike upside down—he was first to flat. He and Nevada worked in tandem—tire off the rim, tube off the inner lining and a new one out of the box. He knew how quickly the tubes could go. He pumped it until it was close to eighty pounds. "You guys go ahead."

"I think we'll stay and make sure everything's all right." Scott had an old, long pump and handed it to Cody. "Try this," and the tire inflated to a hundred pounds of pressure. He knew things could go south very quickly and wanted to make sure Cody was okay. Cody handed the pump back to Scott and gestured thanks. The connective tissue started to grow on the dirt road into the Painted Hills.

The rain let up and the clouds lifted a bit. Up ahead was a long, open valley. More hayfields and ranch houses. I looked down at the gravel and kept moving my front wheel back and forth to keep the heavy bike righted. We rode about seven miles before turning into the John Day River basin. The moisture had limited the dust and each of us found a rhythm in the dirt. I took off my rain gear and started to enjoy the colors—deep red, rust, olive, amber, ochre and colors that seemed more than these—to the canyon's rim. We rode uphill and the only sound was our tires on the dirt. I wondered how many other bikes had come this way. Pat alluded to several but it seemed quiet with the occasional raven, cow and sage, nothing like a route that was traveled. The clouds kept the light low and turned the minerals into a fan of subdued color. It was like riding into a funnel of red-brown dirt: some hardened path to the ridge. My sons were far ahead on the burnished trail with nothing to prove, no one to impress. Both of them had come up for air—literally and metaphorically they were on the rise. You spend your time as a father winnowing the choices, and when the door closes you choose at last to begin the way forward without them. You pretend they have the tools they need. You pretend not to watch as they disappear into the striated canyon. You ride without them, with two old guys like yourself and listen, as they pedal, to what *might* be said—"He slow you down?"

"Nah—it was an easy ride. Mostly. He hit the wall outside of Newport. Laid in the middle of the road. Lights just went out. I walked around, not sure what to do. And he got up, said let's go and we did. ...How's it feel, cutting the cord? That's a long way to leave home."

"Not sure—it might be right—just not sure. But I had to go. It was time. They were going to swallow me whole."

"And your lady?"

"She's good with it. She wanted a change a long time ago."

"So we're doing this—"

"Yeah, we are."

"Un-frickin' real."

"Just like riding through Patagonia when we were kids in that beat up old van."

"Just like that, except it's only on two wheels this time."

"Thanks bro—"

"For what?"

"For coming out here. It was a stretch for you. I didn't have to give up as much. I didn't have to quit to break free."

"We never would have done it."

"Yeah, that crazy old man of ours and Scott and Joe. They put it out there and here we are—riding into a little rock of heaven."

The sky was starting to clear. I couldn't register the beauty of the canyon walls. Photographs of the canyon look painted, as if some other artist had been here. But the artist was not a person; it was many millennia of geologic layers, rivers running to the Willamette Basin, the lethargy of time scored these walls. And here we rode—specks in the universe—pushing two wheels up its red dirt road. I did not know whom I was serving, only that the canyon's layered light let us through. At the summit, we turned onto Highway 207 and rode up a long riparian area. Bear Creek ran alongside the road. There were almost no sounds and we were alone. Cattle crossed the ridges on either side. I looked back for Joe and Scott—we were each in our rhythm—out of sight in the steady uphill climb. I saw a white van about a hundred feet behind me. I slowed for him to pass on the windy road, but he did not. He traveled on as if my speed—five miles an hour or less—were adequate. I didn't understand why he wasn't passing. A flicker of worry came by: was he here to cause trouble? I quickly pushed it out of my mind. The canyon would keep me, keep us, if not from harm at least from something outside its domain.

I saw Cody up ahead. He filled his water bottle in the creek but the Steripen wouldn't work—it was dark with sediment. "Pour it out," I yelled and gave him one of mine. The cattle had sullied the water and nothing we had would clean it. The extra weight on my bike had finally been worth it—there was water when we needed it. The cattle had crushed much of the sage and other low-growing shrubs. It was a used land, not permanently harmed but for a year or two the plants would be down. I wondered how this arrangement took place but knew that it would end in the livelihoods of the ranchers whose canyon we rode in. I scuttled any more thought—it was not the place. I couldn't be on the bike and find reclamation in a creek bed. Answers were hard to come by. The fouled water was no harbinger of high desert health. If that made it less than I imagined, it was nonetheless a truth of the West: we want the open space, we want the wild, we want the river like it was. And yet—there will be a reckoning.

The climb to the T at Highway 19 took it out of us. Scott looked at his phone. "Service Creek is about seventeen miles north. We could stop there and see how we're doing." The clouds returned and mercifully kept the heat from our backs. Cody and Nevada shot out in front of Scott, Joe and me. I was grateful Cody didn't have to wait for me any longer. He could ride with his brother and not hesitate or wonder if I was close behind.

Our second day together. The boys were hitting their stride and to be fair, so were the three of us who were no longer boys. We rode in the afternoon cool for ten miles—more gradual uphill in the pines on Butte Creek Pass. Whatever I had imagined the ride to be, it had come to us on its own terms: if you want this quiet, you must surrender and then I understood: there was no ride without letting go. The rhythm of home—the work, the routine, the daily scrub of staying in place was not here. I reached for those things more than once. The book of essays that had just come out was on a desk and the friends, the people I love—Debby whom I had not seen since leaving and my mother in her Southern California room watching daytime TV—I had to let them go to the climb up the pass. A conversion of focus that kept me pedaling into the parallel journey of contemplation that I imagine each of us felt at one point but could not describe.

The bike pulls you through the physical and into a threshold of stillness. Nothing outside of the movement, the pace of wind on the knees, the flutter of spokes below. It comes without notice, after hours of pushing against gravity. Pushing weight that should not be on a bike into mountains like this. At the top of the volcanic pass, we looked down to the John Day River canyon. A descent that was a first of many for my sons, who could not find the brakes and chose instead the howl of wind in their faces. I tried to ask them to slow down, but they disappeared before I heard any response. Scott turned to me—"They're gone."

As they should be, I thought. I put them in my bubble of light so they would find the center line and swerve hard into the curves dropping down to Service Creek. Scott, Joe, and I joined them at the bottom of the canyon. There was a sign for the campground and Spray—our initial destination—was another ten miles. The dirt road had taken longer than we thought, but it was worth it. We pulled into Service Creek with its infamous sign out front: Warm Beer, Lousy Food and Bad Service. Some places live up to their reputation.

The beer was cold but costly. We set up our tents by the creek, washed our riding shorts and hung them on Scott's makeshift laundry line strung between two Lombardi poplars. Nev found a couple trees creekside and stretched his tented hammock between them. This would be his first night in the hammock. The grass was about six inches high and the clouds were giving way to sunlight. There were two canvas tents on platforms; they cost more money and we opted for the comfort of stars.

Cody got out his stove and boiled water for mac and cheese, which by now had become an expectation. Scott brought chips back from the store with the IPAs—"New York prices," he said. And we opted out of a second six-pack. I tasted a swallow of Cody's—it was a good, hoppy, pale ale. Joe got out some jerky and we snacked in the late afternoon sun. I looked at the clouds in the West—the light was suffused with pink and orange. A sunset of clouds and broken sun. All of us stared up the canyon into its changing light. I tried to capture it on my phone. I wanted to paint it but I was too tired. I'd try at the next rest stop.

This was our second time camping by a creek. The water again, the water of mountains and snowmelt. It literally flowed beneath Nevada's hammock—a sound to rest by. Cody and Nev found some wood and stacked it for a fire in the rock pit. I walked back to the store and asked if there was any dessert I might take out. The young waitress pointed to cheesecake and I shook my head no. I used the bathroom and dodged the eyes of her older brother. It was hard to tell if they wanted guests. I wrote it off to being too long in the canyon. We texted our spouses from the picnic table and told lies until the fire took over. Joe nicknamed the place No Service Creek. The smoke kept us moving and I worried that Scott's tent would get the brunt of it. We said goodnight and closed the day. The creek at our sides, the fire burning down. Nothing broken, nothing lost. The five of us had come up two passes and were almost ready for the day ahead. I made some mental notes for my journal and a last haiku before I slept:

Red dirt and gravel—
fourteen miles to lie
in the Painted Hills.

A Chronicle of What Was Lost
XV

Distance: 53 miles
Elevation: 1,963 feet
Service Creek, Oregon, 2019

The sun hid behind the canyon wall. It was our first night of sleep below clouds and the threat of rain. I looked around—Scott was in his tent and Joe was still sleeping. Cody crawled out of our tent and went to find water. I laid there thinking about riding along the John Day River into Spray. I tried to write in my journal. My legs were sore. I imagined everyone was sore. The ride had registered its presence in our tissues: lactic acid was part of the rising. I rolled the Tenkara rod over my calves, thighs and AT bands to loosen them up. Cody reached in the tent and handed me a cup of coffee—"Here you go, Pops." I wrote a little longer and fetched some oatmeal from my panniers. We kept them inside the tent flap to keep the moisture off the gear.

Joe crawled out of the tent. "How you doing, my friend?" I asked him.

Joe nodded, "Pretty good but my back was stuck on this rock. I couldn't find the sweet spot on the ground."

"I've got some ibuprofen if you want it." Everyone had some ibuprofen.

"I'll be all right." And he was.

Cody turned to Nevada. "How'd the hammock work out?"

"I was out, didn't hear a thing." We stood over the stoves while they warmed water for breakfast. Cody put the peanut butter on the picnic table—it was a staple of the morning. Most of the clothes had dried and Scott put the drip line back in his panniers. He had almost every requisite device. I know it made his load heavy but like him, I understood the road was unforgiving. When a spoke broke you either fixed it or hitchhiked. That was the agreement. Take what you need. Nothing more, nothing less.

I walked over to the restaurant to use the bathroom. There were no eyes to dodge this time. The owners were sleeping and I walked back to the campsite. Sun had finally stretched to the canyon floor. It felt good on my skin. There was moisture on the tents, on the table. Cody broke down the tent and we packed our panniers with the last of the food. I pinched my drying riding shorts under the bungee cord and was almost ready. I looked back at the canyon to the west, tried to remember those clouds for a painting but I knew they were ephemeral.

We walked out of the campground with our bikes, forded Service Creek on a few 2 X 6s, and started to pedal to Spray. The John Day was green and the fly fishermen were out early. Some had John boats, some were in waders. I wished I were with them. I wished we could stop for a day, maybe two and find the trout below. The fishermen were the lone outposts, whipping the line, tranquil in the morning dew. The river seemed larger than I remembered. I had seen the John Day when I gave a reading near Pendleton years earlier; it was over a hundred feet wide and several feet deep—not a river to fool with. And yet the fishermen stood on sand bars, in eddies, in the cool shadows stripping the lines, a methodical rhythm to stir the trout from the pool below. I rode on but I wanted to know them, these few who stood in the water, these few who rose early to get here, these anglers whose time was spoken for by a river, by the temptation of a pull on the line. It's hard to explain why this tether to a mouth with gills is real, but it is no less difficult to explain this tether to the road, the one we rode on now by water. We rode into the market in Spray at the junction of Highways 19 and 207. There were probably twenty motorcycles outside. I heard a Canadian accent and we started to talk. "Where you riding to?"

"Just doing a little four-day tour. Down from British Columbia. What about you?

"Jackson Hole." Nev shot back.

"On a bike?"

We laughed. "We've been getting that a lot."

"I'd ride there but not without an engine."

"We'll swap right now—straight across. You can have the pleasure of a slow ride, almost no gas and a little more food," I teased.

"We'll keep our cycles. Be safe. It's a beautiful country," the old guy said as he put his helmet on. Those words would come to us from many bikers—the two-wheel world, whether motorized or not—who understood that the road was not just a road. It was a place of extremes—heat, wind, cars and curmudgeons.

"We will," I promised for all of us, "we will," and we rode off toward Kimberly.

About an hour later Scott popped the question: "Time to get out the rods?" The river had slowed and it was shallow enough to wade with our sandals and cast. We looked at each other and decided to stop. Like the dirt road in the Painted Hills, the river had other demands and we listened to them. I was grateful for the morning respite, to stand at the river's edge and watch the swallows dart from the willows. Nev headed upstream. I followed him to the first hole. A snag and then a small rainbow. It was early in the season; the fish had just hatched months before. I cast downstream and let the line drift. I couldn't get the line across the river; it was too short and that side was deep. They were jumping for flies in the shadows. The splash and circles moved away from them. After a half-hour I came back to the bike. Cody found the right fly—he had one on every other cast. "Come on over here, Pops."

"What are you using?"

"A Parachute Adams—I have an extra if you want it."

"I'll be there in a bit." I thought there might be enough time to paint. Joe was writing in his journal. "You don't want to fish?" I asked.

"I'm not a fisherman."

"Really? This is the best kind of fly fishing—almost no one in a quiet elbow of the river."

"I've tried. Just not my thing."

"Well, your bike's lighter. I couldn't stand the thought of being by a river and not having my rod." Scott worked downstream, casting with each step. He was the only one with a reel and could cast farther. One after another, the small trout bent his rod. Scott was the consummate angler, spent time scrubbing the shallows of creeks and streams. I was in love as well but fatally spoiled: too many times I had been in the presence of large trout.

"Come on in, Shaun. Take my rod. They're biting here." Scott walked out of the river and broke his sandal before handing me his rod. I deferred at first, not done with my painting and then waded in. The river was cold. Water rose to my waist. I cast into the willow's edge. A riser but he didn't take it, then another who shook the hook. Most of the trout had been scared away, but it was good to cast Scott's fly rod. The Tenkara was a mid-length rod that telescoped down to a couple feet. There was no reel, just a fixed line to whip. A compromise for our bikes, for the river. The trout swam on and we snacked, cajoling the shadows left behind. Cody's $100, out-of-state Oregon license was down to $10—having released at least ten trout. The rest of us would have to gather a few more to reduce its annual fee. Joe set off before us—he wanted to get a head start, not feel rushed. There were at least another thirty-five miles to go. I tried to finish the painting but there wasn't time and put the brush and watercolor paper in my pannier.

Cody and Nevada were sitting on the cement that held the cables for the small freight box that went across the river. It was tempting to stay. This was the moment when having time was such a luxury. We did not *have* to arrive, only to see the day through its course. We started back up the dirt road with hay in the ruts and then pedaled away, our first day of fishing as five. We rode for more than an hour before we caught up to Joe. Always, when the distance became over-long, I wondered if something had intervened. He was fine, just pedaling in a pine grove. "Was wondering where you were."

"I wanted to get out in front of the boys," he said. "They ride pretty hard."

I smiled. "Hoping this trip gives them the leeway they need.

They've both been running, especially Nev, and the bike runs at another pace. I think they're coming to that awareness. It takes a while, you know. This is only day three—after a couple weeks you can't think about other things. This is the star above and below you, this is the lone galaxy in which you reside."

"You damn poets. Where'd you learn to speak like that?"

"I don't know, Joe. It wasn't something I tried to do. The words came tumbling in. I had to figure what the hell to do with them. And started writing."

"Prose or poems?"

"Mostly poems but it was stories that kept me quiet in school. I wrote for days and the teacher, my fourth-grade princess, let me fill those blank pages I stapled together. I had no idea what writing meant. I just liked it. Like standing in the stream. Made me feel good."

"I wanted to write," Joe said. "Long before I taught, I fell in love with words. But work and school got in the way. I went back in my thirties. So did my wife. She became a doc and I got a degree in English. Guess it's good for something but the teaching is only half of what it means. If the kids don't read, then I kind of sit outside, waiting for them to come back. I don't know how much longer I can go but that's what you get for going on. Getting that piece of paper. Some other way to work. But I read, goddamnit. Like it was the only thing left."

"They get that," I replied. "The kids don't always tell you but what you say, what you do in that classroom matters. They read the lines in your face."

Joe smiled. "I don't know—sometimes I don't know what they get."

At the Thomas Condon Paleontology and Visitor Center we read maps of geology, saw plant, and animal evolution from the Eocene to the Miocene eras, saw "terminator pigs" whose shoulders were six feet from the ground (entelodonts). Whose canyon was home to such species, I thought, filling our water bottles at the drinking fountain. An owl's nest was overhead; the white dung shaped like watery stars below. I wondered if there was an owl to guide us up the canyon's interior. I listened for the ahoo, ahoo, ahoo, hoo but only heard rims turning in the dirt. A William Stafford poem, "Earth Dweller," was posted in the kiosk, his words like the owls who visited at night.

> Now I know why people worship, carry around
> Magic emblems, wake up talking dreams
> They teach to their children: the world speaks.
> The world speaks everything to us.
> It is our only friend.

The light slipped through the spokes. After a long time by the water, we were trying to get to Dayville, back to Highway 26. It had been good to get off the main road for a few days. The small roads were like old friends you met in a café—something unspoken let you in, let you experience the quiet, the landscape on either side of the blacktop. The John Day was a green tail we followed south. This river was one to record—there was a subtle strength below its surface. In the winter, in the spring runoff, it was not a river to be ignored. Another tributary of the Columbia, it is the third longest free-flowing river in the U.S. at 284 miles, nearly a fourth of the distance to Teton Pass. It would take six days to ride its length, but we rode its flanks for two of those days, pressed to the highway downstream.

We rode through hayfields with harobeds (automatic baling wagons), tractors, and the occasional house pitchforked on the land. There was a private airstrip so large a farm abutted its edge. Cars and machines of every kind. This life was rural and for some, it was good, very good. For others, it was way to make do. Some of the houses were barely houses and some were trailers or a hodgepodge of both. I wondered what brought their owners to this agrarian coast, what kept them inside. Was it the frame of place and time in which their beliefs found comfort? Was it a storm they left behind? Some choices are not rational, some choices move out of the dark and come without recourse. Some choices leave us where we stopped.

This land was a place to stop. To let go of what was expected and take root. The cheap, political slants that scattered the highway were no different than other small towns. But these words were living under a tent of misplaced fears and dreams. I saw kids bucking bikes in the yard, patterns stitched on the lawn.

Nothing was free here, nothing worth keeping public save the outlaws and the busted pews in church. I lived next to a man for twenty years who brought home that same reckless carnival every night—"You think I give a shit—ain't my fault the government's so f---ed up." I watched who got on and who got off. It wasn't pretty. And just as quickly, I looked up from my tire to a house with a border of straight and simple lines, a flower bed, a hay fork, a tractor idle in the shed. Someone carved a niche from this land. Someone claimed its broken heritage—we were still in the ancestral West of Shoshone and Sahaptin peoples, the West that was never really the West. Like all colonized rivers and wildlands, it was suffused with other tributaries, other roots. They moved beneath houses, hayfields. They chronicled what was lost. No house afforded such witness.

We stopped to snack. The light was drawing low. Somehow in the hope of arriving in Dayville, we forgot to eat lunch, complicated by the fact that the road stops were thin on real food. The distance wasn't over-long, but the energy bars wore out quick. I swallowed a few more chews, asked Nev and Cody if they wanted some. They each took one, a kind of chicory for the gums. Scott and Joe pulled up. "How much farther?"

"Can't be too far—should be there in an hour," Cody said, looking at his phone. "Y'all good?" he asked, and they rode on. By the time I caught up to them, they had already scoped out the town. There were three campgrounds. One was filled with young people on a retreat. But the ice cream store was close by—damn, I thought. I bought a cone just to be safe.

"You go to the one up there, I'll head to the one by the river," Nev shouted. I turned up the road to a church. There was a hostel inside. A lone biker stood in the doorway. "What's it like?"

"Not too bad. A place to sleep."

"You riding by yourself?" He nodded yes. "Can I take a look inside?" I got off my bike and took a peek. It was pretty spartan. "Thanks. I'll see what my sons find."

Nev motioned to the campground by the river. "There's showers and grass. Think we should stay here."

Scott and Joe pulled in—"Looks good to me."

We took turns in the single shower, thankful for the hot water and a commode. We spread out by the river. There were motorhomes, expensive rigs, trailers, and tents. I walked to the entrance and saw a thin man who seemed familiar. I couldn't place him and let it go. We were starved, but the river called. Cody and Nev got out their rods. I loved watching them on the riverbank. This was the silent movie I took, the screen a father sees when his sons have run to the river. A parallax image of two apart from him and close to the wetlands down the canyon. A piece of film I will take to my chest and share when the sun returns for those standing apart from their sons.

Scott came out of the shower and announced, "Better get to the restaurant. They close at eight." We walked our bikes up to the highway. The sun was nearly down and we rode the quarter mile to the only open place. At least we were clean. The waitress pointed to the table by the wall. We ordered the same thing—flank steak, baked potato and salad. She brought out a pile of potato skins and cheese. They were gone in minutes. They didn't serve any booze but we probably needed water more. I have never tasted a steak like that. It was grown in those same fields we rode through. As tender as slow-cooked ribs. We swallowed dinner without a thought. Empty of all things but hunger. I was hurting but after having ridden all day, I couldn't stop. She brought us homemade apple pie á la mode and we ate that too. My stomach was gorged.

I confessed to the dark outside—best meal, best damn meal—and rode back to camp by headlight. Cody made some tea and we talked over beers at the picnic table. We didn't last long. Another day of rivers and hayfields and mountains, begun and ended in places small and dignified. Places of origin. Places you return to, whatever the cost. I said goodnight, brushed my teeth under the light bulb outside the showers and walked to the river, the riffles in the starlight. Joe was reading. Scott was trying to hang the laundry line. Nev was in his hammock, reading too. We were distilled of all movement, all effort spent in the lacquer of exhaustion.

An Unintended West
XVI

Distance: 61 miles
Elevation: 3,476 feet
Dayville, Oregon, 2019

Absence. I was acutely aware of the absence of noise, news, music—
the folderol that wept in a mind. I could not remember a time when
so little was in my cranium. The miles had rid me of thoughts that
otherwise scampered alongside. All of my focus was on the wheel,
feet from my face. Every pedal stroke took supreme attention and,
in the mountains, effort. There was no other route, no other path
to day's end. A routine solace yes, but a further quieting: the mind
stopped needing, wanting, stopped that insistent pressure to require
of a day more than it could give.

    This was not in my purview when we left. I had no idea that
this relative silence would accompany me. I thought the fog of effort
would be filled with other fogs—ones I left in the work and rhythm
of home, things you cannot run from. But I was wrong. The silence
was a comfort whose presence was slow to yield to other intrusions.
Maybe it didn't need an explanation. It wore into me, into us and
became a habit of hours in wind or cold or whitened sunlight,
a weathering of tissue and vision. The sweat formed rings on my
sunglasses and I just looked a few feet in front of the wheel. I stopped

worrying about trying to see. What I saw was before me, nothing more, nothing less. Absence became a correlate for presence. That was the line we rode on—nothing in between. A silence of mayflies, honeybees, mosquitoes. A silence of light wind, tire gravel, chain stretch. A silence of looking out, looking in.

This ramble-down thought is what I awoke to in Dayville. My stomach still hurt from the dinner. I imagined we all hurt and summarily promised not to go without lunch again. I walked to the men's stall and saw the same man from the night before. A flicker of recognition—he was a friend from home.

"What are *you* doing here?"

"We're riding the other way," and we hugged hard. He was on the TransAmerica Bike Trail going west. He'd ridden to Missoula the year before but had eye problems and had to stop. So he finished this summer. His wife was in the car. I yelled at her and we hugged.

"What a coincidence!" She didn't think we'd meet up. Debby had texted her our approximate location but due to the changes in our schedule, it was doubtful that we'd connect. And here they were. I couldn't have staged this gathering in a campground miles from anywhere. We went back to the same restaurant for breakfast and stood with them for pictures. He rode off, alone, for his sixty-plus miles that day. His wife followed in the van. There was a solitude about his journey. "I wish I had some friends along," he said, but he was determined to get to Astoria, Oregon, to plant his wheels in the Pacific.

Nev and Cody walked to the general store, pumped their tires and bought another tube. It seemed like every store on the highway doubled as a bike shop. We looked at the map and suddenly felt an ease. The ride had divided into thirds—morning, noon, and night—and the first hours were the best. The body was fresh, mind waking, belly full. The first hour was like watching the sun rise: little to consider, little to abide. The town of John Day was halfway to Austin, where we hoped to camp. It was a lazy pedal through hayfields and rusted cars. We followed the John Day River, our guide for easterly direction. Joe and Scott were behind me. I looked back, could see their outlines, and kept riding. Nev and Cody were out front, pedaling in the warm sun. I imagined they were shedding the obligations of home. I never asked, didn't want to. So often, when Nevada called home, there was exhaustion in his voice, as if he had run for miles. Debby and I listened—the final stop for a parent. The regimen of early morning flights and late nights was spinning across the air waves.

He talked to Cody sometimes—"A lot of perks—kind of—if you can keep learning," when Cody wanted to get into consulting, "but sometimes the sting isn't worth it. You wake up with ashes on your pillow. They told me I'd make partner but you never know what's out there, what's in the rear view mirror that I flew by? It's a crazy up or out culture—not the non-profit the 'rents stood up. You'll figure it out. You've got a lot going C-bear, you'll sort things, you watch." They broke the rhythm together, comparing what it took to leave, to stay. Cody chose a different firm, a different culture, but at the end of the day the work came first.

The road took and the road gave. You were not far from its outline. The river was a jade string at our sides. We threaded the black top above, the green below. The sun rose in our faces. Sweat, water and salt on our skin. A sign perched in a yard—something about prison and Hillary—I didn't need to read more. Nev turned and rode back to take a picture. The houses bent with belief in renegade posters. The closer we came to John Day, the angrier the signs grew. More right-wing, more hard-line, more offensive and, I thought, just like the signs of home. How the country has split open like a melon! But I live with my neighbors; I don't ask their beliefs or they mine. We straddle the widening of a time together, a time with vehemence. An agreed-upon place of reckoning. Some kindling of respect for other points of view. It's not required in big cities. In small places, places close to the earth, you track what your neighbor does, how they mark time. I choose to mark it with them when I can. When I can't, we just—

I heard Joe—shaken, whitened, short of breath. "That sonofabitch skidded—that's the closest I've come—"

Scott got off his bike. "They jumped out and started to pick a fight. I told 'em we didn't want one. The dog jumped out in front of me. I had nowhere to go. Joe swerved into the street. They cussed and heaved and got back in the truck and drove off."

I looked at Joe. He was stricken with other images. He was tangled in a barb of what might have happened—he was the first to edge the wheel of a car—the one that hurt you and yet had no feeling. The loud, barking diesel. The quiet Chevy. The Saturn ready for the wrecking yard. They came out of hiding. One nearly drove my friend off the road. One nearly drove him to the well of quiet. Joe was looking into the parking lot. Not seeing much. Trying to find his way back. Nev and Cody came out of the store with food. We tried to eat in the cool of the grocery store awning. Tried not to think about what other dogs might spring from yards, what other men might spring from cars. Men who didn't need a reason. Men who got their rocks off doing the dirty.

Highway 395 went south from here. The road home. The road we drove to Susanville to find that first night in Portland. The road that went south to more open pasture, more BLM land. I looked at Joe quiet with his thoughts. He looked at Scott. The road into Malheur National Wildlife Refuge. The Bundys. The whole damn sad mess of a squalid chapter in the West. Or less. And then it wasn't so hard to fathom the brakes, the skid marks, the deafening pitch of a car at your back. It wasn't so hard to remember what we left, what we came from, who staged the rampage in the desert of home. Bundy and his group were armed when our senator showed up at their southern Nevada ranch and they were given a weary permission to roam. A stalemate of ideas and dead weight in the corner of blame. I have no use for guns in the sage. It has nothing to do with beliefs. It is a definition of place I refuse to countenance. Joe was trying to refuse it too. Nev and Cody didn't have words. They wanted him to know. They wanted him to be all right.

I wondered how long it would take to tempt the light that kept us thus far. And thanked what gods were with us for Joe's safety. We looked across the street, the mountain to the east, the climb into Prairie City. Joe looked into the distance, "That was the closest—"

Clouds were coming in. We filled our water bottles in the store and pushed the food into the panniers. Something had joined us, had wedged its way into our path. We rode out of the parking lot. I didn't want to look back and kept pedaling, hoping the mountain would assuage the sudden swerve. It was a good ten-mile climb to the covered wagon rest stop. The valley stretched below. Oregon's long green river valley to the west. The wind was picking up. Scott and Joe pulled in. Nev and Cody were already in the wagon—repurposed here to signify the passage of settlers. We took a picture on the knoll above the valley, the Malheur Refuge not far below. A truculent light of cloud-sun broke from the south, southwest. We ate some bars, tried to laugh and crossed the four-lane to start up Dixie Pass. An afternoon of climbing. What we needed. What the clouds could not say.

In the radius of the American West, it's a pretty straight line from the Malheur Refuge to the corner in Deming, New Mexico. A corner I was trying to forget. A corner whose anonymity kept things from memory. Like the buses that unloaded the delirious faces of the children seeking refuge in this country. Somehow they crept into the signs that leapt from the front yards coming into John Day. Somehow they wrangled the universe of tough talk on range land. Somehow they became friend to the object of derision. And the refuge became its canticle. A refuge I would never outrun. We tried to let the place go. The valley we looked upon to the south was just as beautiful without knowledge of its discomfiting history. But it was not a knowledge that would leave us. The mountain was ahead. That was the only certainty. The pines, the wind, they kept the aberration at bay. I wanted to take the moment away from Joe, from Scott—peel the ribs of the morning but all I could do was pedal and look south when I stopped on the ridge.

By now, the newly arrived children had fanned to the desert of churches and people for whom the corner was home. The Bundys had switched places—from courthouse to ranch, absent a few whose guns brought them to dust. A radius of proportion, of outlines in the barren land. Not a place that was wanted, not a place of comfort. Exactly what a place in the West might be without us. Without the temerity of too many warring opinions. Without the guns in the saddle. Without the straight line to the river south of Deming, the river that people crossed to find a home without violence. The cure, it seemed, was not far from here, if only we could abide the endless sage, the outliers lying in wait. I thought of Kittredge leaving his Oregon farm roots: the West was founded on a mythology of conquest.

Cody pulled out his phone—it was another five miles to Austin. It looked like there was a restaurant. We could eat before riding on to Bates State Park. The mountain was starting to cut the noise from the mind. It was a 2,200-foot climb to the summit. Somehow that was just enough. The sun was low at our backs and the wind picked up. I listened to it in the lodgepole and ponderosa pines. Joe was in front of me. "How you doing?" A grunt and not much more. Cody and Nev pulled away.

The miles distorted any notion of calm. I was hungry again and tried not to think about food. The wind pulled at my side— the campgrounds on the ridge would be cold tonight. But there was wood and some campers had the coveted shelter of a trailer. I heard Cody yelling—something about "way to go—" and looked up. They were in the parking lot of the Austin House Café and Country Store. We pulled up behind them. Nothing could have been more welcomed. A place to eat and breathe before the hustle of camp at nightfall. We ordered beer and dinner and the owner brought us clean towels for showers. A thimble of kindness in the mountains— it was early in the season and we were lucky she let us use them. Joe held up his namesake IPA—Joe—and we took a picture for the spouses who didn't know what had gone on. Eddy Arnold was on the radio playlist—"Make the World Go Away," apropos of the evening. One by one, we changed and felt as if the salt of the day had gone down to another place.

A group of young motorcyclists rode in from Corvallis with stoves, hatchets, wood, and beer strapped to their bikes. This was respite from the week. We looked at each other—not so different but for the conversation. One of the guys had just rebuilt his motorcycle. He insisted on showing me his paint job—a canary yellow. It was an old Harley but running now. What circumstance brought us together? They were hungry and happy to be out of the cold.

We ate more food than I thought possible—again—and staggered to our bikes. The proprietor asked us where we were going. Nev and

Cody pointed to Scott and Joe. "They're going back to Mitchell. We're going on to Vale." We thanked her and her husband, who was still cooking for the others who had driven up for the weekend. The restaurant had been on the market for a couple years. No takers. They were going south for the winter. I waved to the bikers and we rode off—about seven miles downhill to Bates State Park.

We picked a couple sites on the grass and began to set up camp. I went for firewood, which, unbelievably was stacked with a wagon nearby. Two dollars a load and it was dry wood *with* kindling. I started a fire and looked down at the Middle Fork of the John Day. The sun was behind the mountain. We were standing in shadow. Joe emerged from his tent. The temperature dropped. A young woman joined us—she was camped below. A New Yorker, she smiled when Nev told her he was from Brooklyn. She'd moved to Portland a year and a half ago. We put the Oreos on the table and took turns revisiting the day. Nev and Cody were happy to have someone their age in the conversation. "I try to get out on the weekends," she said.

"Queens is not a place you get out of easily." Nev joked. "I grew up out here. I still miss it but tell myself I don't. Moving to the other coast when I get home. Maybe I'll get to see a little more of this." The Harleys followed us to the campsite. The howl of pipes was disquieting but soon they were in tents, by a fire, letting the day down.

The flames were outline to some other day that whipped in the ash. I fumbled for my pen in the panniers but let the thought go. The night ebbed to a close. A young man was in his tent when we arrived. His bike, belongings and towel were perfectly sorted outside. I hoped we hadn't kept him up. I saw the Brooks saddle—and wondered if it helped him. Once worn in, the leather seat was something to be envied. We never talked about it—but our seats were light, hard and not always easy on the arse. One thing you learn on a bike—forget the ease. It's more than an equation of weight and use, closer to a spoon or cup you might favor in the morning. Closer to being in a chair with a lump in the back or a spring gone. You ride with it and sometimes you let it go to the flames, to the stars that, however blighted they may have been, were luminous tonight.

It was cold when light came in the tent. I didn't want to get up.

Cody pulled on his pants and went for water. The spigot was next to the table. I found my down jacket and stood outside. Mist was on the canyon floor. The river was a dark brown wedge to the southwest. A car drove in and the ranger went into the office. A half-hour later he drove up in his golf cart. "Good morning. Where y'all from?"

Scott shook his hand. "Mostly Nevada and a little New York, California."

"I'm Larry. Been running this park for thirty years. Going to retire next year. Figure it's enough."

"I'm Scott and these are my friends, Joe, Shaun and his sons, Nevada and Cody."

"This place is nice—the bathrooms are heated and clean."

"See that building down there? Last year we had two bikers who stood in it all night, it got down to seventeen. And they were fine. Thankful for the heat. This used to be an old lumber town. But the septic tanks bled into the water and they had to leave. Some of them moved their houses to Prairie City or John Day. A good number of those folks grew up here. They were the ones that saved the place. Helped turn it into what it is now. They wanted something here to signify what they had, what they grew up with."

We looked at each other. A lumber town that closed in the '70s and now was a campground? The nicest one we'd been in. "You boys have a good ride—" and Larry drove off to start his day. The sun was just creeping over the ridge. Down below, the bikers were waking and the lone bicyclist emerged from his tent.

"I saw you in the church in Dayville. Hope we didn't keep you up last night," I said. He shook his head. "Didn't hear a thing."

"You riding alone?"

"Yeah—going up to Baker City. You guys?"

"Three of us are going to Vale—and the other two back to Mitchell. We're trying to get to Jackson Hole."

"I'm riding the TransAmerica Bike Trail—another couple months I'm guessing."

"That seat help?"

"Not as much as I thought."

"Well, if it's any comfort, ours hurt too." We laughed and sipped coffee in the chill morning. There was a palpable weight in the air. We had grown close in a very few days, and now Joe and Scott were riding away. Their presence, their string-theory and existential alchemy gave way to something larger and I wasn't ready for it to go. Nev and Cody weren't either. Scott and Joe ate oatmeal from their cups and weren't exactly sure how far they would ride downriver. Fishing was a certainty. Joe would look on, journal and say his goodbye to the day before. We hugged hard in the cold light, packed the panniers with the last of the food, said goodbye to the young woman and rode back to the Austin Café. Larry told us about spring water half-way to the lodge. We saw the pipe but didn't stop—I'm not sure why. He said people drove with five-gallon bottles to fill for their homes in John Day. We had filled our bottles from the spigot—some things you just let go.

We walked in and the owner was there, brewing coffee, her husband over the grill. We ordered eggs, bacon and toast. She asked again, "Where you going? There's nothing between here and Vale. Why don't I make you some sandwiches?" We looked at each other—saved again. "Sure—" and she walked back to the kitchen. We ate in silence. Eddy Arnold was sleeping somewhere on the radio dial. She brought more coffee. We were alone in the pine room. The sandwiches were big enough for five. We hoped Scott and Joe had enough food, but knew they had everything they needed. It was what we couldn't say that was left behind.

Zodiac

Noun:

1. A circular diagram with 12 parts, each named after a constellation, used in astrology.

2. A circle, circuit, etc.

Etymology: from Latin zodiacus, from Greek zoidiakos, shortening of zoidiakos kyklos

(zodiac circle), from zoion (living being) + kyklos (circle, wheel).

Earliest documented use: 1390.

A Further Toll
XVII

Distance: 88 miles
Elevation: 3,142 feet
Austin, Oregon, 2019

"Tolstoy takes a long time to lay his trap," Joe again, his echo lodged
deep in the refrain of four short days. His scant remark about the
Russian novelist was indicative of a mind that didn't let go. Two more
winters after that he stopped teaching, the grain of old books having
lost their readers to screens. Three summers later we rode into Big
Hole National Monument, none of us feeling very good about it.
Joe asked me to write about it but I couldn't—what can be said of
the ghost tents lying in the fields of loss? I thought about him and
Scott, whose hydrologic surveys might keep us from further climate
harm—these twin stems of learning we left behind as I stepped onto
my bike outside the Austin Café. And remembered Joy Harjo.

> It's not easy to say this
> or anything when my entrails
> dangle between paradise
> and fear.

I said goodbye to the ephemera of their friendship.

My sons were out front in the shade of the pines, pedaling to Blue Mountain Summit. It was almost the right amount of cover from the morning sun. We had hoped to make Unity the day before, but the delays kept us from the regimen of a schedule. By now, distance was approximate—what we found as we rode became the day's cartography. Ours was closer to a map of insurrection and it kept us from taking our route too seriously.

I didn't look up to see my sons but once—it was about an hour from the café to the summit and we let our thoughts go to the wind. I wondered if my sons worried that the three of us might get too quiet, but I knew also that the quiet came from family. The earned quiet of years, the relative quiet of not needing to ask why.

Cody was atop the ridge waiting for me. It was mid-morning. "How you doing, Pops?" I smiled and felt almost alive. We'd been in the saddle two weeks, our muscles stretched to the routine of long climbs. I looked east to the valley below. A distance of hay and hills and small buildings, the outlines of an east-west highway. We coasted past Unity Lake State Park, the hills dotted with sage and juniper. It looked like the landscape of home and there were almost no cars. I was grateful for the time without noise. The singular fragrance of sage crossed my nose. There was comfort in the sparse vegetation— this is where you belong, this is how you define the soil.

My thoughts drifted. In three days my mother would turn ninety—an almost unthinkable threshold. I imagined she could see us, take pleasure in the long expanse to the east, her grandsons nearly free of the regimen of work and stability. Not unlike her when she was a vibrant woman, when she knew what the open road meant. Had she been able, there would have been another bike beside us. I remember her in her fifties. We were in Mexico and she took off from the beach to paraglide. Just as free as the two men in front of me now.

I knew we would call her from a phone in a mountain town, try to send our thoughts into her board-and-care home. I knew that my son's voices would elevate the day in which she was sitting. I hadn't received any texts from my sisters so I trusted that my mother's health was fair or at least not worse. I thanked them for watching her in my absence. There was a lot of time to thank those around me.

By now, the exterior varnish had pretty much worn off. I had little to hide behind—I was just a rider with my sons. We never talked about it but they were rubbed clean too. You couldn't be on a bike for days and not become finite, scrubbed to one purpose, to one elegiac note, a symmetry of being in the wind-driven miles.

We stopped for a drink in Unity then pushed on to El Dorado Pass, crossed Willow Creek and coasted into Ironside, an empty town of faded, clapboard buildings. I was starting to understand what the woman in the Austin Café said—"There's nothing between here and Vale." We found some shade and ate the sandwiches her husband made. I tried to imagine doing this segment without her counsel. The road would have taken a further toll.

We were still in Malheur County and I hoped the unknown would keep its distance. Joe probably had a hard time getting back on the bike today. Yesterday was more than a close escape. Yesterday was a feral shot in the ribs. To keep riding he had to push the image from consciousness. Scott was fishing the Middle Fork of the John Day. In his journal, Joe wrote long about the screech from the truck. Or so I believed. He did what was needed to let it slip from memory. The Malheur River, a tributary of the Snake, took its name from the French-Canadian trappers—misfortune. A place name that kept its meaning. The bramble of too many taking its land for granted.

"I miss them," Nevada said to no one. "Miss their banter. Wonder how they're doing today? If they rode back to Mitchell?"

We nodded in agreement. This was our time to turn to each other, to the miles of rolling highway and we pedaled on to Brogan Summit. Cody looked at his phone: "From Brogan to Vale, Willow Creek parallels the road. Water's close."

There just wasn't any place between for food and drinks. The owner was right—we were on our own and miles from Vale, in the hayfields, the dusty irrigation ditches and little shade. The heat was firmly overhead. Nev and Cody put water-soaked bandanas on their necks; I was still hoping for a miracle of sunscreen protection. After fourteen days we had skin the color of walnut—striped from the gloves to the shirt sleeves, from the bike shorts to shoes. My face was a grizzled beard of dry skin. I stopped caring about my looks. It made no sense. Each day came over the horizon and if we had no water to wash, so be it. We rode whether or not there was a place to bathe. It seemed almost beyond credulity to imagine a bathroom outside of a hotel, let alone some semblance of cleanliness.

At last we rode into Brogan—a small agrarian outpost on Highway 26. Founded by Dennis Brogan in the early 1900s, it was intended to be an agriculture hub close to the short-line into Vale. Three dams were built and canals brought water to the farmland. But the droughts of the '20s and '30s closed that dream and Brogan drifted off. It felt like there were a lot of these dreams riding this highway, like there was more here than what we saw. Things unspoken. Towns that curled up in isolation, skinned of what they once stood for.

We bought some Gatorade and ate some energy bars and Cody looked at his phone: "Still have twenty-four miles to Vale." We wished for shade. It was an untenable heat—like the heat coming over the Coast Range so long ago—but save the lone cottonwoods and an occasional rest stop, there was only a dusty distance in the sun. Not much else to point to. We filled our water bottles and guessed another two hours to Vale. We made Jamieson in an hour— home to handmade yarns—and kept on. The heat wouldn't let up. The wind was at our backs and without its push, the day would have felt eternal. The water kept my throat from drying but I could not drink enough. The two outlines in front of me dipped their bandanas again. I finally put a wet one over my scalp, beneath my helmet. The sun radiated—we tried to navigate its presence.

I imagined Joe and Scott riding west, into the sunset, without the terminus of valley heat. I imagined them by the middle fork of the John Day. The night before had been one of the rare moments without intrusion of light or noise. The fire burning to ash, Katie, the New York transplant, teasing us about riding bikes when a car could do the job just fine and Larry proud to share his small corner of the mountain. They were not far. Nev was right—I missed them. I wanted to know that their road held no surprises, that the travel back to Mitchell was without incident. It would be days before we heard from them and we had to trust that silence was its own reward. Still, I could see them with us, in the rows and rows of hay cut for the second time, almost to the Idaho border. They were our shamans, our seers, who had touched down briefly and moved on. They brought some other refrain to the ride and we were practicing letting go. We were listening without them, the wind pushing into the late afternoon.

Willowcreek had one store which, thankfully, was open. We leaned our bikes against the tin siding and went inside just to feel the air conditioning. I threw water on my face in the bathroom. Outside, I held the bottle over my head and let it drain. Of course, it evaporated in minutes but it was cool. A man drove up in a large tractor and kicked the dirt from his shoes. We sipped more Gatorade and ate yogurt beneath the porch. "Ten more miles," Cody shouted. "You ready, old man?" I laughed, not worth much more and got back on my bike.

When we hit Vale, Cody and Nev spilt up to find a hotel. The main drag was a hodgepodge of empty buildings and stores trying to hang on. The farmers grew onions and raised cattle. Out of the corner of my eye I saw a coffee house. The usual double take—they could make it *here*?—and I noted the cross street for the next morning. There was a pizza place too. It looked like it might be open. We rode through town and Nev caught up to us at the Bates Motel. It almost looked like Hitchcock could be inside. I don't think it had seen many patrons. A few doors hadn't been opened for months. The owner peeked up from his living room TV—"Yes, we're open. Let me get you a card. Write your names down. You can bring your bikes in your room."

Done. We found a room and didn't ask how much or how long the weary stayed. Another near-ninety-mile day. We collapsed on the two double beds. Not much to say. I walked into the shower and let the salt pour down the drain. We tried to text home but the Internet was spotty. Nev looked for dinner—we could always hope. We rode back into town and stopped at the pizza joint. Inside, it looked like a biker bar with food. My sons ordered two cold IPAs and we went out back to sit on the picnic tables. On the wall were many slogans—most of them offensive—and we drank slowly, savored the calm before the pizza. They started to talk as men grown from the same stalk. I leaned in, too tired to do much else. "You listen like it was the most important thing—" Cody faded off—"that's why you have so many—"

"I try to treat people—I spent a long time listening to others. It's kept me awake—the concerns of others. I spent a long time before that trying to be heard. We find the place to begin, again, after the days and months of school and home, and—"

"Sometimes it's hard to listen," Nev turned. "It's never easy, standing over there when what you want is to be in the middle of things." We shook our heads in acknowledgment.

"I'm still learning how—" Cody swallowed again.

"Aren't we all."

"You guys have the wings?" The tattooed server set the wings down.

We couldn't find a way out of the sun and went back inside to eat. Somehow, the service just got better. The owner came over to our table. "Sorry it's taken so long. Let me get you another beer on the house." We looked at each other—kindness ushered us into their lives.

"We're good. Been on our bikes all day. Just happy to be out of the sun."

By the time we walked outside, the sun was almost down. Nev's back tire was low. He and Cody took turns pumping to get enough pressure to get back to the motel. Inside the room, Nev took it off the bike and changed the tube. He kept the punctured one just in case he flatted again and ran out of spares. They were good to me, always and slept together so that I might have my own bed. I fell into a deep sleep, the whine of the AC blurring the sound from the highway. The Bates Motel was good enough.

The Midday Silence
XVIII

Distance: 75 miles
Elevation: 1,433 feet
Vale, Oregon, 2019

If ever there was a stretch of highway that reflected its riders, the ride to Vale was it. Tempered with dry heat, wind and dust, I could still see the hazy sky when I opened my eyes in the cinderblock room of the motel. My sons were sleeping. We could have slept until noon. The whir of the AC drowned out the coffee maker. I fumbled with the light on my phone. "It's all right—turn on the light." Cody's words were barely audible.

I sat with bad coffee in my hands, stared at the bike, at our panniers and clothes scattered at the foot of the beds. We had finally started to look like the road we were riding down: disheveled, layered with the day's salt and debris. The news was a long way from us now—I couldn't think of much save finding my bike shorts and socks to start again. My mind was empty. There were some words on my phone and they became less than words. I didn't understand but the world was leaving. We stood outside that awareness without knowing it. It was the cumulative effect of pushing to finish each day and yesterday was a mobile of hay trucks, wind and killdeer.

It wasn't time through which we passed but closer to a gap,

a place outside of time or the regimen of its keeping. The parallel journey that made its presence known in the early days of the ride was now how we lived. Pedaling was all we did and therefore all there was, the slow letting-go of time and space as we knew it. Scott probably had a name for this. Our name was exhaustion.

"I'm going to try and find the coffee house," I told the boys.

"Don't go. We'll go together," Cody fired back.

I picked up my journal and was too tired to write. A lone haiku from the day before that I would not show them until we finished.

Thank you for the time
with my sons. Before dawn
earth scrapes us to dust.

Nev's tire still had pressure—the patch worked. We loaded our things onto the bikes, took a last look through the room and rode into town, hoping to find the Perk Beverage Company. The little things were no longer little—a real cup of coffee, some food that tasted like food began to mark the day. The boys ordered two huge bagel sandwiches. I couldn't eat all of mine but savored the latte and the juice. I wanted to ask the server: how do you sustain an art house with coffee and real food in such a remote place? There were many paintings on the walls and in back they had rooms for community artwork. At harvest time, there were vegetables for sale. An oasis, if an oasis were here, and it was not so different from the outposts all along the highway. Not so different from home. Not so different from community anywhere.

Once, while hiking the base of Annapurna, I slept in a warming hut with a snowmelt creek running beneath it. By candlelight, the owner brought food from the adjoining stone kitchen and reached to pull cold beer from the water, but not before he moved the granite slab that bridged the two rooms. It was a community of five—the owner and his wife, a few hikers in the mountains from another culture and we washed off the hike with the owner's warmth. This is what we found in Perk—a young woman who was eager to learn of our journey, who thought her work was sacred, who made our food with willing hands. We got back on the bikes, our bellies full and turned east for the ride into Boise.

There was a hill leaving town and the morning began. The heat hadn't risen yet and we straddled irrigation ditches riding out of Vale. The morning of farms to the horizon. Cody found a path off Highway 26 and we rode up and down the long furrows that dotted eastern Oregon. I scared the killdeer whenever my bike came into view. I had never seen so many black and white birds nesting in the rows. I wondered how many made it out of the eggs, so vulnerable were their nests. We rode through the alleys of old agriculture buildings, truck stops and irrigation equipment. We rode the alley of another era but paradoxically, it was an era of different attention. An attention to the details of agrarian life. Not the lives from which we had come—or knew for that matter. A transcription of labor spent in place. A reckoning with definition from outside of this time. It was what drew the farmers here—this notion of rural work for rural good. Many collectives to help process the sugar beets, the onions, the long ladders of distribution to the shelf I reached for at home. I had worked for myself most of my life. I understood the attraction: let me live as I can, let me earn what I keep. A thread of this sentiment ran through the land and kept families close. And we rode through the midday silence.

Cody found another two-lane onto Highway 26. We rode too far and doubled back. The little incisions of losing one's way. The shimmer of buildings and trucks in the distance. We rode into Parma, starving and found a Subway in the gas station. Happy to be out of the sun, we leaned the bikes in the shade of the gas pumps. The owner came outside—"Better bring them in. We've had trouble, things getting stolen." She made room for them in the back where the goods were stored. We stood them against boxes of oil, water and cables. It was a ranch store and gas station, a place to refill when something broke on the farm. Cody ordered a foot-long sandwich with four chicken filets. I didn't think it was possible to consume that much but we were tired and there was nothing in the tank. It was the only lunch for miles around—truck drivers, farm owners, mothers, and children were in line, hoping to quiet their hunger. We looked like we were from another planet—our bike shorts and shirts with sweat rings and dusty, bearded faces. They seemed to understand: if you needed to come this way, sit down, have some lunch. Nev looked at his phone—"We have to ride through Notus, Caldwell and Nampa before getting to Boise." It was hot already and Highways 20 and 26 (conjoined for this section) were the main route into Boise.

"We'll ride the last twenty miles in traffic. It'll be rush hour." Cody and I nodded and folded the wrappers for the trash. We pushed our bikes out the door and thanked the woman for letting us keep them inside. It seemed hard to believe that anything could be stolen in this place but I took her word for it. There wasn't much to take in once we left the gas station. A road south, more trucks and irrigation ditches. We kept the taillights on and drank from our bottles every few miles. Notus was small, a tiny farm town of five hundred people. We found some shade, ate an energy chew and looked at the map—another ten miles to Caldwell. Nev had a pained expression in his face. His seat was giving him fits—just like Cody's shoulder and my feet. The miles turned into moments when the physical was all there was.

Nev stood on the pedals most of the way, preferring to ride without the discomfort. This was the fulcrum of the journey—more than halfway but no less difficult. To keep on, I reached for the fifteen yards in front of me. Cody rubbed his shoulder with his free hand and Nev adjusted his music. At one point, he offered the tunes to me but I couldn't handle the buds in my ears. Too much distraction. Hot as it was, I wanted the open air without intrusion. Staying clear of the farm trucks took all my focus. We couldn't see above their tires in the wind gusts blowing by, so we kept our gaze low.

It was near ninety degrees by the time we rode into Caldwell, a college town going through a metamorphosis. The downtown was rebuilt—new shops, restaurants and a river park. Indian Creek was once buried with concrete and now it drew people to its shore. A river from another time when water was a tool to irrigate, not much more, and towns looked upon its surface as something to be avoided. A friend who was born here told me the river was below ground for the duration of her childhood—not until 2009 did the city remove the concrete above this tributary of the Boise River. That something so redolent of life could be hidden from view seems unthinkable when towns and cities across the West have turned water into arteries of rejuvenation, reflecting a cultural shift from wet to dry to wet. We put our feet in the river and sat on the grass. Months later, I returned to Caldwell to read poems at the college in this small town and the river was angled like a piece of driftwood through its downtown. There were sculptures on the grass and foot bridges to and fro. It was a place that drew people in, a place that came into its own because of water.

We didn't stay long; the sun was eating all the moisture from our limbs. I yelled, "Better get out of here. We have another thirty into town." Cody found a back road to keep us off the highway. We joined the highway at the top of a knoll. I crossed the railroad tracks and saw a gas station on the other side of the road. It was a four-lane in each direction and no stop sign. I waited on the side of the road for them to catch up. We tried to cross as a group but it was too dangerous. One by one, we threaded the trucks to the station. The air was smothering on the pavement outside. We bought four large Gatorades, drank one each before speaking and then tried to cross again. Nampa and Boise were in the distance. Not a mile came easily. I kept my head down, put my sons in the bubble of light, tried to keep the truck tires from view. Of course, my sons went on without me but I said what I could: ride safe, ride as if you were alone and needed to land on tomorrow.

We rode about ten miles and I saw a hot rod on the other side of road. It was trailered, mostly restored save the body. A '31 Ford. I thought of my '41 Chevy at home and wished I had a rig to tow the '31 along. I was too tired to cross the road and get a number but I wanted to. My sons thought I was losing it; it seemed the last thing to care about in the heat of the afternoon but that momentary distraction kept me riding, kept the stiffness from my limbs. I yelled to them—"I don't want to leave that rod"—but they didn't hear me. They didn't need to. It was one of a hundred I had left by the roadside. A graveyard of wished-for redemption. The kind without flesh, the metal that scored these streets.

We rode in traffic; it was close to 4:30. Trucks and brake lights were all we saw. I just held them safe, away from the menacing sound of the road. Most of the drivers wanted to deliver their goods, get home. We were a speck in their windows. We were on the same trajectory, but it was single file into the warren of tires and heat. This was not the bucolic route of central Oregon. There were no Douglas firs here. There were no idyll cricks by the roadside. Only machines, things that moved and we had little choice but to move with them. The sound of our tires was lost in the hurry to home. We were reminded: you're just a bike, nothing more. Horns honked and people grew weary of the traffic lines. I pushed my bike between the fenders and set off behind them when the light changed. Sometimes the bike was like a blade and we carved our way through bumpers. Other times, it was like a piece of gauze and we were transparent. "Didn't want to have to do this, Pops."

"Ain't your fault Cody. Just hit the highway at the wrong time."

"The bike path should be here shortly."

Nev was looking at his phone. "Think we should stay on this side of the road."

"It goes to the other side."

I didn't want to get into it with them. Nev rode on and Cody turned left. I wondered how long it would take the heat and the miles to press down between them. I heard the meddling distance take its toll on Nev: "Why won't he follow me? I got the route on my phone. Goddamnit, I just want to get into Boise and get off this seat."

I didn't want us to separate; I was too tired to find one of them if they got lost but could do little more than follow. Nev wanted to get to Boise as quickly as possible. Cody thought the bike path went east along the river. It went both ways but we rode in separate silences for miles.

Off the highway, out of noise and exhaust, out of sight, save the occasional runner and day-cyclists who had no weight on their frames. I hadn't looked that light on my wheels since Portland. Some carried their children in state-of-the-art trailers. Some walked dogs. In the late afternoon, they were lithe and unworried, without encumbrance. Things you let go of on the pavement at the river's edge. We turned and stopped. Cody looked at his phone. "Think it goes this way," and we did. Still no sign of Nevada.

"Should we go back?" We tried calling. I didn't want him waiting at the signal where we turned off. I didn't want him to wonder if we had gone on. The stubborn angle of repose. "We'll ride another five and if he doesn't show, I'll go back."

I nodded and pedaled on. It was ten degrees cooler on the bike path. I was so thankful to be out of the direct sun. I wanted to get in the river but the current was too strong with the snowmelt from the Sawtooths, the mountains we had only heard of before Boise. We crossed a bike bridge and turned again. "Think he'll find us?" I shouted to Cody. He kept riding, reading his phone. "The paths converge up ahead. He'll find us."

By now all I had was trust. The two of them led me here; they would find each other. I followed Cody's turns on the bike path. He was out of my sight but close enough if something went wrong with the bike. At a turnstile, more people joined the path on their walks after work. We were still on the outskirts of Boise, small homes and apartments grew into large lawns, expansive porches and homes that held many walls. A Boise of beauty not seen from the highway. A Boise of flowers and shrubs and collared trees. A way to be at the river's edge. I wondered what happened in heavy runoff years. I wondered if the river had left its mark. But the houses were free of any debris, rooted at its shore. What you might hope for in a valley of a hundred years of farms and labor and leviathan machines to move that product to market.

I remember Richard Shelton's memoir of Boise, *Nobody Rich or Famous*, how he grew up in this town without much, how he found his way to the rough and tumble bars and dirt roads looking for a father in the midmorning sun. Shelton, whose bloodlines led to him write "I needed / your love but I recovered without it. / Now I no longer need anything." A poet whose Idaho roots are tangled in the soil of this valley. It's a miracle he lived to tell his story but like so many poets, despite their cold and desperate starts, he did. I would not have gone into the prison to teach poetry had he not assured me I could. A gift I will not be able to thank him for in my short time here. Even now, his presence looms overhead at the desk, he who, until recently, wrote and lived on the outskirts of Tucson. A legacy of letters, of heft. What you leave in the furrows of this land.

Nev turned the corner in front of us. I exhaled deeply—not that we couldn't have found him or that some other trick had befallen our tired selves—only that he was back, up ahead in the wind outside. Soon the beautiful homes gave way to eateries and more people outside. He stopped to motion, "Let's get a beer." Folks were at the tables, under umbrellas, sunning and sipping with sunglasses and hats.

"Sure." I laid my bike against the steel fence, "so long as we sit away from them. They'll probably 86 us if we get any closer."

We laughed and hung our helmets on the bags. I tried to find my wallet and couldn't remember where it was. "I got this one," Nev hollered and I followed them in. We sipped for an hour and ate some fries. I wanted to eat everything but managed to wait for a shower. The hot sting in my legs and back were ready for water to work its way over my pores. We rode off for the last couple miles to the hotel. Thankfully, Cody had enough points to comp us a room. In the air-conditioned lobby the woman at the desk was happy to see us. Why, I did not know; we stank, looked like hell and had these over-wide bikes with us. She pointed to the elevator and said, "Put them in your room. Have a nice night."

We unclipped the panniers, got out a clean pair of shorts and showered. I fell back to the bed. Boise in the distance. The downtown was quiet. And all I could think of was the noisy storm of Highway 20 we somehow left behind.

People ask me, why did you go on this ride with your sons? In the end, redemption means you have more than one definition of loss. Fathers loom large or small in a child's life. Shelton's nearly buried him, or his spirit; mine did what he could to love me and my siblings. He was not perfect—nor was I. Nor am I now, watching these two grown men, his offspring, my blood-kin, my wife's blood-kin, move down this road. I wanted them to know that fathers could be different— you could have something like this with your sons, your daughters, even though it looked like they would not have children. They were busy with their careers; how could this be, this fathering? For years, I asked the same question—how could this be, this fathering?

My father grew up poor on the dirt streets of National City. His father was a Navy man, gone for long periods. When he married my mother, he started at Cal Tech and worked nights hanging bowling pins. She taught and somewhere in the worry and hustle, I was born. He worked so hard he came down with tuberculosis and spent six months recovering in a Pasadena sanatorium. He had a scar that looked like a scythe across his barrel chest for the rest of his life.

He wanted what was best for us but sometimes choked on his emotions. And pushed into the liming light for answers—and I wanted to be one of those answers but was never right enough for him, or so I thought. What did it matter? The two of them raised four young people, worked until they couldn't and had scant few years to themselves before the cancer took him. I have wandered in those shadows of fathers and sons long enough to want my sons to hold their time precious and be certain of the value in each of us, whether or not they had kids. I wanted them to know that without some certainty of love, they would wither like the dusty crop lines we rode through.

To be vulnerable would take more than any mile on this ride. It was something I could not teach, maybe show, maybe if I was lucky, give them when they weren't looking. I tried in my muddled way to acknowledge the debt of my father, my mother, who broke with their traditions to leave us a little more than they had. It's a fight I will not win. I will go down as one who tried to make a parallel line from their hands to my son's hands, replete with diversions and mistakes. A father of fault lines.

I do not know my sons as they are now. I think they have grown into men that I raised like the shoots of an aspen, never far from the roots of the first tree. That knowledge limits how I see them because it is not knowledge at all. It is perception. I think my sons will morph into something I recognize—the banter, the belief in a moral compass, the willingness to stoop, to be captivated by a force greater than oneself, these attributes of compassion for a globe gone sideways. What I cannot know, because I am their father, is that they will become hybrids of another story, another sapling nearby. A threshold of new origin, new beliefs and they will leave the early story of the aspen. They will branch to take their place in the land and they will do so without me or my influence.

The father does not know that he and the mother will abide in this old country without them. They will stand on a porch of their making and bear witness to what has left. This is the conundrum of all things born—they must leave. A father avows the stars that he followed—in my case—the seven sisters of the Pleiades, the wooden bed of Icarus, inside the galaxy I knew and perceived. The new country has new stars. The sons will wander beneath them until a north emerges, not the north that drew me but the one that is unseen because I cannot find its orbit.

My eyes are not trained to see beyond what I know. The father is fallible like rain. Blind until the sky clears again, the constellations return. The sons return also but with new knowledge, new horizons. And this is the story that erodes what I believe, the vision of them riding down the road. The vision of seeing an eternity of lineage from the father I knew to the fathers they may become. The goodwill jettisoned, the knife-edge of an analogous story to what I wanted and what I had. The way I surrendered to the father before me. And that father too. All of it, a dereliction of duty or what might have been had without this perilous growth into someone else—and I bemoan what it is I cannot see. What I want from the sons I raised but who are now more than that.

They are like willows to the deeper soil, the deeper cognition that I may not fathom. And yet, I am beside them, always. Always. Under the bridge on the bike, below the night sky. I live with the sons, hear them breathe, hear them cough into the early desert light. I hear them struggle to find their way because the way is not what I knew. I live with the parting like I live with others who have left. I hold this knowledge close because it would ruin the silence that serves to unite us. And say nothing to announce what I do not know. Except to lavish the sons with light.

At night sometimes, I awake arguing with my father, the story he told me growing up and wonder if there is a place where he is finally at rest, looking at the three of us, his son and grandsons grown to the age when that story started. Other nights, I toss and let the memory go, thankful for books like Shelton's, like others who keep the ruler righted: it did not go the way you may have hoped, but it went as best it could. When I was born in the dreaded 1950s, there was little choice but to conform.

The innocence of the time became suffocating and when I first saw through the cracks, it exposed fault lines in their generation, like my sons, no doubt, see through mine. This is what I tried to say when people asked me why, but even as I tried to answer it seemed foolish, unnecessary. What possible good could come from veering back to Eisenhower, the mercurial Nixon? What could be done to this moment in time by looking back? The historian would answer with a corrective; the scientist with an explanation; the poet with doubt.

I looked out to skyscrapers in the lowering sun. The city had grown since I was last here. There was a buzz about it—brew pubs and eateries on the streets. They had taken its inner corridors back, remade the muscle of the place into one that welcomed. Nev found the bed and breakfast with a boutique restaurant he had stayed in some months earlier. We rode through downtown to find its open-air dining tables. The sun was hidden at last. We ordered food I hadn't seen since leaving, fancy things with difficult names and it was like eating from your mother's palm. As delicate as light rain on the lips. I couldn't say much. We ate long and it came close to sating.

This was not the Boise I knew. Another community in the West that had arced to a fuller, richer humanity. When I was last here, there were life-size images of the refugees settling here, a source of pride. A nod to more than what had kept it humming all these years, a nod to the variegated faces and lives throughout the West, the globe. On that same trip when I came to Caldwell to read poems, I rode a taxi to the outskirts of Boise. A South Sudanese man drove me to a school. He had been in this valley for fourteen years. He saved to visit his family once a year. The government was shaky but for now, stable. His mother was okay but missed him. And his sons were in college, sending their roots into this soil. He thought of Boise as home—not unlike its oldest residents.

I tried to call my friend Rick, who ran Limberlost press. I told him we would be here for a day, to restock and rest, before the ride out of Boise. I said we could do dinner tomorrow night. I turned to the riders: "You two all right with a meal with my friend? He's a good man; so is his wife. They've run the press here for thirty years. He did that chapbook with the horses on the cover."

"Sounds fun," Cody hollered, looking at the tube.

"I'm in," Nev tossed from the hall.

Bar Gernika at Dusk
XIX

Distance: 10 miles
Elevation: none
Boise, Idaho, 2019

I opened Debby's card that was waiting for me at the desk. There was an egret on its cover with a quote from Blake: "No bird soars too high/ if it soars with its/ own wings." The totem bird that had followed me through many times and places. In Chile, I imagined my father among the snowy egrets in an estuary in Isla Negra and in Hainan, China, my late friend and poet, Stephen Liu, bought an egret to save it from the farmer's hatchet.

Debby wrote to tell each of us she hoped that, like the bird, we had freed ourselves from what we left behind. I thought of her, now more than two weeks apart and wished a totem bird would land in the sage out her door. Wished some flight of wings set down to free her too. She had originally planned on riding cross-country with me a few years earlier, but in the whir of work she could not break free. I asked if she wanted to go on this journey but it wasn't the time. We would ride together in a future summer.

I noodled in my diary, the first time in days I had been able to write. The last two days of riding were long, took most of what I had to finish. I didn't ask my sons if they were tired. The road shone on our faces. We had tried to measure up. It took its share. We threw our clothes in sleeping bag sacks and took them to the laundry. I rode to the fly fishing store to get an Idaho license and a few more flies. The young man at the desk was skeptical—"On a *bike*? You ain't gonna catch—." I handed him a twenty and folded the license in my pocket. Outside, I rode the strip mall street back to downtown. I saw a writer's cabin in a park, wondered what they did there and went under a highway past Boise State.

Back at the hotel, Nev and Cody wanted to find a bike store. We needed some parts and a minor tune-up. We were unclear on the route—it looked like the freeway was the only route east to connect with Highway 20 further on. We rode through the downtown on a Tuesday. The city was moving. "I could live here," Nev said. "We thought about it before leaving New York. There's a lot to like."

We found the bike store and ogled the shelves—the things we couldn't carry: more energy bars, clothes and tools. We told the mechanic we were riding across the West and asked if he could do a quick adjustment on the bikes. There were a lot of people waiting. I told him we'd pay him—just needed a few minutes of his time.

Cody was at the cashier's desk looking at a topo map with another mechanic. "Is there any other way to get to Highway 20? Do we have to take the freeway?"

"You can go into the Sawtooths, but it's a ramble. I've never done it, but friends tell me it's a push. That's pretty much the only way. Into the mountains and down through Ketchum."

"What's the elevation?"

"I'm not sure." He turned and asked one of his buddies in the shop. "It's gotta be close to 6,000."

We looked at each other and shook our heads. "I don't know, that's a lot of mountain. If we didn't have the weight it would be another thing. That's a long day." I was thinking out loud, maybe for all of us, maybe for myself. I'd been able to hang on until now, not quite a rider but a pedaler. I liked the hills more than the flats but we hadn't done that much elevation in a day. "Is there any place to stop past Idaho City?" I asked, hoping for an obvious way out.

"Not really. Pretty much have to ride to Loman for food and drinks."

I thanked him, paid for the tube, chews and quick adjustments. We found a sandwich place and had some lunch. I called Rick again and he asked, "What about Bar Gernika, the Basque place?"

"Sounds great. We'll see you at six." I told Nev and Cody we'll get some real food tonight. We folded clothes and watched some golf on the tube. Too tired to object; it was calming in that surreal way. Cody called his wife, and Nev tried to find his but she was still working. And then I remembered: tomorrow was my mother's ninetieth birthday. We'd have to call her—wherever we were. I promised her we wouldn't forget. For the first time in two days, I wrote more than a sentence in my diary and transcribed the haiku from my phone.

> Now we are three—
> father and sons—how we shift
> from piñon to juniper.

I'd stopped reciting haiku to my sons as the days melted into one another. I couldn't remember what I had shared and so kept them in the notes on my cell. A seventeen-syllable record of the day. I sent a card to Debby, let her know we were doing all right. Jackson Hole still seemed possible. That's all I could say. I didn't tell her about Joe and Scott's scare. I knew it would worry her and that worry would trickle to Nev and Cody's spouses. We went down to the outdoor patio flush with the beautiful people and drinks and hors-d'oeuvres. A big man walked up. "Mind if I set here?"

"Have a seat," Nev pointed. "What are you here for?"

"A convention. A forensic convention."

"Really? What are you learning?"

"My partner and I are detectives in Omaha. Trying to find a way to keep the bangers from killing each other."

"In Omaha?" I asked, incredulous.

"Been at it fourteen years. You think it's gonna end and someone else throws a straw on the fire. It's like a damn snake but you can't get the head off."

His young Black partner sat down. "I was just telling my friends here, it can get a little rough out there."

He nodded and sipped his beer. "Sure enough can."

Just when I thought it was going to get awkward, his partner asked, "What are you guys doing in Boise?"

"Riding our bikes," Cody laughed, "to Jackson Hole."

"You kidding me?" the young guy popped.

"Nope. We're about two-thirds of the way. Doing all right. Glad to have a day off. Real glad."

"Damn, you got some balls."

"Could say the same about y'all—don't think I could break a day in your line of work."

"Yeah, you get used to it. The hustle, the games, the tin man at the top."

"But you keep at it?"

"Yep, maybe do some good before it's all over." The big guy reached for the pretzels. "You never know, do ya?"

"I guess not," I said, "I guess not."

"We got to get back upstairs," the young one said. "Good to meet you. Ride safe. Stop by if you get out my way."

Just like that they left to join their colleagues for dinner. I wasn't going to start. I'd seen the chancrous walls of prison too long—the men elbowed out of sight. The boys weren't going to start either. Some things were better left unsaid.

We went up to our rooms, grabbed our jackets, left the hotel and walked to Bar Gernika. The pretzels were already gone or so it felt and a good Basque meal would settle us for the ride out of Boise. Rick was waiting at a table on the sidewalk. The restaurant was in the Basque part of town, a favorite watering hole during Rick's many years as the state humanities director. His friend walked by, teasing him: "Are these the guys on the ride," looking at us. "Kind of like Zen and the art of bicycle maintenance, right?"

"Yeah, just like that," Rick joked, sipping a Guinness.

He kept walking and I introduced Rick to my sons. They stood up to shake his hand.

"Welcome to Boise. How are you guys holding up? I can't imagine doing what you're doing. The West is a big place and you're riding through it. I'm happy to get thirty minutes on my stationary bike!"

"We've been getting a lot of that," Cody laughed. "Not quite like it seems. The miles kind of roll into one another."

"Yesterday was a long one. Too much sun and traffic. But that was unusual. It's been pretty good most days," I added.

"So Dad tells me you have a small press," Nev said. "You've done many letterpress books. And you're finally able to spend more time with them, right?"

"I retired about a year ago. I'm still getting used to it. We did some pretty good things in my time. That's how I met your dad. There was a conference in Reno and we were at dinner with mutual friends. That was ten years ago?" Rick asked, looking at me.

"About that. I'd known about your press for some time. You've published some heavyweights."

"Where you heading tomorrow?"

"Trying to get to get back to Highway 20 but we have to take 84 out of town," Cody answered. "You have any suggestions?"

"Well you know, Idaho is known for the Sawtooths. It's the most beautiful part of the state. If it were me…"

For a second time in an afternoon. Nev and Cody looked at me. I turned my head—"It's not up to me."

"There's some mountains. You go through Idaho City and over Mores Creek Summit. I've driven to Stanley, Ketchum many times. We used to run programs out there."

The waiter set four big, open-faced shredded beef sandwiches on the table. The hook had been set. I knew we were going into the mountains.

I've had to be careful not to force the literati on my sons. When they were growing up I read out loud to them, thinking the words might set in, might come back to them when they needed them. Twain, Swift, Dahl, Nguyen, London—the usual fare—but I knew, too, that pushing literature on them was fatal. It would kill their pleasure faster than Black Flag. Like so many fathers, I let the words sail into their lives. If they arrived, so much the better. That's why sitting at the table with Rick was special but I couldn't take for granted that it was equally special for them.

I wanted to take them to his house and show them the presses, wanted them to see the art he made of handmade books, the stitching, the hand-set type, the actual imprint on the page—things that could not be seen in offset printing. Things that made it an art. But I trusted them to know what it meant to both of us, Luddites in another time, two people who fell hard for words and were still trying to wade into the digital era. A mixed metaphor but it might not be mixed enough for these two old guys sitting with two young ones who make their living trading knowledge with very smart men and women on a screen. Rick could see that and did not need a script. "It's not a place you'll see again. I won't tell you what to do but it will leave you breathless."

We ate like we'd never seen food and Rick ordered another Guinness and the boys an IPA. I had my crappy non-alcoholic beer, but it was cold. With very little effort, the boys intuited what this moment was: this was tantamount to opening an artery, a carefully constructed place where literature and books and love of art funneled to feed our mutual passion. Now in their thirties, they could watch and not worry that literature would infect them, but rather take heart that the two old guys at the table could still laugh about things like misplaced periods, or the three misspellings in my last chapbook that both of us had been over a dozen times. They could watch the reverie unfold and if it didn't mean the same thing, it was all right. Their understanding of literature was defined by a father who hollowed out time to make stanzas in its margins. Like any other poet who had a job. They watched him from the stands, trying to get on base.

Rick shook our hands and said we should stop by but I wondered—if we really had to climb near 6,000 feet, there would be little time to do anything but ride. Rick's house was up the canyon and we would reach his dirt road mid-morning. I'd let the miles do the talking.

We thanked him—I thanked him especially—for finding time to meet us and tilt our itinerary north with insight the maps could not offer. This route would kick our asses, but we would be so impoverished on the freeway that little would console. This was the time you retooled, let go to see what might not have been visible without a dinner with an old friend in a Basque restaurant. This was the time you turned to your sons and said, what the hell? This was the time you rode a little farther just to see if you could. And maybe, just maybe, you could find a summit in the pines and clouds to the north.

Back in the room, quiet gathered us. We packed the Trader Joe's food, the bike parts, and clean clothes. We filled the water bottles and put the panniers near the door. Tomorrow would take us in its hands and we would surrender to mountains. We knew, without even making our first mile, that of all the choices we could have made, this one was the right one. Turning away from the mountains would have kept us in a routine, albeit a dreaded one—miles of three-lane freeway—and if I'd learned anything on this trip, routines were made to be broken. On a bike there was little more than the moment to idle away. We'd been pushing pretty hard for over two weeks. If we couldn't make it, we'd camp on its flanks. I wasn't worried about them. I was the pony trying to keep up with two mustangs out front. I looked over to them reading from their phones. "Goodnight you two. Thanks for being willing."

Rocks on the Outhouse Roof
XX

Distance: 76 miles
Elevation: 5,744 feet
Boise, Idaho, 2019

I tried not to disturb them—they were still sleeping. I dressed and went downstairs to sip some coffee in the quiet of the morning. The businessmen were staring into their laptops, phones, trying to square some unfinished deal. I thought about the day—my mother's ninetieth birthday. A milestone we would celebrate when we reached Idaho City. I ate some cereal and fruit. The boys came down and filled their plates. I laughed, "You'll never eat enough."

Nev smiled. "You ready for this?" he asked.

"I don't think I have a choice—we're heading out. Go as far as I can. If we don't make Lowman we'll find a place to camp." We still couldn't find anyone who could tell us the exact elevation or the grade and we decided it didn't matter. A road was a road was a road. This one went up and we were about to start. We went upstairs, changed into our bike clothes and put some sunscreen on. I opened the small fridge. "You guys have room for this?" There was a half sandwich and a yogurt on the shelf.

"I'll take them," Cody said, grabbing them from me.

"You've got too much already."

"Here, give them to *me*," Nev fired back and took them from Cody.

We pushed the bikes to the elevator, out to the lobby and said goodbye to the desk clerks. Outside, Boise was rushing to work. We rode east on the main street through stately homes from another era—two and three stories with grand porticoes. My friend who grew up in Caldwell taught swimming to some of the kids who lived in these homes. These families were not strangers to her; they were elders of the community, people who had rooted here long before Boise was known beyond its borders. The beautiful homes gave way to modern homes that climbed the hillsides. An architect's footprint followed in every direction—wood, glass and steel that looked like it was from a magazine. The new Boise had settled into the east of town, become its quadrant of poise and certainty.

Further on, we stopped at the Coffee Mill, the same coffee house I was in when I read later that fall. It was our last time to use a bathroom and get food before the climb began. I sipped a latte in the eastern window, the sun on my face. Mothers and fathers raced from their cars, their kids like kites behind them.

We rode past the Riverstone International School, where I also read in the class of a friend's sister. When the cab driver dropped me off that morning, it looked like an Exploratorium, an interactive museum of ideas. Never had I seen such a place for learning—resources and art and smiles on the staff—things you couldn't take for granted. I watched the parents drop their kids off in the lobby—parents who knew what a special place this was. Parents who might have lived in those homes on the hills. In the classroom, I read poems to the students and they were rapt. Then they read—eager, thoughtful, unafraid to risk the flight of a poem. I thanked them when I left and thought about what the world would mean to them in twenty years—a possible tomorrow of solution, of choice, of things we had not yet found our way to. The code for peace, the comity of dialogue among people who differed.

Cody yelled, "You ready, old man?"

We rode along the Boise River for another few miles and then turned to start up. Lucky Peak Dam rose out of the ground to the east. An imposing wall of cement that regulated water flow into Boise. It was a gradual climb up the flank of the highway. Now the talking was over, the road was real. As long as the grade was 5 percent or less, we would be all right. About five miles up, a young cyclist flew by mumbling something like hello. I barely looked up in time to see her back. She must have been training. In a couple hundred yards she caught up with the boys and passed them too. Lithe, she was a pointed wing on wheels. And we would never catch her. Nev and Cody pulled into the dam turnoff and I followed them. We ate an energy bar and walked out to see the cloud shadows on the water below. There was a drinking fountain in front of the restrooms and we refilled our water bottles to be safe.

We started back to the highway, turned and rode until Mores Creek Bridge. The canyon below was steep, the water blue-green and tranquil. It made me feel diminished, like I was a speck in the sky above. We kept on for another several miles up the grade until we reached a plateau. More houses in the hills to the west. I recognized them from my earlier visits to Rick's place. There was a lone gas stop and store on the west side of the highway. We crossed carefully; the oncoming traffic was out of sight. I drank a Gatorade on the porch. The boys looked at their phones. "Maybe twenty miles to Idaho City," Cody offered. "You doing all right?"

"Right as I am." About all I could come up with. Nev got back across the road first and signaled for Cody and me to start. And then they were gone. When they reached Rick's dirt road I yelled to them, "That's the place, just down from the highway," but they didn't hear me. They were too far in front to be deterred by any literary outposts. I promised I'd take them to see the press in another time, a time apart from the spokes on a wheel. We followed Mores Creek through the canyon; the road thinned to two lanes. It was just us and the occasional camper trailer. I looked down to see if the trout were surfacing for flies. I thought I saw a silvered presence below, but I wasn't sure. The sun was hidden by the canyon walls. I heard Nev's voice and looked up. He was pointing to the other side of the road. I couldn't see what it was and kept riding. "Everything all right?" I hollered.

"Elk!"

I looked and saw the bull in the pines. It looked like there were one or two more, but they were too far away to be sure. "Your first bull sighting, Nev. Not bad. I'd have missed it just trying to keep up with you two," I joked. The elk was a good sign. Some other wild presence was among us. We were riding with the ones who were here long before. It was unusual to see them at this time of day. They came out at dawn and dusk—it was a momentary flight from the ascent, a marker I silently recorded. I got back on my bike. As long as the stream was in sight, water was close and provided a subtle pull up the canyon, a possible gravity we relied on.

Idaho City was another fifteen miles. The entire morning was spent on a gradual climb. The sun cut through the pines. The boys were out front when she flew by—the woman who passed us at the bottom of the dam. She had already been to Idaho City and back. She must have been riding over twenty miles an hour up and down. Training for a marathon or a distance ride. We were summarily put in our places. She probably didn't weigh a hundred pounds and rode like she came out of a slingshot. I remembered the man and his wife on a tandem recumbent bike on the beach in Oregon, gathering salt water. These were the poles on the continuum—a rider whose blur was all we would know of her and a Portland couple whose bike was a mule for ocean water. They would take days to travel the distance she had already ridden that morning.

We came out of the canyon and turned into the rising sun. Nev spotted an artery off to the left and I pulled in behind them. We leaned our bikes against the ponderosa pines. There was a campground farther up the dirt road. Another creek flowed into the Mores. We sat against the bulk of the pine trunks, sipped water and ate jerky and dried fruit from Trader Joe's. Dust particles rose in the late morning light. From here on, we'd earn every mile. But it was still a relatively mild grade. We'd all ridden much steeper grades; it was a question of distance. How long our legs could go before the saturation of effort took over.

Back on the highway, the pines shrouded us from the cover of the sun. Heads down, we rolled through the cabins on either side of the road. Some were occupied, some only in the summer. You could see the attraction—close to Boise, to culture, to what you needed to stay in a remote area but quiet, far from the tentacles of the city. Mores Creek crossed below us when the canyon walls were steep.

Debby had always wanted to live close to the sound of running water. I would relent over and over until we found the checkbook and couldn't find enough zeroes to make it work. I rode on, imagining us in some tranquil place like this.

The houses became closer, more cars, signs of life, on the way up the hill. We rode into Idaho City about noon. The sun wasn't too hot. We found a general store and went inside to get some water but no dice. If you didn't buy anything, you couldn't use the tap. Fair enough—trying to make a living in the mountains was always a crap shoot. We opened the sandwiches from Boise—our last taste of good food before Lowman—and started to eat.

An old truck pulled up, the dog howling at these spectacles in tight shorts. "What the hell you doing on the damn road? They won't even let me ride my ATV on it." Must have been the welcome party. He staggered into the store for more cheap beer, already gone by noon. The next car pulled in, barely running, bumper hanging on a last bolt. "You got any spare change?" and we looked on as they walked in and out with another six-pack. Wasted. And on and on it went—the willing selling of goods for the last dollars to be found.

Our phones were dead—no service—and we rode to the visitor center. The woman inside was kind and I bought a postcard from another time—the Idaho City brass band. A source of pride from 1870, something the mining town held onto for occasional celebrations. I lived in one and we had a community band, something we looked forward to hearing in parades and school functions. But the musicians grew old and the instruments weren't picked up by the young people.

"Is it time? Do you have service?" Nev hollered.

"Yeah, let's do this," I answered.

Mom's thin voice came through the speaker: "How are you Mom? How's things in Southern California?"

Predictably, she crooned "I'm fine. How are you?" It was her go-to deferent kindness, gathered all these miles to reach us on her ninetieth birthday.

"You going to do something special? The kids going to take you out?" Cody asked.

"I hope so," she laughed.

"Guess what Mom? Do you know what the caregiver said? He said they're taking you off hospice. That's your ninetieth birthday present—no more hospice care. You're doing better. Your oxygen, pulse, and pressure have stabilized," I told her as if it was wrapped in a box for her.

"If you say so," she said.

"I do, but what really matters is we're talking right now," I smiled.

"Where are you?"

"In Idaho, in the mountains above Boise. A friend said we'd have more fun in the Sawtooths and we listened. Not sure it's fun, but it's stunningly beautiful."

"How's the boys?"

"They're keeping the old man on his pedals."

"I miss you."

"We miss you."

"When will I see you?"

"Home in about a month. I promise I'll visit."

"Cody and Nev want to say goodbye."

"We love you Grandma. Thanks for being there."

She was ninety, almost ready for the new decade. Off hospice—something we never thought possible nine months earlier when the doc stopped us in the doorway of her room, intimating that her quality of life was down to palliative and soon to hospice care. She had turned, just like us, into the mountains. Such conviction on a path she could not have known. Such willingness to soldier on without a guide, without a template for how to be in the undulating present. For how to be with her children, their children, her eight decades of doing framed in the room she now spoke to us from.

I said goodbye and put the phone away. We filled our bottles in the fountain and said hello to the locals gathered outside the post office. A little kinder, a little more willing to embrace the strangers in tight pants.

Cody turned to me, "You ready?"

"Doing all right. Just have to keep on."

We set off for Mores Creek Summit, elevation 6,118, thirteen miles away. "A false summit," Rick had told us. "You think you're on the ridgetop but you head down to another plateau until you start climbing again. It's deceiving."

That didn't seem too far a distance. The grade was still relatively gradual. I saw trout in Mores Creek. More than once I wanted to stop, to call, "you want to dip a line in?" but they were gone, two shadows I saw around the occasional hairpin turn. I felt pretty good and the two of them were strong, their prodigious climbing was relentless. They took turns waiting for me, no words, just a nod until I caught up. And then back on the bike. The unspoken took us from our places and into the hands of each other.

The trucks and travel trailers had almost disappeared. We were in the mountain quiet, the sun at about two o'clock. All the edges were gone. I depended on them like the links in my chain. I couldn't say what it was they depended on, but the thrall of the day kept us close, like points on a star. It was a star of our own making, of blue-green crayons drawn in the motion of pushing uphill. A star they might have drawn for my mother when they were young. A star she might rely on as we pedaled away.

"You think he's going to be all right?" Nev asked.

"Probably ride into the night sky before he drops."

"I think he wants to do this for us."

"He wants to do it for himself."

"Maybe. But you never know. It looks like one thing and then it changes."

"Like coming up this ridge. Never thought about a climb like this. You?"

"In New York? Lucky to climb out of Manhattan, let alone a mountain."

"Yeah, how's that feel—coming West—back to the place you grew up in?"

"Should be good once we get things sorted—the job, a place to live, you know—"

"Yeah I do, but we've been in L.A. for a while so it's home. But I miss this—these granite vistas, this sky that breaks your heart, this air."

"I think that's why the old man's on the bike. He does too."

The trout were schooled in the shadows—maybe ten inches. If we had to stop, dinner was fresh. We pulled into another campground. It was almost empty and Cody got out the rest of our sub sandwiches. They were gone in minutes. We stood over the stream. It was cold, snowmelt from the ridgetop. I put my hands in and cupped a splash to my face. Took my socks off and dipped my feet in the shallow pool. I leaned back against the bank. "Maybe we should stay," I half-joked.

"Pretty nice, Pops," Cody echoed.

"How much longer to the false summit?"

"Another couple hours, I think."

"All right. I'll make that."

We loaded the bikes back up, stole fresh water from Mores Creek, and started up. The canyon was thinned to the road edge, the ponderosas gaveled us to our places. We grew smaller with every mile. The Sawtooths, conversely, became mountains we could only imagine. Winter had strewn boulders and tree stumps across the highway's edge. The mountain was slow to greet us, to acknowledge our ephemeral presence and we had to trust the hot afternoon stasis. I leaned down to grab my water bottle, took some of the cold liquid into my mouth and, not looking, put the bottle back. In an instant it flipped from the frame to the highway and on down the canyon to the pine duff. The boys were gone. I laid my bike down and walked back to where it left the road. I couldn't see it below and started down the canyon. At the creek I kicked the pine needles and saw the yellow rim—I didn't lose my fourth bottle. I wouldn't have to climb without extra water. I walked back up the river gorge, dumped the needles from my bike shoes and started to ride. Cody was waiting for me around the bend. "You blow a tire?"

"No, just lost the bottle. Missed the rack and it rolled to the creek."

He motioned ahead. Nev found a campground for water and a bathroom break. I nodded and kept on. When I pulled in I couldn't tell where they were. The road angled down, away from the creek and the highway. I stopped at the outhouse. A young woman got out of her diesel truck and trailer rig. "What the hell are you doing here?"

"Uh, riding my bike."

"You crazy? Nobody does that up here."

"Good to know—" and walked into the can.

Must have been kin to the boys in Idaho City.

Nev and Cody came back up the camp road to find me. "You won't believe—" I stopped, knowing they would and kept filling my water bottles until the cold ran over my hands.

"Think we have about five miles to the false summit," Cody said, looking at his phone.

He took a screen shot in Idaho City, knowing we wouldn't have cell service. I was so grateful for his and Nev's technical wizardry unlike me with my highway map, torn, folded, and stuffed into the window on my handlebar bag. Me, who couldn't read it without glasses. Me, who would have just kept pedaling, knowing the road only went up. And sat when I couldn't pedal any longer.

"Got it," I mumbled and started on the access road. I took the lead for the next few miles, which only meant they slowed down. I wanted to see the summit unfold. I kept looking back to Boise, the Treasure Valley, wondering what we had ridden into. The mouth of the canyon opened wider. The granite on either side gave way to the high alpine flora. It was an environment I had hiked for most of my years. In the Sierras, the Sequoias, and so many other ranges. A place of sanctuary—the wind, the deep southern light, the crisp pine air.

At the rest stop, there were boulders strewn across the black top, pine stumps the size of cars were upended, guard rails bent like tin cans. An avalanche had sent them down canyon. They were cleared from the highway for passage but stopped among the debris I could hear the echo of a winter, the scrape of stone and wood from the earth. When Nev and Cody pulled up, the three of us sat, looking at the boulder field. Some serpent of deadly snow and ice broke from the ridge and leveled every green thing in its path. We didn't need to hear the ground shudder. It was all around us, drying in the first days of summer. This was the detritus of a broken ledge of ice. And we were waiting for the opening through which to climb.

"How much farther?"

"A mile or two, at most," Cody said, looking at his phone.

I started again, determined to make the false summit and soon the sound of Lycra came close. I pulled to the right so the boys could pass. We were into the switchbacks, each turn another couple hundred feet up the grade. It was steeper now, more like climbing the grades at home. All I could do was focus on the next hundred yards. Each of us pedaled like it was the only stretch of highway, because to look farther would have slowed us to a crawl. I turned and stood on the pedals, the sun in a haze over the valley below. Late afternoon, the sweat on my sunglasses in salt rings and I had nothing to assuage the thirst. At the elbow of each hairpin, one of my sons looked back to affirm my presence and sometimes, our eyes met—I'm still here. Still here, the crank moving slower on the smallest chain ring, my granny gear the last mechanical resort.

The mountains started to turn black, whole stands of pine forest dark with the residue of ash. Some green shoots poked up from the soil. The sky was a cerulean I could only hope to paint. I could hear the boys' voices up ahead and occasionally, a red-tail hawk overhead. It felt like we had ridden since dawn. I looked up and saw them, against the side of the road, bikes leaning on the Mores Creek Summit sign. And I smiled. We had made it. We had made it this far. We were going to be all right. We got some food out of our bags and sat in the scraggly pines. Snow was so deep here the trees had a few months to grow before winter returned to freeze them in place. The mosquitoes buzzed us and we took some pictures with the sign at our backs. Proof of our silliness, our determination to be on this mountain.

We set off down the highway, heading to the final summit of the day. I was thankful to coast, my legs spent of all reserves. There was a man cutting wood on the west side of the road, furtive looking, hoping no one would notice. I yelled at Cody, "Remember that time—" and he did. We were cutting wood at home and a man stuffed his truck so full of rounds he stuck it. The ranger had to pull him out.

Before long we were back into the switchbacks for the final push. It was another thousand feet to the summit. I didn't know what reserves to draw on so I pedaled, each turn of the crank a slow, monotonous rhythm. The boys looked back; we were all worn. The mountain was sizing us up, taking its time to measure these three who came calling. As if the stumps and boulders weren't sign enough, we had to braille its surface beneath our tires to know what it held. At a long stretch of straight highway, I saw the outline of a bike on the side of the road. When I pulled up Cody had his tire off. His rear rack was slipping from the mount and he was worried that it would cut his tire. He adjusted the brackets and tightened the hex nuts. "This should hold it," he said. I handed him my extra tube but he waved it off. "I've still got an extra one. Should be good to Ketchum."

I waited until he was back on the bike. He looked back, "Maybe another couple miles."

I promised not to notice and started again in the late afternoon shadows. The wind blew up-canyon, sending dust into our eyes. I heard the trees moan with each gust. We were almost above the reach of earth. A hawk crossed in the sunlight. I couldn't tell how much farther it was to the summit. My legs were like sticks below. I kept the tires rolling over the tiny gravel shards on the road edge. And then the boys screamed—the last switchback before the summit. I exhaled and tried to find the strength to sing but gave up any coherence and hollered a resounding "Yes," into the forest. Their torsos came into view. They held their palms up as I rode by. Some part of me was released to this passage. We were going to make Lowman. Cody held up his phone: "A nine-mile descent!" I smiled.

Nev gathered his arms around our backs. "That was a climb I won't forget—Beaver Creek Summit, 6,041 feet."

We each ate a last energy bar—by now they tasted like cardboard, but they eased our hunger. I tried my fatherly best to ask them to go slow—it was near an 8% percent grade—but there was no hearing it. They were gone and rightly so. They had earned every mile and if there was one joy on a bike, it was the descent. This was the longest descent so far. I thought of Scott's description—a truss on a cheeseboard, the DOT signs signaling the grade. I just put them in the bubble and hoped the deer, squirrels, and the elk kept their distance. All I heard was the yelling from the canyon below. I put my arm warmers and windbreaker on, tightened down the panniers and started off. There were no words left for the goodness of this last, long sail down the canyon. The broken, early evening sun came through the pines as I leaned into the switchbacks, both brakes on to keep me upright. I knew they were flying and I held them close—in that place they cannot know, not watching their sons careen the mountain below. Time peeled away to the details of pine pollen, rooftops and the occasional view of the valley. The wind in my ears was a flutter of nylon and tires and brake noise. It was preternaturally still, like the calm you feel at dawn. I had nothing left to surrender and I let go of the boys. They were also in this unwinding of effort, this choreography of slow-motion.

The bikes pitched to a gravity we rarely enjoyed. We were heading into the last minutes of concentration, our bodies weightless in the air. I looked below to the green patch with a lodge and a river—and hoped that was Lowman. I could ride no farther. When I turned the last switchback, Cody was out front, Nevada walking in the parking lot. I pulled up, completely spent and tried to rest my bike against the wooden posts. Cody looked at me, incredulous, "You won't believe what happened. The second I arrived, my back tire blew. The brake pad had slid down the clamp and rubbed the sidewall till it popped."

I looked at him, at Nev and couldn't say anything. It was grace that saved him from a hard fall and each of us knew it. We tried to walk inside. There were a few people still eating dinner. It was past 7:30 p.m. We'd been on the bike more than ten hours. "Do you have any rooms?" Nev and Cody went to find something cold in the snack bar.

"I can put you up. One room or two?"

"They're my sons. We'll take one."

"Are you still serving dinner?"

"Till eight."

"Thank God."

"Tell him to leave the grill on. We'll be back." And we rolled our bikes to the rooms in front of the river. We set them against the pine exterior and took the panniers off. The mosquitoes were howling in our ears. "I'm so glad we're not camping."

They looked at me— "You got that right."

They let me shower first, so I could try to find enough energy to walk back up to the lodge for dinner. We ordered three large burgers, nachos and beer. The pine lodge had vaulted ceilings and a huge fireplace. The heads of elk stared down at us. It looked like a lodge in Glacier. We were the last to leave the dining room. The boys showered, washed their clothes in the sink. I laid on the bed, nothing to say, to do but rest. They asked about the bikes. I waved my hand; leave them outside. If someone wants to steal them *here*, let them have 'em. There were some bicyclists in the room next door, middle-aged guys who looked far too happy to have pedaled here. It must have been their car in the lot.

I looked at the boys trying to text their brides, to let them know we were in the mountains. The service was spotty. "Maybe at the lodge in the morning," I said. "This was the mountain you'll remember. This was the climb that let you into the circle. You don't have to worry anymore. The mountains will no longer ask why you came."

The Payette Blues
XXI

Distance: 61 miles
Elevation: 4,416 feet
Lowman, Idaho, 2019

I looked through the window shade to the soft light outside, pulled my pants on and made some coffee. I heard the guys in the room next door. I had a few minutes of calm before it began again—the day's turning from stasis to motion. I found my journal and wrote down the day's haiku. I'd nearly lost it on my phone.

> Look what's been given—
> green needles reach for light.
> We coast the forest floor.

I walked outside and stood in the grassy meadow that stretched to the south fork of the Payette. I knew we could fish here and I wanted to, wanted to stay. It seemed foolish to go on when the water was feet from our room and we were almost alone. The sun was starting to crest the eastern ridge. I walked back to the room, my shoes wet from the dew. What I would give to be here long enough to know the cut banks downstream. I threw some water on my face. Cody stirred, "How you doing, Pops?"

"I'm trying to move the legs. Not sure anything is going to help today." I grabbed the Tenkara rod and rolled my thighs, my AT bands for a good ten minutes. They were leather, just old, worn leather. Most of the clothes felt dry—"Think they're close," I said, pulling my shorts off the coat hangers. This would last for a few more days in the mountains. Cody and Nev walked outside. The guys next door were getting ready. "Where you heading to?" one of them asked.

"Jackson Hole," Nev said.

"How long you been gone?"

"Two and-a-half weeks."

"What are you doing up here?" Cody asked.

"We're staying here and taking day rides, out and back."

"Maybe next time," Cody laughed.

"You came over that ridge with bags—?"

"I think so," Nev laughed. "We're still trying to figure out what we did."

I hollered something about food. We grabbed our jackets and walked up to the lodge. More eggs, bacon, and toast, food that seemed to disappear as soon as we started. But it beat the hell out of oatmeal. The boys were ravenous, but I couldn't eat as much. I was still coming down the mountain. I asked, "How far today?" Nev thought it was about sixty miles to Stanley, another pass and then a long plateau. Sixty miles sounded like a distance I could manage.

We loaded up our bikes, said adios to the day cyclists next door and pedaled off. We started up an incline and pushed for the first couple miles, past more cabins and people who lived there year-round, the occasional signs of commerce, a store, a post office, not much more than the basics. In Bar Gernika, Rick had sealed the deal when he mentioned Kirkham Hot Springs. He insisted that we stop, insisted we wouldn't regret it. Nev and Cody found them first. We circled around the camp sites and rode to the stone steps leading to the springs. They threw on their bathing suits and yelled, "We're outta' here. You coming?"

"Not this time. I don't want a headache."

"Come on, you'll enjoy it," Nev screamed, running down the stones.

"Next time, I promise." I was thinking about the road ahead and relaxing right now would have taken me out of the game. I grabbed my fly rod and started back to the bridge.

A man and his son were standing in full camo, a hatchet in the father's hand. "Like this," he said, "like this," throwing it hard until it thumped into the pine. I turned as he handed the axe to his son who was not more than six.

"You can do it, hold it back and let it go."

I looked at him, at his son, as if it might have been a scene from a bad movie. The boy could barely hold the axe. He let it go. It cart wheeled across the dirt and laid at the edge of the campsite. The father yelled and I had to leave. If I heard any more of the sick, Payette blues, the father's romp through that young boy's head—and I promised not to forget the bluster, the rough outback we'd ridden through, the radius that stretched from here to Deming, from the carnal crowd that pushed this place to its limits.

I threw a fly in the riffles. A small rainbow leapt for it. I played him for a minute and released him. A few more hit the fluorescent line and then I coiled it back up. I started up the bank and saw the ranger's truck cross the bridge. I motioned to her. "You have a minute?" I asked. "Some guy's down there throwing an axe into the pines at his campsite. He's got his son with him. One of them is going to get hurt."

"Where at?" she said.

"The last site before the steps down to the hot springs."

By the time we got there, they were gone. "Is this legal?" I asked. "Can you throw an axe into the trees in the campground?"

"Hell no," she replied. "You should have seen the camp last summer. Had a guy kill ten squirrels with a .22 standing in the front of his tent. Stacked them up like a trophy. I wrote him a ticket and he just laughed. Said he'd kill 'em again if he could."

"Well—thanks for your help. This can't be easy."

"Those squirrels were my friends. I'd given names to them. I buried them after he left. I've been doing this a long time. You see things. You wonder. You think it just won't happen. And then…" her voice trailed off.

The boys started yelling. "You should have come in, Dad. The hot springs were so fine. Nev sat under the hot waterfall."

I was jealous of their hot soak. I wished, for a minute, to be rid of the scenes that followed us into the mountains. I wished, for a minute, to be without reasons to make sense of it. I watched my sons change back into their bike clothes. They were the reason, I thought. They were the reason to keep on. I started to say something—

"You catch anything," Cody asked.

"A few small ones. It was good to stand in the stream. Good to be alone in the current."

I pushed my rod into the panniers and waited for them to catch up. They were ecstatic—refreshed from that hot, soothing, water. "Everything all right?" Nev asked.

"Yeah, just more goofiness in the campground—some guy trying to teach his kid to toss a hatchet. They must have saved the home movies for last."

"What the hell—"

"Yeah, let's get going. I want to be on the road edge, near the Payette. Near what I can see and hear and touch." Nev understood the litmus test of riding through the West—you had to let it go. If Joe were here, he would have probably punched the guy but maybe not. Maybe he would have looked into the father's eyes, tried to dig down and see what was rooting in him.

Sometimes the eyes let on, I heard Joe saying. I imagined their house, cantilevered on hillside, a few busted cars, the one burner on the stove that still worked. And I tried to see the boy outrun those green and yellow camo spots, tried to find him in a future without spots, without something to kill. And none of it worked. So I just started riding. "You guys holler when you catch up with me." They knew I had to leave. By now, we telegraphed what each of us thought before we spoke—the elegance of effort born in the successive daylight of switchbacks. "We'll see you in thirty Pops," and I rode off.

It was about thirty miles to Banner Summit, elevation 7,037. That should be sufficient, I thought—a 4,200-foot climb. That should be enough to take away the noise. There were days when I didn't hear a thing—nothing in my head but the clean air I rode through. And then there were days when the noise was loud, intrusive and emptying. My butt hurt from pushing hard on the saddle the day before. I stretched my legs against the seat to find enough leverage to move the bike up the last switchbacks. The repeated, strained motion bruised my sit bones. I could feel them now—they were like wedges on my backside. There was little to do—you just rode through it. A bike store? Forget it—there were more bears than bikes in the next hundred miles. Nev's seat was giving him fits too. We were stuck riding on our pedals. This was the sweat you gave to arrive, and the time without choice—we were in the middle of a long climb across the mountains. To turn back would simply add to the pain and then what? Stare at a hotel wall? I didn't have an answer save to move one leg up and the other down. The monotonous transfer of weight to hub to wheel.

I looked at the ponderosa forest to distract myself, the peaks from the Sawtooths to the south, snow still on their flanks. This was not the Buddhist temple of no-thought; it was the intentional strain of leaving thought, leaving physical discomfort. Each of us found this well of determination. I never tried to explain to them how badly they would need it. They would find their way to it when the road stretched out before them and there was only road, not convenience. I trusted what they had inside—some fortitude of will to gather in isolation. The bike pushed them to that focus, that moment when, with no other choice, they reached deep to pedal on. We all reached deep. To keep the physical effort from view, to keep the other things at the forefront of concentration.

I looked down to my gooseneck and read the words again—"All work and no play is no fun at all." I imagined there would come a day when I needed those words, when those words were a comfort I relied on. I hoped my sons did not regret this choice. This was the ride within the ride, the time and the place I could not explain when we sat on the couch so long ago. Where there was only sheer effort, wind and a dry throat. Where there was no outside looking in. Where there were three men, alone, shadows on the highway, northeasterly, in a high plateau of cattle and sage and lupine. In a place whose beauty was elemental, was here first, without us, was of another time—and we were given this time to experience it, sweat and all. We heard the skin against the cross bar, gloves on the down-curve of the handlebar, leather on pedal clip, sounds that might otherwise be lost in the press to keep on. Sounds that isolated the mechanical from flesh, sounds that meant no metal thing was breaking or about to, no skin scabbed with road rash, no smoke from the diesel combustion.

I heard the boys behind me and angled upright: I wanted them
to know I was with them, especially now, deep into the mountains of
no looking back. I wanted them to know we were going on.

"Hey, old man—" Cody slapped my back riding by.

"Hey, little man—" I fired back. "You see the Payette? Damn, I
want to fish this.

Maybe when we get to Stanley. Maybe we can take an hour
before we start in the morning."

"You wish," he teased.

"Damn right I do."

"He giving you shit, Pops?" Nev chimed in.

"Is there any other kind?"

"Don't let him talk shit to ya."

"Yeah—I'll let the mountain do the talking."

"Let's stop for lunch at the summit."

I broke open a chew from the pack and swallowed. The sweet,
gummy-bear flavor. Probably all sugar and food coloring. No wonder
I liked them.

"You good on water?"

"All good."

That was the nod I needed. The nod from the two of them: they
were all right. Stiff, sore, but all right. We were over the niceties. We
were stripped to the essential—the grunt, the sigh, the motley hair
and three-week growth. And still—this was what Rick wanted us to
see. The Sawtooths came into view. They reminded me of the Tetons,
of the spiked ridges in Glacier. The absolute tectonic fissures of the
Intermountain West. The glacial divide of ice and rock. My vision
was fixed on the outline to the south. An outline I wanted to hike
on another trip. Maybe with the boys. Maybe with our spouses. An
interior land we had not wandered.

When they were young I took them up many peaks in Nevada.
I trusted the trail to lead us to small, alpine lakes. In Great Basin
National Park we camped at the upper-elevation site. I woke early.
There were three deer, a doe, and two fawns not more than a week
old. I made bacon and coffee on a stone fire circle. When the boys
came out of the tent I told them about the fawns. They could barely

see them in the creek bed below. A creek bed of memory, of stamina, of boulders. At 12,000 feet, the two of them were tempting the elevation. At the summit, we looked east and turned back to the Great Basin of home.

The mind of a young man about to unfold on a mountain, reach for the height of his five-foot self and push into thin air. The mind of two young boys about to touch a boulder field for the first time and recognize this was home. This was where I belonged. I couldn't give them the material things that might have been nice but I could share these peaks in an open sky. I could sit with them, look east into the Utah desert and the brown ranch valleys that flanked the ridges and later, descend to that same campground and sleep with stars as if that were enough. The visceral edged through the physical, the viscera of love. That was preparation for the day star we rode under now.

"Let's eat here," Cody waved from the ridge top. I laid my bike on the roadside. We got out some bagels and peanut butter, the last of the dried fruit and jerky from Boise. There wasn't anything to say. We ate slowly, no cars, no distractions. I'd forgotten the morning, which by now seemed part of another day altogether. "You doing all right?" he asked.

"Yeah, just here, just sitting here."

Nev looked down the valley—another big descent—more wind time, floating with the bulk of our bikes, floating into the valley on the other side of the ridge. "How far to Stanley?" I asked.

"Looks like it's about thirty miles." Cody took another screen shot on his phone. We wouldn't have cell service until we reached town. "Probably a pretty steady push through the valley but not much uphill."

"Good," I muttered. "My butt thanks you."

He laughed. "How you doing, Nev?"

"About the same. Whoever made bike seats must have been a masochist."

"Yeah—guess we'll be riding on posts after this."

"Might feel better."

They started down the ridge. I put my windbreaker on—it was a little windy and clouds were clinging to the peaks. I started to coast, a sudden freedom again, letting go to wind, to the unspoken things that distance had kept from us: the good, harsh effort washed from our limbs. When I got to the bottom of the descent, they were way out in front. I settled into a steady rhythm of about fifteen miles an hour, not much more—I was too tired to think about it. But it was steady nonetheless, a long horizon to the east into Stanley. The soak at the ponds would put us in later, close to 6:30 or 7:00. We'd just have to play it by ear, whether there was a place to camp, or not. This was the new route. The boys were waiting on the side of the road. "Think we have about twenty miles, a couple hours I'm guessing," Nev said.

"I think I can manage—so long as the elk and the bear stay clear," I joked.

"Any moose up here?" Nev asked.

"I don't know—"

"Remember that time in Jackson when he nearly pulled the apple tree out of the ground?"

"I could wait here for that."

"Bet you could."

"You two get something to eat?" It was the perennial question—food, did you eat and drink enough? They hadn't hit the wall yet—the physical stop that came with too much exertion and no hydration. Save my bodily crash on the second day out with Cody, I had done okay. But it was always a guess. We just had to pour the liquids down and eat, even when the food tasted like wood. "Why don't you two head out? I'm going at my usual pace. I'll catch up in an hour."

"Got it," Cody said, and off they rode.

I was ready for Stanley and hoped that last twenty miles wouldn't be over-hard. It was already late in the afternoon. The wind started to pick up, a headwind we hadn't been in since the long day coming into Boise. I put my head down. This stretch was going to be at a slower pace. I just didn't have anything left in the tank to make up for the loss of speed. A muscle is a map of origin, of effort, of exhaustion. I was leaning heavily on the latter. I imagined the boys were too but they were still moving through the wind. The cattle to my left grazed without looking up. Miles of open grass pasture, an occasional barn, a dirt road with cattle guards. This plateau must be buried under five feet of snow in winter. But it was lush and verdant now, a country of ranch land and short seasons. Seasons here were defined by otherness, not self, seasons outside of our reach, a compromise of external use and interiority. Time spent alone. As we were now, windswept, finite objects, almost rolling in the powder and dust from the roadside.

The boys were standing up ahead, bikes leaning on their thighs, facing me, trying to keep out of the wind gusts. "You had enough of this yet?" Cody yelled.

"Think I have."

"We saved it for you, Pops."

"Mighty kind of you."

"Make the world go away—" and we laughed. "Where's Eddy Arnold when I need him?"

"In Austin."

"You smartass."

"Make my sons go away."

"Not until we reach a bar in Stanley."

"Okay—just get me there."

And we started into the wind, the only sound a persistent buffeting. Like rain might have sounded under our nylon parkas. I didn't look up for miles. I just stared down at the red, round ring on my goose neck. "All work and no play…."

Joe had daughters—and we talked a lot about our respective offspring. One was an entrepreneur and the other in finance. He wondered if he had done enough to launch them from the nest. He wondered if they would find their path away from home, from what he and his wife gave them—succor and belief and rudimentary ideas for living.

That was all any parent could do—lean on the broken road map they'd been given and trust that the young ones would find their way. Still, each of us had trepidation. There was never enough preparation. Long after college, the wind buffeted wherever you were—on a bike in the high plateau of the Sawtooths, or in a city hunkered at a computer, trying to find the exit sign. Another long essay you hoped they understood, even though it was never spoken, directly. There were the pointers—the boss might lean hard, the money might not be enough, the daylight might lose out to the rearview mirror.

Two fathers riding down the road. Fathers of daughters and sons. There were other things you just didn't say, other things you left on the table, other things they'd knock into, whatever soiled belief led them to discover. You'd love them like an old silver dollar. Close, cherished, solitary. As near a thing of beauty as you could imagine.

Scott and his wife wanted this too and I imagine he watched Joe and me with a glow—when it worked, the young ones were just about as ruggedly beautiful as the peaks to the south. I was grateful when Scott reached for them like they were distant kin—no effort, just the single purpose of being together. And we put these conversations to sleep when the three of us caught up to the boys, pretended they were like stage sets for a performance we might see. I thought about my two friends, where they were now—most likely home but perhaps streamside, with a journal and a rod.

The roofs of Stanley started to appear on the hills outside of town, rough angular wood structures staring straight at the Sawtooths. The town was bustling. Cars and people walking on the dirt streets. I was spent and said the hotel's on me. We split up and rode to each neon sign we could find. There was a stage in the middle of the street and it was blocked off at both ends but there were no rooms. The river-rafters were in town and every room was taken with those about to leave in the morning. We might be camping outside of town. Nev rode up to the last hotel before the T at Highway 75. There was one room left—with natural hot springs, a must in the morning. Damn! Good fortune smiled on us again. The boys let me shower first and I tried to stand my crooked legs in the hot water. The bikes wouldn't fit in the room but we were too tired to care. My phone rang—I was startled. I hadn't heard that sound since Boise. It was a good friend who'd called to ask if I would review a book. I wasn't sure what to say—miles from home on a bike, without so much as a poem. "Thank you. I can't believe you found me." I told him where we were—far from all things convenient.

"I thought you'd have a better sense of the manuscript," he said. They were poems by a Basque political prisoner, a poet he had translated. I told him I'd read the manuscript when I got home—and home seemed very far off in that other life I led. I thanked him again and looked at the boys. "You won't believe what happened—" but they already knew.

When they finished showering, we started back into town. The rafters were meeting; they looked serious. We found our way to the pizza joint, which was right across from the stage. There was so much noise inside we could barely order. Strangely, the servers were Eastern European, here on H1 visas for the summer tourism. They didn't mind the noise; they were having as much fun as the crowd on the other side of the counter. We sat down with the beer and wings and waited. The pizza was spicy and fresh. We almost ate three of them and took the rest with us. Cold pizza the next day sounded great. Outside, Southern Satellite was practicing before their set began. A free concert? How'd we get so lucky? Again.

They were out of Texas for a tour. Their bus looked like they were doing well. The boys ordered another cold one and I tried to find something to pretend with. "I love the funky, quirky, possibility of this place. What took us so damn long to find it?"

"We should have started here," Nev chimed in.

"Couldn't have gone wrong," Cody hollered.

"I could stay here a while," I nodded.

When the band started, we raised our glasses—good, southern rock and roll. Southern Satellite was a tight band—this wasn't their first gig. The dirt and gravel turned into a dance floor and soon we were stomping our feet with the ones who knew what they were doing. The couple in front of us had been practicing—they danced their boots off. We made it through the first set and looked at each other, knowing the next day wasn't too far off. We made a mandatory stop at the ice cream store—open till ten Thursday through Sunday. My kind of job—a little work and a lot of free time.

"Vhat would you vike?" The Eastern European students again.

"All of it," I laughed.

"Don't listen to him," Nev wrapped his arm around my ribs.

"I'll take two scoops of the mint chip." They tried the chocolate mocha and coffee. We walked outside and sat on the wooden bench. "This may be the best night of the ride."

"Think you're right."

"Rick won't believe us. Better tell him it was a crappy ride."

We found the pizza we'd hidden and started back to the hotel. There was a corn hole game set up on the grass outside.

"Come on, old man," and I gave in. We played a couple of games and meandered back to the room. The sun was almost down. I looked back at the Sawtooths. So this is what we had come for—to lie at the foot of these magisterial peaks.

What the River Portends
XXII

Distance: 73 miles
Elevation: 3,383 feet
Stanley, Idaho, 2019

The sky was overcast. Cool, light wind. I got dressed and made some coffee. The boys slept on. I heard the rafters outside. The nervous chatter before their first big splash in the river later that morning. "Hey, big guy," Nev whispered, to keep Cody from waking, "you going in the hot springs?"

I nodded my head. I tried to write in my journal, transcribe the haiku that were lost in the notes on my phone. I found the last one—

River, ask me why—
a chorus of stones replies—
three weeks in western sky.

And I thought about the call the night before—that strangle oracle from the other world. I hadn't thought of words for weeks and yet, here, last night, walking home there was a used book stand outside the Chamber of Commerce. I found a copy of Emerson's essays. It was thin enough, maybe an ounce and I held it for a long time. I read from it, water from the source and realized how much I'd missed the written word. Just the idea that a thin paperback could travel with me assuaged my longing but I left the book behind. The weight. I just couldn't relent.

We all put our bathing suits on and walked down the dirt path. There was a small building about a hundred yards away on the Upper Salmon. We couldn't see it until we crested the bluff. The woman at the desk gave us towels—the same young woman who had closed the pizza place. I asked if she was tired. "No—just getting to work. You're the only ones using the springs. Just leave the towels in the basket."

We saw the gable in the distance. When we walked in, the steam rose in our noses. The doors to the west were flung wide. The Sawtooths stood up like lunar roof beams. We stepped into the hot water, our feet in the sand. It was the best feeling—my legs were tight. Each of us stretched the back and neck and legs. The river was about twenty feet from the door. Not a person in sight. The steam rose into the ridges. We sat in silence for twenty minutes, a rest that let the soreness disappear for a moment. A moment of hot, earthen calm. Nev walked down to the river, put his feet in and splashed his torso. I couldn't move. It was too nice. I would have stayed, but the weather was threatening. We walked back to the room, changed and loaded our bikes up. There was a bagel place nearby. We all rode over and ordered a breakfast bagel and a latte. More food than I should eat but I did.

I looked south—the clouds were low and the wind was starting. I put on my windbreaker and leggings and hoped we would beat the snow. Galena Summit was 8,990—about a 2,700-foot climb. We couldn't get a sense of the upper elevation. The locals didn't know if the pass was open. We turned south on Highway 75, into the headwind. We rode through the outskirts of town, the diesel rigs towing their trailers into the clouds. Long fields of sage and bitterbrush, the occasional house set back from the road. My butt was still sore. I'd hoped for some miracle of recovery in the hot springs. There was a log cabin, almost fallen to its craters. I stopped to pee out of the wind. "What do you think?" Cody asked. "Those clouds look pretty gnarly."

"I just don't want to ride thirty miles in this wind and have to turn around."

"Me neither."

We took off before it got any colder. Nev was out front. There was a ranger station set back from the road, but I couldn't tell if it was open. We went on for another couple miles and found Nev waiting for us. "You all right?"

"Just worried about the pass."

"Let me try and go back to the ranger station. Maybe they'll know if it's open."

Cody and I waited at the road edge. The clouds were low to the west, blocking the mountains. A small creek ran into the Salmon. I'd never seen so much water. If only—but this wasn't the time for fishing. We'd be lucky to get to Ketchum in this weather.

Nev rode up. "The ranger came over this morning. Road was fine."

"Just gotta keep riding," Cody answered.

"Damn wind. Must be payback for the pizza and good music." I tried to laugh it off.

We set out into the sage. The valley was such a mirror of the landscape of home. I longed to see it in the sun, without the clouds and wind. The boys were ahead of me but slowed by wind. Red Lake Lodge was off to the south—another place we'd have to imagine. All these detours without so much as a glimpse. And my rear end was killing me; I could make twenty minutes or so and then had to stop. I got to the turnout. Cody was waiting. "Why don't you put on your other pair of bike shorts."

"Right now I'd put a catcher's mitt on my butt if I could." I fished through my panniers, trying to find the shorts. I pulled them over my leggings and hoped the second layer of padding might work. We started off again. For the first time since Lowman, I could ride without trying to avoid the precise angle of pain. When pain focuses its laser attention on you, nothing you can do will stop it. I was pretty much shut down. No feeling except the grunt of pedal strokes. Why hadn't I thought of this sooner? I knew, as much as anything, that they pulled me along in wind, clouds and now light rain. I was without my mask, alone in the sage. And the wind brushed me from my perch. The wind would not relent. It was a wind of cold, of weather that I could not deny. My sons saw me grimace. What I could not say to them—and then said it anyway: "I don't have a solution." The father without enough words.

We rolled up to Smiley Creek Lodge and leaned our bikes against a picnic table. I put the cold pizza on the table. Nev walked inside to use the bathroom. I followed. The proprietor was trying to seat the families who were waiting. "It's for the guests," she said. I promised to buy six Snickers if she turned the other way. She smiled and pointed down the hall. Nev got three frothy shakes. They were just right for the crummy weather.

Outside, we tried to eat in the mist. It was stunningly beautiful, even on this gray morning. I wanted to return when time was not part of the journey. When the day could just unfold. "I'm getting cold"—my mantra since leaving.

"Better get out of here. If the rain gets harder we're going to be really cold."

"I don't want to climb in wet shorts." They understood. We tossed the last of the pizza and shakes, threw the candy bars in the panniers and started again. About five miles to the turn east and then north, up the valley to the headwaters of the Salmon. This was the time you let go. There was no other path save going on, into the rain and wind. At the elbow, I looked up and didn't feel the pressure on my face. I kept it vertical, not trusting my senses—the wind had slowed. We were out of the draw from the canyon. The bike almost felt light. The unseen wall had lifted and the slow ascent was before us. The trailer rigs passed to our left. They looked at us like we were lost. Maybe we were—right where we needed to be lost.

I tried to stretch my back by straightening my forearms. At last I could ride with relatively little pain. If the wind held at 5-10 miles per hour, we'd be fine. Just so long as the snow stayed above the ridge. The climb up the canyon to Galena was about fifteen miles, slow and gradual and then the switchbacks. I wasn't worried any longer. It was just pedaling, the rhythm of legs and torso and pulling on the bars. I turned back repeatedly and on the southerly switchbacks, saw the Sawtooth Valley below, a crescent of green with the Salmon running through it. I was eager to see it—raw, jawboned, cut from the ridges after millennia. What a river portends in the beginning.

I read from the Stanley writer, John Rember, whose father was a guide when the salmon were natives and the big businessmen flew in to have a shot at the thrill. "I'd trade anything for your life," he recalled them saying. But it was work, nothing more, a livelihood, a hustle to keep food in the house. Rember doesn't think that much about the salmon now, stocked as they are, and even when the steelhead are running the out-of-towners wobble the drifts to find the hole. It's a valley gone in reverse, but what valley isn't? Still, on the saddle, looking west, it was a jade-green horizon I could not find words for. I was lost in the preamble, the story of what it once held. If anyone held the words, they were in that little paperback of Emerson's essays.

The switchback arced the western flank of the ridge, and I tried not to look up. The boys were up ahead; I saw them at the turns when there was open sky. The grade was steeper but not too much. I just pedaled and tried to stay over the wheel, my focus three feet out. There was nothing more to do. It was the isolating thrum of a few yards and another few yards, until enough distance became another turn to move up again. I was getting hungry and found a turnout to get out of the traffic. Cody was waiting there. "How you doing, old man?" his garrulous greeting. "Nev went up ahead to see how much farther it was."

"All right. A little stiff, a little boney, but the tush isn't killing me, so I'm all right."

"Think we got another five miles or so."

"I can manage that. But not a mile more."

"I got ya."

"You hungry? I gotta eat."

"I had a bar. Let's take a break at the summit."

"You lead the way."

The road was wide, a commuter road. People from Ketchum came over every day. The locals said they kept it open most of the year. On the flats below, an ambulance had driven over from Ketchum to Stanley and by the time we made it to Smiley's, they were headed back. The rain had let up, the sky was overcast and there was a light wind. The snow stayed away. I didn't have the energy to ride back to Stanley. We'd make the summit relatively dry. I took off my windbreaker and rode in the arm-warmers. It was still cool but manageable. I came up on the lookout. Nev was standing there.

"What do you think of this?" he pointed to the west, the Sawtooth Valley spread like a lush green tide below, the Salmon lit in the gray light.

"I've been looking at it all the way up. It's overwhelming. The canyon walls, like two forearms, holding all this beauty inside. And the river—I floated that river when I was kid. Caught my first native trout on that river. Don't think I've been on a stretch of wild river like that since then."

"It's pretty stunning."

"Hey, big guy," Cody shouted from the ledge. "Come over so we can get some pix." We tried to look impressive with the daunting mountain valley below, but the pictures didn't do much except record our exhausted grins.

"I don't think it's much farther to the summit."

"I'm hoping it's around this bend."

"Maybe another mile or two."

"Think you're right. I can see the treetops on the following ridge, a little blue in their tops. We're close." Navigation by hope of forethought—we were getting pretty good at it. The headwaters of the Salmon were just below our gaze—named the River of No Return by the men who ferried cargo to the mining camps in flat-bottom boats—"sweep scows." The boats were built from green wood with a double hull that drew fourteen inches of water. Because the river was too rough to return, the boats were disassembled at their destination and sold for lumber.

The boys started off and I was just able to pedal. I couldn't do more if I had wanted to. Almost to 9,000 feet, I hoped the elevation wouldn't take it out of us. We didn't need any more distractions. I wasn't too worried but I knew we weren't on our first day out. A little less oxygen and a lot of miles could slow us to a crawl. I heard some yelling up ahead and imagined that one of them had made it. All I could see was the bladed roadside to my left and vast tree-laden ridges to the east. The road was four lanes to the summit, and there was a fair shoulder to stay out of the traffic. The boys' voices grew louder. I thought I saw one of them off the bike. Another couple hundred yards. I saw the wooden sign but couldn't read the letters. When I leaned my bike against it, I could see the words *Galena* carved in the wood. Rick told me there was a photograph of Hemingway standing at the summit with a bottle of gin in his hand. I could almost imagine him in the gravel, yelling from his Ketchum roots, *You made it. Have a drink with me.*

We sat down for a snack and water. I let out a long exhale. This was the last ridge before Ketchum, the third in as many days. I looked at the boys and said, "You did it. One helluva ride. I know you'll try to tell people what this was and they'll look at you like, *what*? But it doesn't matter. Those climbs are part of your DNA now. They are what you'll take away when the soreness is over. They'll stay with you."

"Look who's talking, old man. Didn't see you walking up the ridge," Nev teased.

"Yeah, well… I hitchhiked. You just didn't see me."

They were hugging each other. "We did it, man, we did it. Tell Rick he was right. Tell him it was the best climb we've ever done," they echoed.

"I'll try, if I can get this sorry ass of mine off the ground."

We started down the canyon onto the long flat into Ketchum. Cody said it looked like it was downhill on the screen shot. And that would be just fine. I couldn't do anymore elevation. I coasted, my windbreaker flapping in my ears. I didn't have anything but wind and a lazy ride to the bottom of the grade. They were far out front, but it was still a gradual descent. I'd be fine—ten or twelve miles an hour—and no head wind. I thanked the weather gods—we had made it over without snow. We could have done it with snow but it would have been miserable. I'd ridden in snow before; it was a cold ride and hard to see much at all. The front forks gum up with ice, the chain and crank become stiff from the loss of lubricant. This kind of riding was not something to be proud of; it was endurance of another sort, the kind without a flag at the end. The reason to finish was simple— get out of the wet. Change clothes and forget you wanted to do that.

Once we got into the valley, the rollers started and before long I sensed the grade rise beneath me. So much for the screen shot. If we wanted to make Ketchum, we were going to have to push. It looked like about ten miles of rollers into town and we turned to each other—"Really?" and kept on, the lightening of thought and presence. A habitual movement, without otherness, only up and down, up and down, the singular rotation until the next gradual descent. The valley was grass-filled, as much of it as I could see. Large ranches, campsites, more places to wet a rod. And then the homes, beautiful log structures, metal and glass buildings set back from the road. Most of the windows were closed, most of the driveways, empty. These were homes that kept people warm in snow but not now, in late June, when the ski resort was closed. These were homes that people flew into, homes that needed navigation. I saw a yard crew and thought of the crews on the flanks of the eastern Sierra homes when I was training in May—a demarcation of weather and labor. The homes that Joe had said I might look into had shifted, and we were now riding into our reflection on the plate glass. The manicured lawns came right up to the road edge. Where was Deming now? I hadn't seen Ketchum for a few years and the town was pretty empty—still too early in the tourist season. There was a hotel on the outskirts, and I yelled, "That's it," but the boys couldn't hear me. We pedaled past four bike stores in the first mile. Maybe they might have a better bike seat, I thought. The boys were looking at their phones. "Think it's up here. Turn left at the signal," Cody gestured.

Every part of my body was sore. I just wanted to be off the bike. "You sure about this?"

"Supposed to be four miles out of town," Nev said.

I groaned and tried to find the toe clip on my pedal. We meandered through Sun Valley on a bike road, parallel to more beautiful homes and a golf course. It seemed so far from their porches to our bikes and some bags. Maybe I was just too tired. We pulled into the campground. The boys rode through the circle of tables and fire pits. I waited. "Tell me I can unpack."

"They're full."

"F—k!" I lost it. "We have to ride back to town?"

There was a young couple who heard my displeasure. "There's a nice dispersed camp about a mile and-a-half up the road." We thanked them and I looked back at the road. What I'd give to be stinking up one of those beautiful cars winding into Ketchum. The boys were on their phones in a minute, trying to find an open room. There must have been something going on in town because every place was full. I was ready to go back to the first place we rode past, but I couldn't say anything; my joints were leaden. Finally the boys found a room below the square with an Austrian motif. We took our bikes up to the second floor and I collapsed on the bed. I didn't talk for minutes. The shower woke me from my stupor. "We'll take an Uber into town for some food."

I tried to laugh. Suddenly, the ride had taken its toll. I was threadbare, had no more reserves. My resilience was scattered in the Sawtooths like pine pollen and all I could do was mumble. I fumbled with my phone and set it back down. Nothing would operate. I was out, and they knew it. "You gonna be all right?"

"Uh." My one-word vocabulary. Closer to stone, to the ghost of exertion, that finite place where concentration and physical effort collide, the empirical storm of will and fatigue.

We walked down the stairs and into the parking lot. The ski runs were like ribbons down the mountain, swaths of treelessness that emptied into our street. No wonder people came here—it was beautiful without the snow. The sun pushed to the west as we started up to the center of town. There was some noise coming from an upstairs bar. We walked up and tried to find a seat by the fire pit. The wind had returned and it was getting cool. We ordered appetizers and beer, tried to fit in with the regal crowd but there was nothing regal about us. We were worn through to the tendons. I hugged the fire pit, cold again and the light clothes couldn't keep me warm. It was exhaustion. "You guys all right?" I couldn't think of anything else to say.

They turned and nodded. "We're fine."

Thirty years younger and they were ready for the night. The bar was filled with the necessary distractions, but all I could do was eat and sip my fake beer. I needed sleep. We paid up and walked back, tried not to go into the market, a fifth bike store and finally made it to the room. I got out my diary but couldn't write a thing. I said goodbye but meant goodnight, and they laughed, knowing I was gone. They fooled with the TV but I didn't hear much. I turned the light off in my corner and let the day go. This was another day I couldn't explain to the outsiders when I returned. Like the river boats, it had to be dismantled and sold by the piece. I wasn't going to try to make sense of it. If there was sense to be made.

Scorned by the Wind
XXIII

Distance: 5 miles
Elevation: none
Ketchum, Idaho, 2019

I didn't feel too good about losing it the night before. I laid in a dream state for many minutes and tried to focus on the aspens. We were in one of the original Ketchum hotels. There were pictures of the early ski resort and the hotel covered in snow to the eaves. I found the coffee and started to make a cup. This was a ritual the boys put up with. It was my one routine I couldn't forgo. Camp or not, room or not, I started with a cup of coffee. The room was stuffed with our things—we had a rollaway and panniers—but it was dry and the bed was like lying on the beach—it fit every sore joint. We found our clothes and threw some water on our faces. They were serving breakfast downstairs. It seemed almost folly to eat again; the food, no matter how much, disappeared in an hour. There were berries on the table—such a surprise—and I savored them going down, blue and black and red, a cornucopia of flavor to my oatmeal and peanut butter tongue.

It was a day of rest, something we'd given ourselves after the climb. The ride was now divided: before and after the climb. I needed to get to a bike store about a seat and they went shopping for food.

At the second store, the mechanic told me my seat was tilted too low in front. If I raised it, it might solve the problem. I acquiesced, not sure if it would. I rode back to the hotel and we packed up. We had to move again. There wasn't a room for a second night. The boys found a place on the main street and we rode over there. Just as I pulled in, my tire caught a patch of hot asphalt and sank in. The bike turned and fell to the side. I looked down at my wheel—tar on the rim and tire, penance for the thrill of relocating. I must not have understood: you want this? It's going to take something. It's not coming as you imagined. When I walked into the lobby, they looked at me and said "What happened?"

"I found the one three-foot-square of hot asphalt in the whole road."

"You cut yourself," Nev pointed.

"It's just a scrape. Got to figure out how to get some kerosene. I can't ride like this."

We left the bikes downstairs and walked our gear up to the room. It was a fancy place, almost like a vacation, except this was time out from the ride. We could see the Big Wood River from our room. "I'm going fishing," Cody said. "You coming?"

"After I get that tar off my rim. Let's walk back into town and I'll scope out a hardware store. Maybe we can grab some lunch and then head down to the river." Truth is, I was too tired to fish or find some kerosene, but I left the room. They understood. We didn't need to know what each other thought. The wear of the days before was evident. I rode down the main street, trying to find some place that sold kerosene. I rode to the end of town and found the first hotel we rode by. I laughed, or tried to, our plans quickly dissolving like silt through our hands. There was a new bike store adjacent to it. I stopped to see if they might have a seat, still unsure of the adjustment. They were putting together mountain bikes for the opening. "This is literally your *first* day," I asked, incredulous?

"Yep, just putting them together for the big event this weekend."

"You don't happen to have any kerosene, do you? I hit some tar on the way into town."

"I think I do. Let me look around."

He came back and took my front tire off. Then he sat down on the cement outside and cleaned the spokes, rim, sidewalls and tread.

You couldn't even tell that the bike had been dirty. I was stunned. "That ought to do it," he said, handing the tire back to me.

"Can I give you anything? I can't thank you enough. You just made my—"

"No problem, man. Come back through when we get the store fully open. Let us know how it went. Sounds like a helluva trip."

The unexpected affirmation of one cyclist to another. For a minute, the lost turns and dreaded miles seemed a worthy distraction. They led me to his door. I met the boys at a soup and sandwich place off the main street. We sat on the patio out front, the sun in our faces. "This guy literally came out of his shop—which he was trying to open—and sat down and cleaned every bit of tar off my rim and tire. Unreal." They looked at me with that same affirmation, what comes from being so long together, scored by wind and elevation. The soup was tasty. We had landed on another lily pad just as the exit was about to disappear and leave us spinning into the unknown.

We made it back to the hotel and fumbled in our panniers for the rods. Big Wood River flowed east through town into the Malad River and eventually to the Snake. We found an access point just below the last bridge out of town. Cody waded in the river stones. Nev and I went on, through the Lombardi poplars and cottonwoods. The river bank was tough to access. Nev went further upstream. "I'll catch up with you later," he said and followed the riverside path. I tossed my line in, let it drift until the first tug. A small rainbow, still too early in the season, or so I thought. I whipped the line for another thirty minutes and just sat down.

I brought my watercolors and set them on the sand, sketched the ridges out of Stanley and started to paint. They would never be as I remembered them but I had to try. Exhausted and flush to the water, I put some blue down, then black, let them run the way the peaks ran, one to the other. I tried to focus on the distant perspective, painting from memory what no memory could store: the razor-back ridgeline. I dabbed some pink in the foreground and blew on it to dry. The sun did the rest. I laid down, nothing to say or believe, and rested for a good while. I may have dozed, gone to that place without bikes or weight and let the river wash my feet. I looked across the light riffles. The trout rose in the shadows. I was back at the South Santiam River, on a boulder, in the late afternoon, in that first river gorge where Cody and I had slept in so long ago. How could time have elongated in so very few weeks, an elastic skip of mountains and valleys to this moment? There is a movement of sky out here in the West that you cannot see until you fix your vision in the aperture of leaves and the occasional cloud shadow and things slow in the crystalline air until they move, not as tree or river, but as one tree and river under a current of light and wind. It's a sky I'm still not prepared for. Every time I return to its patient threshold, I'm reminded: you're small in this place, you live here and that is all. The river, the sky, go on.

I folded my paints and put them in my bag. I walked back through the ground growth and found a trail to the bridge. Cody was still fishing the same eddy. "Getting anything?"

"Just a few strikes."

"I'm heading back. Going to rest."

"I'll see you in a few hours."

"Bring me some dinner."

"If the damn trout will take the fly—I can see them but they just won't take it."

"Try the elk hair caddis," I said walking away. "Make sure you grab Nevada before leaving."

I walked the main street back to the hotel, stiff and tired. I'd done nothing but sit by a river. My carriage was starting to sag. I wondered if I had enough strength left to make it over the last ridges. And I know the boys wondered the same thing—will we have to drag him over Teton Pass? I opened the door to the room and fell on the bed. It was quiet, cool in the afternoon air. I left the screen door open and slept.

My phone started buzzing an hour later—it was Cody. A fat rainbow in his hand and then he let it go. He caught several nice trout. He'd found the setup. I put the phone back on the dresser and smiled at the window—if nothing else, they had found the river's edge. I could not explain what I hoped the trip would be but this was part of it—an afternoon in the chill snowmelt with a trout on the line. When he walked in the door he was ecstatic—"Did you see that?"

"Pretty nice. You found the sweet spot. How'd Nev do?"

"Don't know. Told him I was leaving."

"Well, your license only cost $2 bucks a trout—not bad. I'm still trying to pay mine off."

"It's all good. Just standing there, watching them rise, waiting for the tug."

Nev walked in. "Way to go buddy. At least one of us didn't get skunked."

"I just couldn't stand in the water any longer. There's still trout down there."

"You want to go shop for the next couple days?"

"Let me change and we can head out. You staying, old man?"

"Flat as I can be."

And it was quiet again. I looked around the room—log furniture in a faux Native American motif. I couldn't say much, even to myself and dozed again. I tried to call Debby but she was gone. I wrote a few words in my journal and laid still for a long while. All of the muscles turned like wood on a lathe. A haiku at the top of Galena:

Ridgetop oracle—
foul weather to Galena
Summit: too bad.

And later, as I thought about Debby on the bed:

Deer in the aspen—
what a woman remembers—
three beloved men.

Another thing I didn't ask of my sons—could they live without their loved ones for weeks? These questions, unspoken, were like small stones you carry to remind you of their presence. I fumbled them often in my pocket, the gravel interior harnessed to each of us.

Witness to the fabric within. They walked back in the room, arms filled with dried fruit, nuts, and jerky. "We got some real food, Daddy'o," Nev said, turning to unpack.

"Thank God. My peanut butter nightstand was getting a little tired."

"The ride into Arco's going to be a long one—not much shade and a lot of sage and lava fields," Nev said, looking at his phone.

"You mean like every day," Cody teased.

"Yeah, like that," Nev fired back.

The banter was starting. "About four or five days and I think we got it—"

"In your dreams," Nev shot back.

"Yeah, mine and two other guys I know. You ain't fooling nobody."

"Hell, I was thinking you might run to Arco." They were off—the bullshit was getting thick. I laid back on the bed and let them go. One after the other, sparring in their best bike standup. I leafed through the magazine on the dresser but it was filled with big homes and large, round numbers, not something I was going to touch this time around. I tried to go back to sleep but couldn't. They were yammering and I knew we had to get out of the hotel. "Let's get a beer before I lose it again."

We walked back to the same place and had a beer on the rooftop. The weather was not as cold and the fire pits were off. My stomach was growling. Nev ordered some appetizers and the boys started looking at their phones. "What do you feel like for dinner?"

"I'm easy. That Italian place looked good."

"Let's try it."

I'd finally found a good fake beer—Bitburger—and ordered another. After we swallowed the appetizers, we headed downstairs and walked to the restaurant. We sat down outside, the sun nearly over the ridge. We took turns dipping the hot bread in the olive oil and balsamic and tried to fathom how far we'd come. "Did you ever think we'd make it to Ketchum?"

"I never thought about it," Cody answered. "Just going on a ride."

"Yeah, I was still in New York when you guys left. Took me a while to catch up with you two. But I'm feeling okay. The seat's still gnarly, but I'm pretty good."

They were both pretty good. Maybe it was I who was amazed. The young waitress set down our plates, five in all. She put one in front of Cody, one in front of me and three in front of Nevada. I thought she made a mistake. "*Three* entrees? I guess you'll get enough to eat," and knew as soon as I said it that he'd be hungry within hours. I savored the lasagna—probably the last good meal before Idaho Falls. I couldn't finish, but they were barely satiated. We thanked the waitress and walked back down the main street. Cody found a gelato store and I got some money from the ATM.

Ketchum was getting sleepy. The two of them found some crossing guard flags at the stop light and started to parody the happy crosswalk elders. I hid in one of the storefronts. They'd lost it—nothing more to say. Giddy with exhaustion and full bellies, they thought it was time to have some fun. Nev tried to take a video with his phone. I was sure we'd get arrested for disturbing the peace. We managed to avoid the lone car on the street and staggered back to the hotel. It was probably time to leave the big city; too long in isolation we were no longer fit for human interaction. Better left by the side of the road.

I tried to watch some TV but gave up. My eyes closed and I knew it was time to let the day fall to its knees. Let the bramble of worry and effort alone. It would all come back soon enough.

Places without Bearing
XXIV

Distance: 83 miles
Elevation: 1,900 feet
Ketchum, Idaho, 2019

Sun was coming through the screen door. Our laundry hung on the patio rail and it looked like most of it was still there. I tried not to make any noise and found the coffee pot. I started thinking about the dynamics of three, not five, how it was different with Scott and Joe. More cerebral, less shenanigans and maybe that was because the five of us weren't together long. Maybe it couldn't be helped. How was I ever going to keep up with these two? Not on the ride—that was clear—but the give and take. I wasn't going to and sat on the bed and sipped from my cup. They started to get dressed and I didn't want to move. Before long, they were at it again.

"You going to hang those stinking shorts on your panniers?"

"Just close enough for you to smell 'em."

I held up my hand and pleaded, "Not now." But it was futile. They were having too much fun. "What's the matter, old man? You need some *more* coffee?" Nev did his best whiny voice.

"Don't worry, you'll live long enough to be insulted by your kids one day." Just like that, the words flew out of my mouth. They didn't have kids. It made no sense and yet, it did. "Where'd that come from?"

I asked, self-consciously and all we could do was laugh. Down to our last words before the ride. We walked downstairs, settled up, got our bikes, came back to the room and stuffed our panniers with food and Gatorade for the long day ahead. I looked at my tire and gave thanks to the bike store owner. I promised I'd come back when the store was open.

We rode to a Starbucks and ordered some coffee and bagels. I couldn't believe we were hungry but by now it was a joke. No amount of food would fill the cavity for more than an hour, not even three plates of pasta. We started out of Ketchum. It was overcast and we followed the Big Wood River east. About ten miles out, we stopped at a gas station for a last food and pee stop before Hailey. It was good to be back in the valley—the town was still a town, not overgrown with the ebb and flow and tourists. You want what the valley holds—the promise of a good life—but not so good it starts to feel tainted. Cody found an artery just out of Bellevue that took us off Highway 75. We were alone in the hayfields. I rode by an old Buick Woody, restored and for sale. I turned around and went back. "Another one. Damn it. I just have to take a picture for later."

"Stand in front of the hood," Cody pointed.

"I just want the grill."

"I got ya."

Soon we were back on the bikes at a good pace, deep in the hayfields. The boys started again and I countered with "Make the guys behind me go away…"—more Eddy Arnold but it made no difference. We were light; the synchronous pedaling had returned. We joined Highway 20 a little west of Picabo and stopped for an energy bar. The morning had gone by quickly, the topo map had been good to us. After all that climbing, our ride was flat, mild and no wind. The days became defined by the particulars of effort and what could be seen from two wheels. "I'm going to run over there and take a leak," Nev hollered. He crossed the street into the cattails. We followed. In and out, it was a constant battle to drink enough water. It was going to get warm and we needed to hydrate. After the long slog into Boise, we couldn't do another eight hours of heat without enough fluids. We rode another ten miles to Carey and had lunch. It was warm, but we found some shade out of town and leaned our bikes against a cottonwood. There wasn't anyone outside. The sun was holding things still. We ate the sandwiches from Ketchum, the last real food before Arco. "How much longer until we get there?" I joked.

"A little over forty miles. Through the lava beds."

"Not going to be any shade."

"Better wet the bandanas."

"I may finally have to give in." We had managed to avoid the worst heat. Save the third day coming over the Coast Range in Oregon and the long push into Boise, it had been mild most of the way. But there was nothing here, only open land until Arco. We'd just have to go slow and hope the bikes didn't break.

"You got enough water, Pops? There's no place to stop between here and Arco," Cody reminded me.

"I'm good. All four bottles."

"Nev, you all right?" Cody turned.

He nodded. We threw the lunch bags in our panniers and got back on the bikes. At the road edge, I looked back at the Sawtooths one last time. That was a mountain range. I clipped in and started off behind them. Again, the journey turned. Now it was a different endurance—the road without a bend. I hoped the heat wouldn't fatigue us too much. We were committed to getting into Jackson Hole by July 3. Our spouses would be there by then. To return to Ketchum would mean another day of biking and the distance would only grow longer. I trusted the boys would tell me if it got too hot. We'd hitchhike if we had to. Although they hadn't said as much, the tedium of the ride was wearing on them. The long monotonous days ahead only exacerbated the obvious—they were running on stamina—and whatever aches they felt were set aside for the day's demands. Nev was still fighting his seat and rode faster so he could stand. He was returning to a new job, a cross-country move and a new place to live. A lot to absorb even if you weren't on a bike and the expectations of this stretch of highway—this endless hay-become-lava field—became a kind of annoyance. At some point, the ride was simply boring, not enough action for a young mind which had been running all the time. And Cody, on a leave of absence from his job, had plenty of time to sweat the consequences of taking a much-needed breath when the office culture wasn't always sanguine about such things. All of this and more was bleeding through the rings of salt on their brown necks and arms. Something no amount of wishing could take away.

"You excited about the new job?" Cody tossed back to Nev.

"Not sure. Have to wait and see—it's a health care initiative that I haven't worked in. Could be a real challenge."

"How you feeling on your team?"

"I'm starting to hit my groove. Think the leader wants me to stay—but you know how it is—" and Nev cut him off.

"I do. Up or out."

"It's taught me to think on my own and I like the problem-solving. The clients can get a little—"

"Like clients. A lot of money to help people play nice."

"Sounds like you got it down."

"I don't think anyone has it down."

"But it's got to be worth something, right?"

"Meaning?"

"It's gotta be more than the struggle—"

"To know what work means."

"When the boss finds his way into your dreams—and Sunday comes like a torrent of laundry and bills."

"I still don't know what work means."

I looked out at the sage fields—lupine was everywhere. We were finally catching up with the season. It was the first time I'd seen such color at the road edge. As far as I could see became bluer and lighter until the lupine and sage became one leaf in the high desert. About ten miles out, I set my bike down to hydrate and eat a snack. Nev admonished, "You're too close to the traffic."

I snarled, "I kept myself safe for sixty-five years," and walked in circles, drinking from my water bottle. A coded remark—and not much room to move from my slip. I offered an olive branch. "Are you getting too hot?"

"We're good."

And they were. I just had to keep pouring water down and hoped the three bottles would be enough. We rode on, into the Craters of the Moon National Monument and Preserve, a large volcanic plateau just west of Arco. The pumice was a deep brown, almost chocolate, and it stretched for more than fifty miles to the south, with occasional trees and shrubs sprouting from its craters. As far as I could see the rock was boundary to our ride. The boys were in front of me and so I just pedaled up and down the rollers. The Pioneer Mountains were north of us. There was a sign for Fish Creek Reservoir. I thought about going up to fill my one empty bottle but was too hot to worry about it. Besides, Cody was in front and he had the Steripen. We'd ride with what liquid we had. If something happened, I'd hold up an empty bottle and someone would stop. At least that's what my bike mechanic told me before we left.

There was a ridge over a long gradual climb up ahead. The sky was light brown—haze from the valley. I couldn't see them but knew they were up there. When I got to the ridge, Nev had ridden back to make sure we were okay. Cody was waiting for me. I unclipped and laid the bike down. The road turned to the north and the traffic was hard to see. "Stay there," I yelled. "Don't cross." But he thought it was clear and sprinted across. I thought he didn't see the car and I was furious, all my resistance gone. "What were you doing? You could have been—"

"I could see. It was good."

I didn't have the strength of mind to look farther down the road. Impetuously, I yelled, "Why couldn't you listen? It might help." And kicked myself the minute I said it. The wreckage that comes from miles of exertion and then one small burst in the sage. The lava was like a giant dark room without a roof and I couldn't leave. Everywhere to the south and east, it grew on the horizon. I wanted to get out of the sun, I wanted to take back my words, let him know I was wrong. But I couldn't pull out of the volcanic room, I couldn't turn away from its endless stare and ride off. Cody tried to pick up the shards of what I'd left and I imagine Nev was furious with me for breaking the covenant: you don't do this, not in the middle of a long, hot, pedal across a volcanic plateau. You find a way to maintain.

Father or not, you deal with it and trust that something will come out on the other side when the real work is done. We still had miles in the sun but that all left in a flurry of words—the reason I wanted to do this so long ago, do this with them. Nothing was ever spoken about the ride getting crooked. We just assumed we were old enough to know better. I was worn out and trying to be there for them but it wasn't working. My worry stood like a wall I couldn't pass through.

I rode for miles without thinking, just pushed through the hot air and the trailers and the happy people on vacation. The lava road moved in and out of the extant mass and the hot, brown horizon looked like the horizon of home that stretched to the Desatoyas, a Spanish word thought to mean losing one's bearings, a name most likely given by the Basque sheepherders. And I wondered if I had lost mine. Lost what I came for, lost what I hoped to see in the boys, what I had hoped we would share of each other. On the map to the east the Lost River Range rose to the north of Arco. This was a losing I did not know until now. What is it we come for, to these empty places, these places without bearing? I had come to mine.

I saw what looked like a building. It seemed like an apparition. Nothing could be in the middle of this plateau. Small tents and trailers were like outposts in the lava beyond the building. I wasn't hallucinating. I pulled into the parking lot and found my way to the entrance, which was a visitors center with artifacts and murals from the Craters of the Moon Preserve. Rangers were outside leading talks. There were vending machines and water faucets. I put my bottle under the fountain. The water was like snowmelt and I had never tasted anything so good. I drank and drank until I couldn't swallow any more. Before long, the boys walked in. I pointed to the fountain—"It's so good."

They drank endlessly. We looked so out of place, the three of us with sweat running down our faces into something we resented but had no words for—the loss of decorum—even as I hoped the right words would come. "You two all right?"

Nev nodded. Cody the same.

And then they knew—I was just like them. No better, no worse, as fallible as rain. I'd pushed too far. We sat by the window, content to be chilled however briefly, before the return to the sun. Flora and fauna exhibits lined the halls. The place was filled with people trying to get out of the heat. Young kids sat crying at the feet of their parents, like the summers Debby and I dragged the boys through the West in the back of our old Jeep. But that image wasn't going to save me from the nexus of now and I tried to put it away until we made it to Arco.

We ate some energy bars and went back outside. I put a wet bandana on my neck. We'd be lucky to get to Arco in this heat. Slowly, we turned back onto the highway, the two of them out front. I needed to ride at my turtle pace, catch up when I could. They'd wait for me when the lava beds ended. There was more sage and lupine to the north and I tried to keep my vision there, off of the pavement and heat below. I looked into the mountains, hoping for a mirage, some height of pine or juniper that might release me.

The landscape was dry and wild—the place people thought of when you said high desert, the place not wanted by those who drove through it, out of harm's way because it was unused land, sage and bitterbrush. I saw what looked like a small bridge and turned to the north—a river in this unchosen place. The Big Lost River—the words on the highway sign. Big Lost River, like us I thought, rolling down the road. I couldn't see where it came from—the headwaters in the Lost River Range—nor where it flowed to the south. But it did go somewhere—into a sink, underground, where the water disappeared to nourish this dry land.

We'd ridden into the very place we left—our poor rivers of home that flowed into sinks. How could we pass such a finite body of water in this remote place and not pass the Humboldt, the Carson, the lost waters of the Great Basin? A circular motion of a thousand miles to claim what little moisture was left. I didn't know this lost river was here when we left, much like I didn't know the two men in front of me. I had thought I did, thought I knew them well but all I knew was what I could see, not what was below the surface. They were their own men now. They didn't need the rules and metaphors; they outlived them. It was I who had disappeared into the land.

We pulled into Arco with its bold sign—"Atoms for Peace"— referring to the city's early use of atomic power. The boys were on their phones. "There's a campground about a half mile off the highway," Cody yelled. I followed, wanting something cold and some shade. We paid for a camping space and bought two tall Coors from the ice chest out front. I settled for a seltzer and took a swig from Cody's can. We walked to the camp site and sat down at the picnic table. Nothing to say. The road had brought us here, not much more. We threw the pads on the ground and set up the tent. Nev found a couple of trees to hang his hammock. The couple next to us were sitting in lawn chairs, sipping beer. I said hello, not knowing if I could say anything more of consequence. They smiled and raised a can—"Welcome."

I walked to the shower, which was clean and roomy. In the middle of this hot alkaline land, we had found an oasis. My face was wrinkled with dust and a scruff of gray and black whiskers. The lines on my arms and legs contrasted like bands on a coral snake. I had earned every inch of them. The sun line on my neck and lower back was brown too. I looked like a brown and white zebra in the shower. Maybe I was both animals. Maybe I was too tired to care. The wires were down.

I took a long time to dry, find my shorts and brush my teeth. I went back to the office, found another seltzer and brought the guys two more cold ones. They were still sitting at the picnic table. Arco had come at a cost. Its name derives from the tonal quality of the bow on the violin. It can be used as both an adjective and an adverb. Today it was a verb, stretching across our road to the Tetons—our road without end.

"That shower was amazing. And they have a free ice cream happy hour!"

"Ice cream happy hour?" Nev turned.

"That's what it says. I can't imagine it doing anything more than melting but hey, I'll try it." I grabbed the last of the gorp from Ketchum. "If I never eat another peanut, it won't be too soon."

"You won't have to. We're going to Pickles for burgers," Cody snickered, pointing at the phone. "Supposed to be the best. And they make their own dill—you guessed it—pickles."

I started to blow up our pads and Nevada strung his rain fly over the hammock. There was a little grass and the ground was flat. I got out my diary and tried to find a pen but I couldn't write. It was just too hard. I walked over to the couple next to us. "Do you mind if we plug in our phones on the electric post?"

"Use the outlet on our camper."

"Thank you. Where you guys from?"

"On hiatus from North Carolina. Decided it was time to take a break. I'm a cabinet maker and I'd been at it for fifteen years. Took my retirement, bought the motorhome and drove away. Been gone six months. Came across the southern half of the US. We're trying to get through the mountains in the West before we head back."

"How utterly civilized," I said, with just a touch of jealously.

"Yeah, not many people do this but it was right for us."

I could see something in them, a contentedness that comes from letting go. Across the path, an older couple spent forty-five minutes trying to get their tires centered on the wood blocks—"Back up, no, too much." I gave thanks for the ease of two wheels, but only now, at day's end when luxury was no longer needed. The boys came back from the shower and we threw our things in the tent and rode into town. Pickles was a loud green building, the only one with cars in front. We walked in and it was jammed. Every farmer for miles was there and there weren't any seats. We stood at the cash register eyeing the gallon jar of dills. "Think we should get one?" Cody half-asked.

The menu had twelve kinds of burgers. We each got one—with jalapeños, cheddar and bacon, more fat and carbs than I'd seen since—well, before we left on the ride. We got an extra side of fries and yes, the dreaded dill pickle came in its own private basket. It was all pretty damn good, but by that time I could have eaten raw eggs on toast. "Damn, look at those things," Nev pointed to the waitress flying by.

The burgers were huge. We might get enough to eat tonight. When the food finally descended on our table, people were lined up at the door. We ate in utter delight and the food restored some balance to the day. On the other end of the teeter-totter, the sustenance brought us back to one another. Then, of course, because we didn't make it to the ice cream happy hour, Cody ordered vanilla ice cream with chocolate syrup for all of us. You could say we were sated—but not too loud.

"Another great burger in the middle of—wait for it—the desert," Nev tossed out like the first pitch in a game. We laughed and rode back to the campground. Houses and trailers were set back from the gravel road. Kids played in the sprinklers. A mother watered her vegetables. The dogs barked at us, strangers who rode through. Cody looked at his phone. There were some clouds to the south. "Going to rain?" I asked.

"No, looks clear after ten."

"Okay. I'm going to head back over to the store. Get some postcards."

"See ya, Pops."

"You two want anything?" I found three cards with the city in the forefront. I wished they had a card from Pickles. No one would believe me without it—a burger and pickle joint in the eastern Idaho high desert. I wrote a few lines to friends and laid down on the pad. The sky overhead was filled with scattered clouds. I tried to put the day away. Nev was reading from a book he brought with him. Cody was sitting on the bench, texting his wife. Each of us was alone with our thoughts. By the time Cody crawled into the tent I was dozing off. "Good night, you two. It was a long, hard day. I hope you get some rest."

It was dead black and I started to feel something in the dream. I couldn't tell what it was. I put my finger on my forehead and it was wet. And then another small prick. I turned to Cody—"It's starting to rain." He jumped out of the tent and put up the rain fly. I couldn't have done it in the dark. Nev had his up, so he was okay. Cody crawled back into the tent and we listened for many minutes, the quiet wind pushing the rain onto the fly. Restless in the dust below, we waited out the storm and dozed off. In the morning I looked out and Nev was on the ground. His pad had gone flat in the hammock and he had to sleep on the dirt in his bag—a long night of waiting, of turning. "When did the pad puncture?"

"Not sure. Just slept on the grass."

"You stiff?"

"Not too bad."

"At least we have a room in Idaho Falls."

"Yeah," he said. "Thank God for Cody's hotel points. We'd still be sleeping in the dust."

A Scrim of Worry
XXV

Distance: 76 miles
Elevation: 1,401 feet
Arco, Idaho, 2019

As memory gets written, the story seeps to other places, into a chasm of things recorded, believed, imagined. I had mine—a full bounty of pictures and images riding out of Portland—gathered in a few short weeks with my sons on a bicycle. No doubt they had their memories as well, each of us weighted with a history of other stories, written and unwritten, lives lived without intent or willfulness. Just like you might as a child. And that child came along as well, came to upend things when it got too serious, came to laugh at our foolish ways. How dare I think this could go one way on a black two-lane road across the West when there were a hundred ways it could go, a hundred roads to run down, return and rebuild? There was no path, not the one we charted in Cody's flat last spring, not the one we relied on to free us from the confines of work and regimen. Those were just trails in the dust at the road edge. There was no boundary out here and yet there was a boundary that came and went, not just the obvious noise and distraction from the road, but the noise and distraction from within. At some point, the road tilted into the roads left behind—a paradox of perspective. The steady effort slowly took away all pretense to expose what was left. And then the boundary bled over. Father, son, nouns without names. Friends who rode with us, nouns we named. This was the distance of blood and it moved through kin who stood in its aftermath.

Cody walked to the picnic table in the morning sun and heated the water. The older couple had driven away from their perfectly parked motor home blocks. The couple next to us were still asleep. I went and retrieved my phone cord and rear lamp. The green light was on so I might make it to Idaho Falls before the charge ran out. I hoped the night hadn't been too long for Nevada. The ground is soft if you don't need to sleep on it. But he needed sleep; we all needed sleep. The rain came as a reminder: in the high desert, the sky changes and at one in the morning, it can let down sudden and abundant rain. We put the tent and rain flies on the fence and hoped they would dry before we rode off. We sipped coffee and tried to feel our limbs. I pulled up to the bench seat to stretch my hamstrings. It was almost a laugh—they'd been stretched in ways unthinkable and the bench wasn't going to change that. We packed our panniers, rinsed the cups, and huddled in the last shade of a Russian olive. Cody put the tent fly on his panniers and I rode with the wet tent on mine. We thought about stopping at Pickles for sandwiches but it was too risky to buy them in the morning—burgers and fries were not going to travel well. There was a gas station on the east end of town. We pulled in for Gatorade and snacks. An old couple were on Harleys beside us, she on a three-wheeler. They'd ridden for days. "She likes the trike—I can't stand it. Need two wheels on the road. But if it makes her happy—" the sonogram of marriage.

The boys came out with three bottles each. We drank one in the shade and started off. Nev pulled up a café on his phone, six miles out of town. It was already getting hot and we hadn't ridden far. A scrim of worry across the pavement. All the time in the saddle until the moment it doesn't matter. Until now. I didn't want to know what the heat would rise to and so just tried to imagine a cool place in which to pedal. The building grew as we rode into the sun. There were a few cars parked outside but not more. We leaned our bikes against the front wall and walked in. The bartender and two scruffy men turned to us, smoking. "We don't do food—" and we looked around again to make sure it wasn't a bad western.

"Guess not." We turned to leave.

And now the ride back to the station. If we didn't turn around, we wouldn't make it through the day. We didn't have enough food. Nev felt bad— "Sorry guys, didn't want to add more miles to the day." In this heat we'd be lucky to make it halfway without pitching a thumb in traffic. We bought five breakfast burritos at the gas station, hoped the beans would last a couple hours in the heat. There wasn't a lot to choose from. I hid them from the sun, and we retraced our brief steps to Butte City. It was almost 11 a.m. A terrible start on the long day into Idaho Falls. If we'd learned anything it was that you had to get out early. By the time the heat and miles mixed, it was a brutal concoction and it could take you down. I did some quick math—there was no way we were arriving before 7 p.m. and the ride just grew by twelve miles.

We could have taken Highway 33 North, which would have put us on a smaller spur but it was a longer route and so we stayed on Highway 20. Again, an apparition grew on the horizon: a roof and then a parking lot. One motorhome and not much else. We pulled in and stood our bikes under the outdoor patio. It was a visitor display for the research at Idaho National Laboratory. How ironic—we were about to ride through the place that researched atomic energy. Now Arco began to make sense. This is where it came from—those atoms for peace. We filled our bottles in the drinking fountain, ate some energy bars and rolled out. The man in his motor home had been on the road for months. His wife was in Texas. He was happy to be out of the news, without any worry. "I do this every couple years. Kind of need to, don't ya think?"

"That's what we thought when we left," I replied and waved to the place he was driving into.

Just before we pulled into Arco we crossed the Big Lost River again. It was flowing north along the edge of the lava until it drained into the sink. A last band of water before nightfall. We rode about ten miles and found a turnout on the side of the highway. There wasn't much traffic, a few hay trucks and some trailers but not much else. We got off our bikes and I poured water down my back and face. This was the real thing—the hot had just begun. We were looking north, into the field, over the locked gate with the Do Not Enter sign—Idaho Labs. A man pulled in on a Harley, black leathers and helmet. We wondered what possessed him to stop in the middle of the desert next to us. He got off his bike and put the helmet on his bars. "How you doing?" he asked.

"Pretty good. A little warm but hey, not bad. Must be hot on that bike."

"Yeah, I guess," but he only had a t-shirt on under the jacket.

"What brings you out here?"

"Looking to get to Oregon. See my lady. And you? On bikes—"

"Trying to get to the Tetons."

I watched the boys trade talk from the fence. They were holding their own.

"That's a ways."

"Yep. It's a lot longer now. Those things you never see on a map, like food and water."

He sat on his bike for another twenty minutes, then rode off. The boys were convinced he was a spy, working for the labs, checking up on us. He might have been. Maybe he just rode in circles all day. Trying to keep the perimeter clean, or at least clear of any person who might be suspect of character, especially out here.

"Did you see that guy? Was he for real?" Nev was sure the posse was coming next. Cody thought we might have to run for it. We were laughing—it was pretty strange. This man in black on a Harley in the middle of nowhere. Just glad he wasn't ornery. We picked up our bikes and started across the road. It was past noon and we weren't even halfway to our destination. I could feel the sundial overhead, ticking on my scalp. The weather of imperfection. Salting us with lines on our forehead, under the eyes, and lips. The fine thread of dried moisture. I poured water on my face and helmet; I couldn't get overheated. If I did, I was done. If any of us did, we'd have to hitchhike. It was too far to ride in the dizzy fields of heat. I was getting hungry. We'd try for another ten miles and stop for lunch. I hoped the two of them were not losing too much water. They didn't have extra bottles. And I'd given mine to cooling. What the hell—it kept me going. Nev was on the side of the road. There was a turnout to the south. No lab, just hay. We could get out of the dust of the road. We laid our bikes on the weeds and dirt. I pulled the last burrito from my bag and wished I had bought two more like them. It was gone in minutes and I ate every scrap of food I saw. The Gatorade was hot but wet and I drank it even as I longed for something cold. A light wind blew from the south. I laid down on the dirt road, the sun in my eyes and let go of the miles, the bands of hay running to the south. I sat up and looked at the boys. "Not to be morose, but I couldn't have done this ride with my father. He was already gone at my age." I paused. "Don't know where that came from. I was thinking about him, wanting to do this kind of thing together. But it never happened. By the time we could, he was—"

"We're pretty damn lucky Pops. That's all I got to say."

Nev chimed in. "What the hell are we gonna do when we reach sixty-five?" as if either of them had kids to worry about.

"If you ever have kids, you're gonna do what you need to."

"I doubt it. I don't know too many people that do something like this."

"Don't worry about the questions. I'm just grateful we're out here. This isn't on a map, this fifty-third row of hay, miles from a lab where the atoms sing to the researchers. This is not a place; it's what we've come to after weeks of turning into the rising sun. It's what happens when you leave a place. You never know what's out there. The only thing I knew was I wanted to do this with you. That was reason enough."

"I'll try to remember some of this day—but it will disappear. And then what? What will I say to those that didn't come? What will I tell them if they ask how it was?" Cody asked.

"Tell them you rode. And you ran into things. Things that weren't on a map."

"Does he always sound like this?" Nev egged him on.

"Only when he does," Cody tossed back.

"Let's get out of here. It's getting close to two. Going to be a long slog into Idaho Falls." I paused and then, "the thing is, my father would have liked this. This would have changed him. He was never athletic, but he was strong and this would have been a test, one he would have given a shot." But the boys were gone. Just as well. I was talking to my Dad anyway. And Mom, wherever she was in the board-and-care home so far from this field. I had this notion they were looking on, trying to see which way I'd point, which way I'd turn. The things you say to yourself in the hot of the afternoon. The things the mind will not let go of. Until it can no longer hold them and the sounds mingle with the hay trucks.

The boys were a ways out in front. I could see their backs on the rollers—it was forty-plus miles into Idaho Falls. The hay was crooked now, little green sticks tossed in the southerly wind. A horizon of particles in the light. Highway 20 bisected the lava fields on the Snake River Plain. Some hint of things beyond the endless rock and hay. This day was going to take its measure of our stamina. It was going to ask if we wanted to arrive by dark. It was going to exert pressure on the limbs, lock our hands in place on the bars. It was going to sweat the day out of us, make us stretch the hot air for more, with nothing between the shoulder of dirt and the late afternoon hay trucks. Nev's bike was leaning against a roadside stop. I saw Cody there too. It looked like a mirage. How could anything but dust belong to this soil? I took my helmet off, and the pads inside were soaked. I sat on the bench outside. "Get me something cold." They were inside a while. A rancher pulled up in his diesel and nodded. Just another day for him. The real heat wasn't even here yet. He'd be driving the hay in August, another ten degrees hotter. They came out with a seltzer and Gatorade. I swallowed them both and poured more water over my head. "You should try it." But they just laughed, their bandanas soaked from sweat and water and road grit. "What do you think? Another twenty?"

"About that. Service is spotty. We've got the highway until the outskirts of town. We're turning there. I'll keep an eye out for you."

"Thanks, Cody." I didn't ask how they felt; any person would have dried to monosyllables by now. They were in for the duration, but the duration grew longer. *I'll keep an eye out*—we didn't have much more to say. I could only hope they found that well inside upon which to draw. That place you reached for when nothing was left. Finally, ranch homes started to appear and things that looked more like lived-in communities—cars and wood stacks and rusted farm equipment. The detritus of living on the land, the land we'd slipped into. I unbuckled my right shoe, my foot was throbbing. How or why it was on fire I did not know. Another anomaly of motion, of fatigue. The boys had theirs—shoulder, butt and neck. It didn't matter what part of the body stood out. It really didn't because nothing was going to change. The city wouldn't come any sooner. I coasted down a long roller into the four-lane highway. It looked like they were stopped and then one of them was heading south. That must be the turn. I couldn't see the city ahead—it must still be another ten miles—but at least it would be quieter off the road, through the neighborhoods to the east. Places we'd grown fond of, looking for a way into the city. A fair amount of residential development—not unlike the outskirts of Boise. Idaho was growing, even as we were passing through. The stop signs and low-tract houses seemed eternal, but they were only a fragment in the eternal day. I could not make out any buildings ahead in the matrix of parks and homes. At last we turned onto a bluff. The Snake was visible to the south. Cody motioned to go left at the light. Without me knowing it, we'd ridden into the parking lot of the hotel. I heaved thanks to many gods and yelled some obscenity at the entrance. "Did you ever think we'd get here? That was the longest damn day—"

"I feel ya Pops."

"I'm not sure I feel anything," Nev half-joked.

"I don't feel much except gassed."

"Let me get the key. I'll be right back."

We waited outside. "Well, guess this wasn't what we thought, huh?" I asked, as much a thought as I could muster.

"Nope—but we made it. We'll get out of this heat and shower and go find some food."

Cody waved us in, bikes and all. An apparition in the lobby. The guests took notice but not too much. We smiled with our best wet, worn out selves. I took the panniers off the bike and sat on the couch. I could hardly move. The boys were flat on the beds. We pounded the cold water bottles from the reception desk. I tried to find my soap for the shower. I kept walking to the window. This river flowing down, into the reservoir below, into the crepuscular light. I stood in the shower for minutes, the steam eating the salt from my back. I was tattooed with lines, my skin like old shoes, nothing to salvage. I

brushed my teeth, found some dry shorts and sat back down again.
"That kicked my ass—"

"Kicked all our ass—"

"Can you have a plural ass?" A cheap shot but the best I could
do given the cranial fade.

"That shower will bring you back, I promise. Besides, Cody
found Mexican food by the river. If we can still walk—"

"I'll buy a damn cab—"

"It's just a block or two, Pops."

"I sure as hell ain't riding."

"I got ya—"

We staggered out of the hotel and walked on the riverside. The
city had made it a place to be in the summer. Families were on the
grass, on bikes—the cruiser kind—and the river was full, running
over the falls. I imagined it was something like the restoration that
happened in Caldwell, days before, a renaissance of place. We walked
in the cool brick room and were seated by the bar. Before I could
speak, the boys ordered a mountain of nachos and cold beer. Our
waitress set the drinks down and asked how we were. We laughed.

"Happy to be off the bikes."

"Bikes?"

"Yep, just passing through."

"In this heat?"

"We took a wrong turn but the beer is great—"

"Be nice to her. We haven't eaten yet," my last attempt at grace.
The nachos were piled with salsa and avocado and jalapeños. We
dove in like it was the first time we'd seen hot food. The waitress
brought a platter of tacos—more than we could eat—and we ate until
it hurt. We walked back to the river and sat in the cooling night air.
The bikes and roller-skaters came by at a leisurely pace. We followed
the lights on the trail to the hotel. The room was cool but I was chilled
from the burn of the day. I couldn't say any more and we stared at the
TV. Finally, I rolled over, unable to keep my eyes open. They watched
the movie a little longer and followed into darkness. Ours were the
dreams of spent men, alone on the fifth floor of the new hotel at
the river's edge. The dreams that wouldn't end—of coming into the
afternoon hay light and cicadas, of drinking from plastic bottles until

they wouldn't give another drop, of lying against a lone chain-link fence separating the traffic from atomic particles. The dreams of letting down and losing the day to stars.

The Water and Wood that Followed
XXVI

Distance: 66 miles
Elevation: 3,481 feet
Idaho City, Idaho, 2019

I opened the card from Debby. It was the last thing she posted before driving to Salt Lake City to see her good friend. It made me think of home—so like the horizontal sky of the last ninety miles—the hue of desert light burrowing at the edges of brown and yellow and red-orange. A color you could imagine being far away, coming from the lungs of a mountain. Of many mountains. She sounded good but tired of the absence. Tired of listening to the wind without us— much as I was—but my time was not checkered with isolation. Mine was tumbling, always forward, into the heat of the day, the heat of our day as father and sons. It was she who was missing, she who was not there and it was an absence I could feel. I thought of her when I sat with coffee, tried to follow the rules of comportment—my sons had seen me reading her letters, missing her. I knew they missed their spouses, missed the people who anchored them in their homes, in their busy lives before this all began. This is what I couldn't give them in the earnest tender of the moment.

"Where we going to today, old man?" Cody was staring into his phone.

"Good morning to you too!"

"Looks like Teton Pass is about eighty miles—but we have two pretty good climbs."

Nevada sighed. "Can we take a cab and tell 'em the crank broke—"

"I say we hitchhike."

"Now you're talking. Except the bikes won't fit in the damn car."

"Shit. You want some coffee?" I persisted in asking even though they drank half what I did. But we made up for it in beer—even if mine was fake. "That's a lot of climbing. Two passes. Can you find out what the grade is on Teton Pass? I've heard things. Which leads me to believe it's a frickin' bear. We're pretty gassed. I can't see us pushing hard another day *and* doing some serious climbing."

They moaned in agreement. We headed downstairs for breakfast, considerably less sweaty than our first appearance in the lobby. The eggs and sausage were cooked right and there was fruit we hadn't seen in days. We took apples back to the room and loaded the panniers. The clothes had mostly dried in the shower. We were getting good at the one-day laundry service. There still wasn't any consensus on the ride. We'd take it slow and see what opened up. The long days had given us some extra time. We didn't have to arrive today; we could spread out the time. Our legs would tell us in about five hours.

We rode north out of Idaho Falls on Highway 26. It was forty-four miles to Swan Valley, one of the prettiest valleys in the West. The morning traffic was busy and we followed the outpost of retail and strip malls. This was the side of Idaho Falls that kept the town running, the places you couldn't see by the river. The weather was good and it looked like it would be cool going into the mountains. Thankfully, we wouldn't have to fight the orb overhead. We were out of town fairly quickly—and happy to be in the hayfields on the quiet four-lane heading east. There was a Sunoco station at the turnoff for Ririe. We pulled in to get some drinks and food. I could feel the weight of the journey lift. We were light again. The day was coming to us, not like the work of yesterday. "You two doing all right?"

"All good, Pops."

"All right so far."

"This valley just feels different. The elevation, the air—it's not the hot hay of that long afternoon. We're not pushing into the heat. Such a difference."

"Think we'll be on a slow incline until Swan Valley but nothing too bad. Should be an easy pedal for the next two to three hours."

"I like the sound of that." We crossed the road and started again. Yesterday's soreness had subsided. It must have been the sleep and the rest that brought us back to a day without memory of the day before. The *milagritos* of being on two wheels, little miracles of moving on without knowing why. I remembered this valley from my earlier trips in the car. The road ran parallel to the Snake River in the gorge below. The hayfields rose up the flank to the south, large, green, shallow pools that tempted you, made you want to run into their midst. A serene calm about the early summer crop. They hadn't had a first cutting yet. It was higher here; they might get three yet, if the weather held. The occasional house rose out of their center— places where you could settle if this was your choice, places where you could root. I thought of Joe again—look into the houses and Scott, who might have paraphrased—look into the rivers, the long, deep, band below us. Look into them if you want to know a place. I wondered, now that they were home, what they were looking into, if they missed the routine, the banter, the morning quiet unfolding. I'm sure they wanted to ride with us—but equally sure it was not the time. This ride funneled, strangely, to mountains and questions of the sons and father. Mountains and questions I had not yet reconciled but knew they were close, to warrant attention.

When I last drove through this valley it was on fire. Eastern Idaho, like much of the West, was burning and the flames crested the ridge to the south. The Tetons were shrouded in smoke. I wondered if any day would open to this sky with the threat of fire in all directions. How quickly the West disguised itself as a last place, a place you leave before dying. At one time, fire was on both sides of the road. I told Debby riding may not be a good idea. Nothing can come from watching this land burn. At Teton Pass we looked into the valley and the smoke flattened the sky to Yellowstone. Jackson Hole was a dark brown cloud. I had hoped to ride the valley. "Not in this smoke," she said, "not in this smoke." This experience frames a vision of two places—equally beautiful and terrifying. If you're lucky, you get to hold these disparate images until they merge into one place of fire and water. And then, summers and winters on, the snowmelt before planting, the broken cones stiff in soil, some particle of green emerges and the disguise falls from the ridges, leaving a valley without smoke, without its acrid smell.

The boys pulled off at the rest stop overlooking the gorge. It was a large brown building with a water fountain and restrooms. The Snake was below. There were drift boats tracking its current. What I would have given to be in one. "You want to stay an extra day?" I taunted.

"Hell, yeah."

"We'll just get there a day late."

"I don't care. It looks pretty damn nice to me."

"You guys want to eat here?"

"I think we can make another ten before we eat." We picked up subs at the sandwich place in the station. "How you doing? The muscles cramping up?"

"I'm all right. Not sure why; all right so far."

"Nev, you okay?"

"I'm good."

"Damn, I want to get to that river."

"Maybe we'll come back with the car. We've got time."

"I'd like that. Let's get out of here before I walk down and throw my rod in."

The incline was growing. We'd try for lunch on the ridge. I could feel my legs burn but my foot didn't hurt. I pedaled without worry and slowed to the climb, content to let the mountain come to me. The Snake Range started to appear in the east—something I had not known if we would see. Even yesterday, the ride did not have a specific destination. We were like smoke in the hayfields and coming into Idaho Falls, the town of Victor seemed ephemeral. But here they were: the jagged cliffs of Wyoming, not unlike the peaks in the Sawtooths. These were the mountains through which we came, the mountains that defined our days of climbing and bending back to asphalt, the days that sent us to our knees. I fixed my eyes on the most distant peak and promised to learn its name but I quickly forgot any calculation of time and space. Cody was up ahead, at a turnout. I pulled in. We looked at each other, at Nev.

"We might have come for this," I said, "we might have imagined this, but I don't think so. I don't think this place existed when we left. Not the place we're in now. It's not on the contours of a topo map; it's a place we rode into that became a place of our making. A place we carry with us whatever the outcome. Let's eat the subs before they go bad."

It probably sounded wrong, it may have been. We ate in quiet, happy to be off the road.

"How you feeling about Victor, Pops? You want to try to make it over the pass?"

"Let's decide in Swan Valley. I think we have a good climb out of there. That will be the test—" and they smiled the telling smile of sore legs and backs. There wasn't anyone left to convince. We were sticks on the side of the road.

We crested the ridge and rode along the South Fork of the Snake into the valley proper. It was green and moist and mountains rose on either side of the wetlands. The air was brighter—we were higher—the Caribou Mountains were to the south. I felt as if I'd come home, back to where I was supposed to be, with the ones who needed this place. The bikes had become currency paid for the occasional splendor of a valley like this. We were on a two-lane road, twisting quietly along the stream. The town and ranches lay in the distance, a valley of otherworldly beauty.

There was a huge ice cream sign welcoming us. We didn't have to think long and soon we sat licking the cones outside the small shop. Pine Creek Pass was to the north. Twenty more miles to Victor. "We'd better break the day up. Two passes might be too much."

"Think you're right. It's gonna take us till four at least to make Victor. We won't make Teton Pass before six or seven if we're lucky."

"Let's try and get to the campground about six miles out of Victor. Just beyond the pass.

"We still have another day if we need it," Nev offered. "No need to get there tonight."

We hit the gas station across the street. The tourists were outside in their motorhomes, stuffing ice chests, smoking. An elderly Chinese woman came out of her van. Suddenly it occurred to me—people were here from all over the globe. I listened to them—they were traveling from mainland China. Some beauty would call them before long, name itself for this day they stepped into. I looked up at the hill—houses and hay and farm animals until the road disappeared. We looked at each other and then the boys rode off.

It looked like a gradual climb, but that changed quick—I was on the pedals in a couple hundred yards—up an 8 or 9 percent grade and I knew we made the right decision. Two big passes would have done us in, especially having to camp tonight. I reached the flank of farms and cattle and looked west—the valley as clear as a sketch before paint. An outline of things I would carry with me—these ridge tops, these evergreens, these watery fields.

I came upon a house of logs that was slipping to dust. An angle of repose for one or two more winters until it succumbed. This was the green that Stegner was trying to forget—the wavy fields at either road edge like an armchair. The boys were waiting at a turnout; the view behind us just kept getting better. There wasn't any place to want, it was an open sky unlike most I'd seen. A sky you cannot turn away from. Sky of light and hale breath. Everything you want in a mountain valley. We rode across a river gorge, hundreds of feet in the air. I saw Pine Creek and imagined wild trout in a gorge without easy access. We rose out of the gorge onto a slow climb to the false ridge. Pine Creek ran alongside the road. I looked in the pools every chance I could. Wildflowers were on the bank and meadow grass ran to the water. At one point I turned and saw a bloated carcass. I stopped and stared. It was an elk, beheaded and tossed from the road. An eerie reminder: you cannot leave, even here. You must pay attention. The wild will only belong if we let it. "Did you see that?" Nev hollered.

"Made me sick. What in the hell were they doing?"

A trophy kill. If that oxymoron must persist, why here, why now?

"Think we got about ten miles to Pine Creek Pass."

"I've still got a little left. How you guys doing?"

"All right."

"I don't care what happens. As far as I'm concerned, you made it. You made it to the edge of Idaho, in the mountains, without much more than blue lines on a map. Whatever else, you made it in my mind." I looked at the river again, at the animal pitched in the grass like a rug. We started back up the gorge, not able to see much beyond the next turn. It was getting warm, the sun at our backs and no wind. "I think it's pretty gradual until the last five miles. We should be okay for a while," Cody hollered.

"Thanks, big guy."

The navigators. Without them, I would have ridden into the mouth of this mountain without a clue. At one point, I wanted to walk the river upstream, follow the contours of rock and wildflowers in the pristine wilderness, not moving, but even now transport of such slow means kept me from the stream. We got into the switchbacks and I could see the next ridge but not much more. There were turnouts to keep the car radiators from overheating. I joked, "Where's ours?" but we just got off when it was too much.

Nev was waiting for me. "Think we're about to get into it."

"Here I thought you were going to tell me the pass was just a mile away."

"In your dreams."

"Damn straight." And dreamed I did, of having legs that had something left.

"You all right?"

"Kind of out here now."

"Guess you're right. Get over this one and rest."

"Looks like the campground's on the other side of the ridge."

"Got it," and he pedaled off. I stood the bike up and started. Down to the granny gear, the switchbacks were cutting into the mountain. I reached for a chew, my energy dragging. This was it—the next hundred yards, nothing more. It was all I could focus on, as if there were an open passage beyond. By now, each of us had gone to the well. I reached back to its darkened cavity, that place you drew upon when there was only one rotation of the crank and then the next. That place of warning and strength. The perimeter of exertion. I tried to keep the boys in my sights but could only see their occasional backs in the sun and I pushed one leg down and lifted the other. My strength was ebbing, what strength was left. I figured another three miles to the ridge. But it wasn't a given, it was only a guess, a tired guess. I was frustrated because I was shot, without transcription, by the water and wood that followed us. And I did not know which was wet, which was dry until I stood between them and knew they were like my sons.

How this journey had ebbed to these two elements—from the outpost of eastern Oregon where Joe was gut-punched, to the striated hills where Scott pressed deep into the volcanic rock to find filtered water. What we took from it, turning and weaving in the hay and fallen barns at the roadside of father and sons. I couldn't put their words to it, these two who left, but I knew they slowed our vision to the essential marks of this landscape: the water, the wood. As we rode on, my sons grew into a further place where I could not take them. They were on their own, seeing the aperture with fresh eyes. The water and wood of two whose limits were nearly fused with mine. We turned into the switchbacks like dromedaries, insistent on the upward movement. I pulled out on the shaded side of the road when my breath was gone, dropped the bike and a zip tie cut my thigh. I cussed the round and certain pines. I cussed the whole damn day—even as the late sun gave a first glimpse of this penultimate peak. How could I feel such joy and exasperation at once? I laid there, looking up at the pines to the outline above us we rarely saw, and let myself drift.

In a few minutes, Nev rode down to find me. "You all right?"

"Yeah, just the damn tie on the cross bar. Caught my leg when I dropped the bike."

"Think we've got about two more miles and we're there. You good?

"I'll be all right." He rode off.

He caught up to Cody. "I can't believe he's still riding."

"He's long past that. This is just another climb."

"Wish I knew what I was riding into."

"You got this bro. There's no job, no place that's gonna take you sideways. Besides, she's waiting for you. She knows what's going down. She's already on it."

"Yeah. She is. Thank God. This bike, this ride—how'd it get so—"

"Freeing?"

"Hardly and yet—"

"You wait. When you get back to New York, it won't look the

same. And going on will look a lot different too. I think that's why he drug us out here, to scrape our knees a little, and look up. To see what-the-hell's out there."

"Yeah, that crusty old fart. He's got some stones."

"You got stones. You're moving on. Just remember that."

I clipped in and rode across the highway with nothing more in mind than the next hundred yards. The push was down to one turn of the crank at a time, an isolated thrust and pull. I stood on the pedals for most of the corner until I was in the sun and it felt good on my limbs, burnished in the winnowing light. I could see what looked like the summit up ahead, but I had been fooled enough to know it might be a summit of my imagination. I kept my head down just in case and reread the words on my gooseneck cap—all work and no play is no fun at all. Not for a reminder but for the resonant presence of what, after all these variegated miles, we'd become. Without a passport, we had crossed a border and surrendered our currency, our language, for another. Learned to speak this new idiom, this translation of what could not be said before we left. And spent ourselves to acquire its full breadth of knowledge. We were in a window of high altitude, air through which we saw this new land. I brushed the bars with my knee and the physical contact drew me back—the ridgeline was a couple hundred yards away. They were waiting there, bikes lying on the road, walking to the place of greatest sight. I looked up at them and turned back to Swan Valley, the valley of last reckoning. "Damn, we made it. So glad we're only going to Victor. You have no idea—"

"Oh, I think we do—"

"Just a little eighty-miler—"

"Smartass. Damn, this air tastes good. Pine Creek Pass. Help me remember this name. I cussed all the way up—well, only the last four miles. The river after the bridge—what a gorge to ride through."

"I think the campground is about half-way down to Victor. Should be on the left. I'll pull out and wait for you."

"Thanks, Cody. I'm going to hang for a few and coast in after I say adios to the valley."

They rode off and I turned again to look south into the place below—a place of serene quiet that I took with me. I put my arm warmers on as the shade crowded the pines and was relieved to let gravity do the work. Occasionally, the boys came into view on the turns, but for the most part, I followed in the rustling air, content to know the day was closing like it began—in relief—not more, not less than what it was. Cody was standing on his bike as I rolled up. "Not going to fly. There's no water here. They had a light snow pack last year and the creek is dry. The ranger said to head into town. Might find something there."

"At least it's downhill. Okay. I'll follow, see what we find."

It was another six miles into Victor. Most of it was downhill and despite the rollers, we were fine. We'd get a room, if nothing else. They were on their phones, trying to find a campsite. We rode past a place outside of town and turned around. "Maybe they'll let us camp there," I said. "Looks like there's a few tents between the fancy motorhomes." We rode up to the office. Inside the reception area was cool. "You have any campsites?"

"Sure, how many?"

"Just need one, the three of us are on bikes."

"Showers?"

"We got it all."

"And ice cream in the freezer," Cody added.

"Twenty-five bucks."

"We'd pay double that in most towns." We walked out of the office with two cold ones and a seltzer and sat on the picnic table. Teton Pass was in the distance to the east. "See that notch. We'll be up there tomorrow." They smiled. The circumference of a journey. "All the way from Bend, from Portland." We laid in the grass, content to do nothing in the waning light. I went to the shower to let the hot water steam the dirt away. The stalls were clean—we'd landed on a lily pad again. I went into the store and bought some jerky to throw into our last mac and cheese. We put up the tent and Nev strung up his hammock. The boys went off and showered and I started cooking. The meal was filling; we made more than five people could eat. But always, the food looked small when it was dry, without water. We weren't far from town—the buildings were a mile, maybe two away—and decided to stay in the campground; the thought of riding another mile was too much. We'd see it in the morning. I brought three ice cream sandwiches from the store. We ate them in the dark. There were a few clouds overhead. "If it starts to rain, come in the tent."

"I'll be fine."

"In the tent." And I rolled over, nothing more to say, to feel. Even the idea of painting was distant—a vision from that border we had crossed. I slept hard, didn't hear Cody get up in the six a.m. light. The damp air was cool. We would be riding under clouds.

The Portal
XXVII

Distance: 20 miles
Elevation: 2,301 feet
Victor, Idaho, 2019

I couldn't make out the ridge—clouds hung over the valley. I tried to turn without waking Cody, but he was snoring. I stared into the distance: our last day to the summit. It still seemed like an idea: yes, we had ridden, but how far, and had we really come to the Idaho border? I tried to imagine the day we left Bend and could not. All I could feel was the damp overhead. I crawled out of the tent, put some water on the stove. I grabbed my down puffy. The boys were still sleeping. The motorhomes were idling; people were getting ready to drive the passage east to Yellowstone, the one we would soon ride over. I started to make some breakfast but thought better of it. We didn't have that far to ride. It was going to be a push, for sure, but we could take our time and eat in town. I sat on the picnic table, content to not be moving. "Hey, old man?" Cody said, popping from the tent.

"How are you doing?"

"Well, I can still feel my limbs. That's a good sign."

"I'm not too bad. But we made the right decision. That second climb would have killed us."

"I was thinking—never a good choice at this hour, I know—we should eat in town. We don't have to hurry. It will be a climb, but if we leave by ten we'll be fine."

"I'm up for it."

Nev staggered out of the hammock. "You get some rest?"

"I slept well," Nev answered.

"Thinking about going into town for breakfast."

"Sounds like a plan."

I walked over to the store and bought some juice, then grabbed a cup of the coffee from the counter. I walked back and started to fold the tent but left the cold weather clothes out for the day. "You think it's going to rain?"

"Nothing we ain't seen before."

"I'll ride with the rain gear into town. See what happens after breakfast." Cody looked at his phone. "Supposed to lift by midmorning."

I got dressed in the heated bathrooms—a luxury I hadn't expected—and splashed some water on my face. I looked at my weathered self in the mirror and announced to no one, this is our last climb, as if it were a furtive glance into Wyoming. I tried to contain my rising joy—this daily submersion of body, bicycle and sun that had taken hold of us. This was an altogether different way of opening the morning. Each day required us to leave what only yesterday had seemed impassable or a long ride. For days on end, the drum beat of Now called our names. We were slow to listen, slow to acknowledge its demand on our lives. But soon the mirth took over, the restless waiting, the wanting, as the tiring miles bore down. Soon we were malleable, without origin, without compass. On a black line through mountains, swallowed by canyons and still we did not know its code. Its revelations in the roadside elk and deer. Its antecedents in the cracks of sleeping on soil. Its disconsolate stars that draped our nights. Today we would ride into the coda—the strenuous echo of final exertion.

We pushed our bikes against the trees outside the Butter Café. It was stuffed with tourists hungry for something other than dried food. We waited outside until there was room. Unbelievably, the waitresses wore t-shirts although the temperature couldn't have been above forty-five outside. We ordered coffee and juice—the eggs and bacon came in quick rotation—and the breakfast drifted into the cold mountain moment we were riding into. We idled longer than usual, waiting for the clouds to disperse. We still didn't know how steep the climb was, so we rode around, hoping to find a bike store, but it was too early. "Let's just go before it gets warm." The first ten miles were a gradual climb and the sun broke through. On the ridge to the north, I saw some motion in the trees.

"How far you going?" It was a woman on a mountain bike. She was on a parallel trail in the dirt.

"To the top," I yelled.

"Good luck."

I didn't know whether that was good luck or *good luck?* but decided it was the former. We followed the stream coming down from the pass. The houses began to thin out—Victor was a place to be in the spring and fall and it was home to most of the workers in Jackson. There wasn't any affordable place to rent in the beautiful valley. Victor was like Hailey—people commuted to work from there. All these outposts of desire built in the gathering West. I looked up and the two of them were yammering—their excitement was palpable. Whatever the grade, we were climbing our last mountain, which only days earlier had felt imaginary. How could this mountain finally be in front of us? A mountain we had thought of, studied and prepared for. A mountain that moved closer, drew us into its quarters. A mountain we would not name. A mountain whose flanks we repaired to at last. A mountain that remained the portal, the entrance to what we had left to find: the revelation of the twenty-fourth morning in the saddle.

But revelations rarely come and if they do, not nearly as they are imagined. And so we rode on, grateful to be closer to the final ascent but still with reservations. No climb had come to us easily. This was the final one. And it was steep. How steep we did not know but it made no difference. We turned into the morning sun and kept on. After an hour, we stopped for a snack. There was a road to the south and I wondered who was lucky enough to live there. "The climb is about to start."

"Got it. You keep close to the mountain. I'll find ya." They rode off. The highway stretched to long sections of 5-6 percent grade, nothing too challenging, nothing we hadn't ridden many times. I saw a wide turn-out on the right with a building and a plate of steel in front of it. I couldn't make out what it was until I got closer: truck scales. No one was inside. I rode onto the plate and looked at the display: 240 pounds. All of me—bike, bags, water and self. I weighed about 165 and the bike, about 20. The rest, well, it was the rest. I'm sure Cody and Nev were carrying more. They were on lighter bikes but we may as well have been on Pogo Sticks—we still had to go up before reaching Wilson. It was the first time we had weighed our bikes—probably a good thing. I'm sure I would have dropped the weight had I known, eliminated the things you carry for comfort, the things that crowd the thin tires of a bike. These things you learn too late. I came around the corner to look up at the first real incline—as steep a hill as I had seen on the trip. No more than a couple hundred yards long. I could see nothing beyond it—just pavement at an incline. The trucks and trailers down-shifted. Diesel smoke buffeted us at every turn out: this was the beginning of the steep. The boys waited for me at the top of the incline. "Yowza!" Cody hollered. "That's an ass-kicker."

"Now I think it was *good luck?*—like I hope you make it?"

"Yeah, that had some teeth."

"*Poco a poco.*"

"Not much else to do. I'll walk if I have to." But walking wasn't any faster.

"You got enough water?"

"I'm good. Just taking it slow."

"Gotcha, Pops. We'll catch you at the next turnout."

And they were gone into the morning shadows. I tried to see this place in winter—this pass with its banks bladed to the snow markers. I tried to see what the locals drove through but could only make out the next hundred yards. The spiraling ascent, the way forward. I had climbed mountains on foot and this reminded me of those treks—one step, one step, one step—to the ice ridge or the cornice or the waiting snowfield when depth perception faded into less and less contrast. When the difference of light was liminal, as it was now—one turn of the pedal, one turn of the pedal. I wanted to stop again after the turn, but the boys were still on their pedals so I stayed upright. In the flurry of day-motion that culminated in this immense labor, there was no other time. Each of us bore down the only way we knew how—not stopping, not now.

I looked up again and they had pulled off into the shade. My breath was hard. We didn't say anything. The words were gone. It was oxygen, nothing more. Just breathe. Keep the heart rate at a reasonable level. They had special watches that knew these things; I had a pulse and heard it deep in the well of my chest. It was telling me that this was it—I could do no more, but I could keep on. That well inside of every chest when the incline is greater than thought, that's what we were in. I looked at the two of them and hoped they understood: I didn't drag them up here for this crucible. I only wanted to share some part of what a passage meant, a passage into what could not be said. Had the passage come sooner or with less struggle, they would have been bored. As it was, we were on the lee side of ready, they more than I, but we had to ride through it. That was all. I clipped in and rode on, if riding at one or two miles an hour was riding. They followed, each at his own pace. The stones in Trail Creek were an outline of some other shore, a place I tried to keep my eyes on. There was water again, the wood, and now a light wind brushed the pine tops. A wind of the Rockies. Our first taste of this air I knew from other mountains. I blew the air through a circle in my lips, straining to keep the wind inside for a few seconds and then out again. It was the only way to move up without turning away, into something I did not want. I stopped thinking, the road became the pedals, my dance with slow, micro-rhythms. I hoped—and then knew—the boys were in a similar rhythm. This pass we had waited for was now waiting for us. They would tell me if something was wrong, if it was too much. They were there—without obfuscation, trying to catch the next few yards standing on their pedals. And while no thought could make its way through my lips, I heard the hard breath, those spikes of heart and pulse, the witching hour that kept us in its grip. A grip of ending expectation and steeling oneself for the minute or more that legs and arms resisted. A grip of no doubt and every doubt. The grip when you either let go or hung on. I rode past the shadowed corner to see the incline in plain sun. We had no wind, no dream of circumvention to help us. I felt like Alice looking through the glass—a diagonal crossing my upward vision—and still the words fell down. I looked again and drew hard from the inside. I could not see beyond the crest—that was the point. Our road was no longer an extension of hayfields and valleys. It was a stream of low-flying wheels and us in their midst, then the wheels disappeared. There was only the motion, the strenuous *must*, kicking at our spokes, insisting on the turn of the axles, carving inches from the unknown distance to the next stop. The mind could not make sense of such things and gave in to the requirements of lesser balance, the lower register of sound without a definition. We had nothing left but a hidden recourse of *must*. I reached as far as *must* allowed.

Cody yelled, "About halfway, Pops—" and smiled. The inches were crawling down from that threshold to meet us. I pulled out and looked at them. Straining, drinking, breathing. We were in a maelstrom of the weather that comes in the higher gorges. A weather of our own making, like the weather on mountain peaks. We stood in its enclave, without assurance or with it, I did not know—but we stood as three who had tried to get here. It seemed foolish to ask why when the reason was the doing, not the questions. The breaking-down of mile to half-mile to quarter-mile and the oxygen waning. This was so small an action, this idea we had undertaken. And we felt its birth in our legs, lungs, hands. We had turned the axis of no motion into the increment of necessary motion. We were balanced on this beam of rock and sweat and nearly perfect trees, river, calm.

The switchbacks stretched on, into the stair-step ridges. We did not know how far—the cell service was gone, the screen shot gone, all of it gone to exertion. We tried, without more than trying, to focus on that far horizon, on that hot black highway, the three of us, spidering up the grade. I stood with them at about 8,000 feet—still below the summit—as if this was a place we arrived at. We looked back to Victor, our little corner of the morning that had started in clouds. I stood next to them knowing we were close. I was enervated by the writhing of thin air in my capillaries and looked back, as I am wont to do when the crest is near. We three, however far the ride took us from each other, returned for what rights old stems. The stem in each of us ran deep, ran into this mountain that we had not known and yet pushed up, pedal stroke by pedal stroke. The mountain weathered us to the skins of more than father and sons. We had not come with this knowledge of effort. We had not relinquished anything so necessary as this stem of bone in a stand of soft wood and water feet from the road edge. This stem that two wheels eroded only to paradoxically, strengthen. It was living without the regimen of roles in the wood and water that drew the stems to circle as one. A stem of others, a stem of selves as men, not father, not sons.

I was half-way up the switchback when a woman honked in a white Jeep. I wasn't sure if it was someone else or my love, the her I had left in Portland. And the her pulled off at the turnout. And the her jumped from the door and stood, resplendent on the ridge and I started to wave, tried to wave, and put my hand back on the bar and rode to the taillights of the idling Jeep, and her, the her I had spent all these miles to embrace anew, wrapped me close. She was like the her I met in college when none of this was a thought, the her without the me or the two ahead, in the waist of a thinning mountain road. "Are you all right? It's so good to see you."

"I'm all right." And kissed her with what strength I had. "A little bit more and I'll be there."

Her turning, at the taillights, at the idling car, her movement away up the switchback.

I heard Cody—"Three more, Pops—" and tried to feign enthusiasm but the sweat tears were all I had. I pushed into the crevice of will, again, as if it were about to give way. These last inches of a place you leave and then return, leave, return in the light of late morning, the two who rode alongside and her and the honking at the summit, Cody and Nev screaming. There was no other switchback, this was the last, and I rode into the vast black open on the summit, the three of them clasped like they had been pulled to the center. I let my bike fall—

"We did it!" I yelled to no one and everyone. To the tourists parked in the pretty cars, to the minivan chauffeurs with cameras and top hats, to my sons and her, alone and for the first time not alone but solid in their company. We joined at the waist for pictures in front of the "Welcome to Wyoming" sign, Jackson Hole in the valley to the east. Our helmet's outlines stuck to our hair, the salt signature of the grade. Then I did what I knew best: lay prostrate on the pavement and gave thanks to what we had done—and for the long arms that kept us upright and kept us from harm. And I wished Scott and Joe this same exhilaration, wished they could ride into Wilson for the beer to come. A stocky man walked up and pronounced, "I'm too old for that." And before I could say a word, Cody leaned on the baritone and gave it away—"He's sixty-five."

"Jesus, that's my age—"

"I just needed to do this. With them," I said. He understood, a father whose son or daughter was far from here but not so far. He knew that kin ride with you wherever you are. Deb gave us the tee shirts she made and we took more pictures. The downhill beckoned—a last free ride. I started to say something but let it go. "See you at the bike store…" and the boys rode off, five miles of good, hard racing into Wilson. They'd be all right. The scattershot trucks and trailers, beefy tourists and daylight lookers had given them a wide berth. This was the formal crowning, the return to what had begun for each of them on their respective shores, New York, Los Angeles. A cord to the place they left behind. And soon their spouses would grip them just as they had been gripped by the climb. Debby turned off her camera and put the phone away. The words had been spoken. She closed the car door and slowly drove off.

I walked over to my bike, looked down the path I had ridden two summers earlier, the old highway before they paved this four-lane into Victor. Tourists walked the ridge line. The village below floated in the green and brown outlines of houses and fields. I clipped in to coast down the mountain, the final descent into our last day, still incredulous that we were here, without injury, without delay. As far as we'd gone in other directions—the Sawtooths, the errant twists of the road from our path—as far as we'd gone, we were riding into Wilson almost as planned, almost as envisioned. And the plans were what we told others when we needed excuses for going out of our way into this mountain valley. I pulled my bike into the stand and walked to the bike store. My family was out back at the picnic table by Fish Creek. We took our shoes off, put our feet in the grass and then the water, the cold, forgiving water. Debby brought drinks to the table. I laid for a long time on the grass, lost in the euphoria of coming in from the road.

The bike store owner remembered me and smiled: "Where'd you come from?"

"Portland. We left about a month ago."

"Sounds like a ride—" and he looked away, wanting to leave the register, the business, for a time on two wheels.

"It was—and this pass with bags—"

He looked again, "You got some heft there."

He was one of the stoic ones who manned these outposts we relied on: a chain of bike stores throughout the West, spoke-stops on the blue highways. I asked how business was going and told him we'd be back. He smiled again, the affirmation of those who ride. The ones who don't need explanation. He understood. We had entered that place where the ridges did the talking.

I walked back out to the grass and looked at the guys. "What do you want to do? Can't get into the condo until four."

"Let's load the bags in the Jeep and go across the street to the taco place and get a beer."

"That's about as much as I can imagine doing—"

Cody laughed. "About half that—"

Nev cut him off. "Not nearly as done as I am—"

"We're just done. Let's get over there." And we lumbered out to the Jeep, stuffed it haphazardly with panniers and helmets and sweaty bandanas. We found a picnic table in the shade of the poplars. I looked at the two of them—"Can you believe it? It's still not real, not in a way I can speak."

"How are you doing? You guys want to eat now?" Debby asked.

"In a few—just trying to take it in. I'm a little overwhelmed." I looked at my hands without the bike gloves—brown and white stripes at the wrist and last knuckles. My haggard face in the reflection of her sunglasses. "I'm not much to look at," I tried to laugh, but it was still too early to peel back the layers.

"I'll bring you some tacos—" and she walked to the shed-roofed building and ordered.

"Bring a few dozen," Cody hollered.

"Damn, we don't have to ride to six or seven tonight. What the hell will we do with ourselves?" I half-asked.

"Lie down by Fish Creek and do nothing," Nev answered.

"See if we can get an early check-in, Cody?" I asked.

"On it."

"Think we can hang here until two or so and then head that way, buy some groceries, and just wait in the parking lot."

"When do you pick up—"

"Four-thirty. Think I'll go to the airport alone, if you don't mind," Cody said.

I turned to Nev—"And she flies in tomorrow evening, right?"

"Yep. It'll give me a day to shower." They laughed and settled into tacos and a good IPA. I looked at Debby—and stared long thinking of what to say. She smiled, as if the words were understood. Cody's phone rang and he let out a small yelp: "We can get in early. I think Nev and I will ride over there. Not enough room in the Jeep for all of us and the bikes."

"You guys are crazy. I'd hitch before I'd ride." And we ate slowly and bought another round. Debby tried to ask again, "How was it? Did you enjoy it?"

But the adjectives were lost in descriptive space—lost on the mountain we had just ridden over, lost on the picnic tables of ten different campgrounds, lost in the muddy trough of stream banks and eddies. Lost in the turns in the Sawtooths, lost in the foreground of what, only yesterday, was Portland. When Debby left us there, in that gas station, bright, clean, ready for anything or most anything and drove off with Laurie, my light and pump were still in the back of the Jeep and I waved at her frantically, tried to get her attention, and she saw me and pulled to the right, not knowing if the ride had ended prematurely, if the journey had come to a halt. I grabbed the pump and missed the light. Cody and I started for the Oregon coast and she and Laurie left for I-5 south and on to Hayden Mountain Summit, the first pass with snow the night before and the old man sitting with his house plants on the porch wondering when the next tourist would stop. And telling us the snow was up to the roof this winter, like it was in Stanley, like it was in so many places we had ridden through and then, the valleys that scorched the back, the valleys that held these mountains from border to border and the one that bent us like the forked stick of a dowser, to soil, that long day from Arco to Idaho Falls, when the ninety miles could be no farther and we lay on the roadside like splinters, all thought of water gone to dryness, and the last gas station with some ice and cold drinks, and the ag guy climbing down from his cab, the boots worn to the edges, the hat brim a sign post for sweat. And we looked into the valley and said why, why did we do this? And had no answer. Just as I could not answer her now. We put our things in the Jeep and held one another as they rode off and she drove into this valley green enough for almost any eye. And left us to our stoops, wooden and watery, and without explanation.

Better to Right the Stems

Epilogue
XXVIII

Distance: sixty-five years
Elevation: steep
Jackson Hole, Wyoming, 2019

Toward the last morning in the condo, I sat in the window reading from Donald Hall's memoir of losing his beloved Jane Kenyon to cancer, *The Best Day the Worst Day*. I had craved literature for so long it felt eternal and Debby found this book knowing I had closed my book of essays, unable to share it with him. Donald had died just as I had written the last pages and my editor, wisely, suggested I write a postscript to him by way of thanks. It was Don's encouragement throughout writing the book that let me proceed until I found my way and he was there, waiting for my return. I read those pages in the morning sun, grateful for his presence once again. The words were rhythmic intonations to a life shared over middle years, not unlike the ones I'd shared with Debby. I wondered who was waiting for me now as I'd finished this ride, to send me back into the stream. Like Don with Jane, death turns its X-ray to you to ask what was said and what was left out. Cody came downstairs and sat with his coffee on the other side of the room. Debby joined him and sat sipping her coffee. And then he said, haltingly, "Mom said you graduated from another high school."

Taken aback, I looked at her, at him, and stuttered, "Yes, in a county east of home." He looked perplexed and I must have looked the same. Not much else was said. I looked at Debby, at the poplars in the window and then I turned back to the book, to return to Don Hall's long, anguished goodbye to Jane.

In the fall I visited Cody and asked if we could talk. I started to tell him what I wanted to say that morning in Jackson Hole but couldn't. How my father had been the man I hoped to be for most of my life but for a part of it he was not. How we fought, never finding common ground. How other things blew into the room and made dust of our lives. How I could not live with him in that time as a father and son. It became an axe that broke us in two. We lived with that pain for many years. After I languished, waiting for the big minds to decide, they put me in a school in the mountains and I studied there and learned who I was with and without him. My family suffered. It hurt them, all of them. Then I came home, somehow changed from the time in the mountains and I started college too young and didn't know a thing.

What I remember was how hard I'd fought to change—to interact with my father as a man, an equal, with respect, and how I vowed never to disagree in anger again, no matter what. And I didn't for the next twenty years until he, most sadly, after four short years of retirement, died of lung cancer. Then I found a box of his letters to me and they became the letters to my sons. And the river asked me why. This was the register of filial well-being I carried with me until the day I met Debby and we saw in each other some part of that relinquished childhood that made it all right to be together. But I never knew if I could be a father and I resisted because I did not want to fail.

There were weeks and months where my mother cried to me at the wreckage of home. And my father, buried in his work and intelligence, cried in other ways. I could not bear to do that to my sons. I told Cody about what fear I had trying to raise him, hoping he would be the young man he wanted to be, without reservation or anger at some provocation by me. What father has not wanted this for his children? Even the imperfect, which is all of us, have wanted this. I see this every day in the faces of those I live near and work with—they want their children to aspire to more than they had and have what it takes to do so.

Cody was grateful that I had shared with him this unspoken chapter of my life. By now, he had inferred much that I said. Again, he knew more than I gave him credit for. In trying to shield the image of my father, not wanting to tarnish his memory, I had overstepped. It was better to right the stems.

Months later, at Nevada's apartment, I asked in the hallway if I could speak to him. He, of course assented. We sat on the roof of his complex and I tried to share the same story I shared with Cody. I tried to use the same words because I did not want it to vary, wanted it to be the extant version. He slowly began to cry. He too knew there was tension between my father and me and had not heard it explained. I tried to piece together for him the subtle ways my aunts, my father's sisters, raised me too with their loving, blue-collar hands and what my mother, with her hands, had given me. Those same hands I held when I visited in her board-and-care home. I tried to assure Nevada that I didn't want him to feel any anger toward my father, who did the best he could.

Trite as it sounds, he was a man with exorbitant intelligence and courage and it was all I could do to keep up with him in any way. Most of the time I did not, which was apparent to us both. It made me fear being a father, fear loving a child. This was also something Nev understood long before I spoke it and he thanked me for coming back to the beginning of our journey together, these few weeks across the West, to gather ourselves in the grand expanse of mountains and valleys and water, water that always disappeared, to share those others things I could not share. There was nothing to hide. We had ridden for days and days into the land and sky. And he sat there, tears streaming down his face, a crack of a smile at the edges of his mouth, filled with uncertainty and joy: his wife had told him she was pregnant when we arrived in Jackson Hole.

Elemental—Notes from A Ride

Lupine scatter to the horizon, sage too,
how we see them on two wheels,

the blue petals like stars in the sage,
a galaxy of floral hints at beauty,

and the black skin behind us, this strip
of asphalt we travel to road's end.

In the distance, the Sawtooths stare down.
We leave them like you leave a lover—

with regret, with respect and move to the
southern Rockies, supplicants of the open

highway. I have stopped wanting things,
stripped to no desire, a monastic order

of pushing a bike over ridge and plain.
Sunrise compliments sore calves, sweat,

and we enter each day like rain—open,
ready for its revelation. Maybe this

is the birth of joy—a monarch at our
feet, immigrant to another land.

Also by Shaun T. Griffin

Poetry

The Monastery of Stars
This Is What the Desert Surrenders: New and Selected Poems
Woodsmoke, Wind, and the Peregrine
Winter in Pediatrics
Bathing in the River of Ashes
Snowmelt

Nonfiction

Because the Light Will Not Forgive Me, Essays from a Poet
Anthem for a Burnished Land

Limited Editions

Driving the Tender Desert Home
Under Red-Tailed Sky

Editions

From Sorrow's Well: The Poetry of Hayden Carruth
The River Underground: An Anthology of Nevada Fiction
Torn by Light: Selected Poems of Joanne de Longchamps

Desert Wood: An Anthology of Nevada Poets

Translation

Death to Silence (Muerte al silencio). Poems by Emma Sepúlveda

Printed in the USA
CPSIA information can be obtained
at www.ICGtesting.com
JSHW060824070324
58584JS00002B/4